Isn't This Bathsheba?

Princeton Theological Monograph Series

K. C. Hanson, Charles M. Collier, D. Christopher Spinks,
and Robin Parry, Series Editors

Recent volumes in the series:

Paul G. Doerksen
The Church Made Strange for the Nations:
Essays in Ecclesiology and Political Theology

Lisa M. Hess
Learning in a Musical Key: Insight for Theology in Performative Mode

Jack Barentsen
Emerging Leadership in the Pauline Mission: A Social Identity Perspective
on Local Leadership Development in Corinth and Ephesus

Matthew D. Kirkpatrick
Attacks on Christendom in a World Come of Age: Kierkegaard,
Bonhoeffer, and the Question of "Religionless Christianity"

Michael A. Salmeier
Restoring the Kingdom: The Role of God as the "Ordainer of Times
and Seasons" in the Acts of the Apostles

Gerald W. King
Disfellowshiped: Pentecostal Responses to Fundamentalism
in the United States, 1906–1943

Timothy Hessel-Robinson
Spirit and Nature: The Study of Christian Spirituality
in a Time of Ecological Urgency

Paul W. Chilcote
Making Disciples in a World Parish:
Global Perspectives on Mission & Evangelism

Isn't This Bathsheba?

A Study in Characterization

Sara M. Koenig

PICKWICK *Publications* · Eugene, Oregon

ISN'T THIS BATHSHEBA?
A Study in Characterization

Princeton Theological Monograph Series 177

Pickwick Publications
An Imprint of Wipf and Stock Publishers
199 W. 8th Ave., Suite 3
Eugene, OR 97401

www.wipfandstock.com

ISBN 13: 978-1-60899-427-4

Cataloguing-in-Publication data:

Koenig, Sara M.

    Isn't this Bathsheba? : a study in characterization / Sara M. Koenig.

    xiv + 186 pp. ; 23 cm. Includes bibliographical references and index.

    Princeton Theological Monograph Series 177

    ISBN 13: 978-1-60899-427-4

    1. Bathsheba (Biblical figure). 2. Women in the Bible. 3. Bible. O.T. Samuel—Criticism, interpretation, etc. I. Title. II. Series.

BS1335.2 K55 2011

Manufactured in the U.S.A.

Dedicated to my parents,
Jon and Jean Malmin,
the first to teach me the biblical stories

Contents

Acknowledgments

This monograph is based on the dissertation I completed at Princeton Theological Seminary, and I remain profoundly grateful for the assistance, advice, and advocacy of my committee: Dr. Jacqueline Lapsley, Dr. Chip Dobbs-Allsopp, and Dr. Dennis Olson. They struck the fine balance between challenge and encouragement, pushed me to find my own voice and ideas about Bathsheba, and patiently waited during the process. I am still thankful that Dr. Dennis Olson was my chair. All those who know him are aware of his kindness and generosity, but those qualities are complemented by his scholarly rigor and incredibly careful attention to detail. He continues to be a model and an example for me of how to read texts and bear witness to the God about whom those texts speak.

I am honored to have landed at the School of Theology at Seattle Pacific University, where I am surrounded by such fine teachers and scholars. The conversations are always lively, and the support is strong. Indeed, I have benefited from material resources as well as from personal encouragement. There are too many people at Seattle Pacific University who have cheered me on to mention each of them by name, so I will have to thank them in person. But specific mention must go to Dr. Rob Wall and Dr. Bob Drovdahl, who were my professors when I was an undergraduate student. It is a great privilege now to be their colleague. I am also grateful to Dr. Jennifer McKinney and Dr. Karen Snedker for providing me research accountability amidst teaching demands. Librarian Steve Perisho has tirelessly and enthusiastically assisted me in finding references and resources. To many others who have given me written and verbal encouragement, and supported me through prayer, I will continue to say thank you as long as I can.

My husband Matthew is my best cheerleader and companion. His belief in and love for me is a foundation on which I stand, and I am grateful for his ability to love me so well. In the process of creating this work, I have also given birth to my daughter, Madeleine, and my son, Maximilian. Their own complexity and development have been a source of delight! Paradoxically, they provide me with clarity and focus, reminding me of what is really important. I am grateful to them for being living parables for me of the love of God. My parents, Jon and Jean Malmin, were the first ones to teach me the biblical stories. They have continued to give me love, support, encouragement, and practical help, without which I could not achieve the things I have. It is to them that I dedicate this monograph.

Abbreviations

'Erub.	*'Erubin*
AB	Anchor Bible
'Abod. Zar.	*'Abodah Zarah*
ABD	*The Anchor Bible Dictionary.* 6 vols. Edited by David Noel Freedman. New York: Doubleday, 1992
ANET	*Ancient Near Eastern Texts Relating to the Old Testament.* 3rd ed. Edited by James B. Pritchard. Princeton: Princeton University Press, 1969
Ant.	*The Antiquities*
b.	Babylonian Talmud
B. Meṣ.	*Baba Meṣiʿa*
BBE	The Bible in Basic English
BDB	Francis Brown, S. R. Driver, and Charles A. Briggs, *Hebrew and English Lexicon of the Old Testament.* Oxford: Clarendon, 1907
C. Ap.	*Contra Apionem*
CBQ	*Catholic Biblical Quarterly*
Eccl. Rab.	Ecclesiastes Rabbah
Ex. Rab.	Exodus Rabbah
Gen. Rab.	Genesis Rabbah
HALOT	Hebrew and Aramaic Lexicon of the Old Testament
HRCS	E. Hatch, and H. A. Redpath, *A Concordance to the Septuagint and the Other Greek Versions of the Old Testament.* 2 vols. 2nd ed. 1897. Reprint, Grand Rapids: Baker, 1998

Int	*Interpretation*
JBL	*Journal of Biblical Literature*
J.W.	*The Jewish Wars*
JPS	Jewish Publication Society
JSOT	*Journal for the Study of the Old Testament*
JSOTSup	Journal for the Study of the Old Testament Supplements
Ketub.	*Ketubbot*
KJV	King James Version
KTU	*Die keilalphabetischen Texte aus Ugarit.* Edited by M. Dietrich, O. Loretz, and J. Sanmartin. Neukirchen-Vluyn: Neukirchener, 1976
Lev. Rab.	*Leviticus Rabbah*
LXX	Septuagint
Meg.	*Megillah*
Moʿed Qaṭ.	*Moʿed Qaṭan*
MT	Massoretic Text
NAB	New American Bible
NASB	New American Standard Bible
Ned.	*Nedarim*
NIB	*The New Interpreter's Bible*
NIV	New International Version
NLT	New Living Translation
NRSV	New Revised Standard Version
Num. Rab.	*Numbers Rabbah*
Pesaḥ.	*Pesaḥim*
Rab.	*Rabbah*
REB	Revised English Bible

Sanh.	*Sanhedrin*
SBLDS	Society of Biblical Literature Dissertation Series
Song. Rab.	*Song of Songs Rabbah*
Taʿan.	*Taʿanit*
TNK	Tanak
VT	*Vetus Testamentum*
YLT	Young's Literal Translation
Šabb.	*Šabbat*
ZAW	*Zeitschrift für die alttestamentliche Wissenschaft*

1

Why Bathsheba?

Bathsheba is the woman King David saw bathing when he was walking around on his roof. He knew she was married, but he sent messengers for her, and when she came to him, he slept with her. She conceived, and sent messengers to David to announce her pregnancy, and then he attempted to get Bathsheba's husband Uriah—one of his soldiers—to sleep with her to cover up the adultery. When Uriah refused, David had him killed on the battlefield, and then took Bathsheba as his own wife, and she bore a son. God sent Nathan the prophet to confront David and to convey the consequences for David's actions—consequences that included the death of the child of Bathsheba and David. After the first child died, Bathsheba conceived and gave birth to a second child, Solomon. Bathsheba faded from the story until David was nearing death, when she reminded him of a promise he had made that Solomon would succeed him as king. Solomon then took the throne in lieu of his elder half-brother, Adonijah. Bathsheba's last act was to be the intermediary between Adonijah and her son. She disappears from the story before Solomon had Adonijah killed.

Why Bathsheba? There is not much to her story: it can be summarized in a paragraph, as I did above. Though I tried in my summary to focus on her role, so much of her story is tied to other male characters: David, Uriah, Nathan, Solomon, and Adonijah. Though I wanted to highlight what she did, so much of her story consists of things done to her. Indeed, Bathsheba has been neglected in biblical scholarship, and not without reason. But, there is so much of interest in both what is said and not said about her in the biblical text. The way the text about her is written is significant—though biblical narrative is often more reticent than revealing, more laconic than verbose, and more opaque than clear, the narrative about Bathsheba has been described as "frugal to excess even relative to the biblical norm."[1] Because the text is so open and so gapped, the different ways that people have filled the gaps regarding Bathsheba have been wildly and widely different. On one end of the spectrum, she is pictured as a seductress who was at least complicit, if not involved in her husband's death. On the other end of the spectrum are those who view Bathsheba as an innocent and helpless victim. Recently, Bathsheba has been compared to both Anat *and* Paghit in the Ugaritic legend of Aqhat (KTU 1/ 19 iv. 18–61),[2] and both Desdemona *and* Othello in Shakespeare's *Othello*.[3] Indeed, there have been so many different interpretations and pictures of Bathsheba that it is easy to find oneself asking, along with the anonymous informant in 2 Sam 11:3, "Isn't this Bathsheba?"[4] These varying interpretations point out how salient Bathsheba's story is as a place to examine hermeneutics.

My desire is first and foremost to respect the text by paying close and careful attention to what is said. Because of that, I offer a reading of Bathsheba that critiques some other readings of her, specifically those that see her as simple, stupid, seductive, or unchanging. I offer this different reading, first, because the text suggests it. But second, those other readings of Bathsheba are misogynistic, with harmful and even dangerous implications for the way women are viewed. Of course, in giving my second reason, I am revealing my own biases and perspectives. Yet, again, because the text about Bathsheba is so gapped, it is paramount that readers pay attention to exactly what the text does say, but also are aware of their own biases as they fill in the gaps.[5] Instead,

1. Sternberg, *Poetics*, 191.
2. Moore, "Bathsheba's Silence," 336–46.
3. Kirk-Duggan, "Slingshots," 37–70.
4. It is possible to translate the Hebrew word הלוא as a definite statement, as some English translations do: JPS: "She is Bathsheba . . . ," NRSV: "This is Bathsheba." Waltke and O'Connor explain it as "a double negative used to indicate that an affirmative answer is expected; in English such an expectation is shown by a tag question, e.g., 'isn't that so?'" *Introduction,* 684 n. 48. I prefer to leave it as a genuine question because it points to some of the uncertainty surrounding this enigmatic woman. Other places where this interrogative is used in the Bathsheba story (2 Sam 11:21; 1 Kgs 1:13) should also be translated as a question, instead of a positive affirmation.
5. Bal argues for an interest in the precise wording of texts while at the same time denying that there is an immutable meaning for each text. Instead, she acknowledges that a reader's own cultural framework and conceptions will affect how connections are made between the text and their contemporary world. *Loving Yusuf,* 4–5. The balance between text and reader will be discussed in greater detail below.

in the pages to come I will argue that Bathsheba is complex, generally positive and shows development from Samuel to Kings. I will revisit what has been said—and not said—about her, and will explain how I will characterize her.

Bathsheba Neglected

In 1978, Seymour Chatman began his discussion on character by stating, "It is remarkable how little has been said about character in literary history and criticism."[6] Three decades later such a comment is somewhat laughable, as there seems to be no end to the making of many books, or articles, or monographs exclusively devoted to the topic of character. Chatman's quote, however, only needs slight modification to still ring true, for it is remarkable how little has been said about the character of Bathsheba in biblical literary history and criticism. She is noted and mentioned, of course, by most scholars who discuss David, and often fills a chapter of a book or an article, but she has not occupied center stage. Even in the books where Bathsheba's name makes it into the title, she still is not the main focus.[7]

Bathsheba's neglect can be explained through two broad categories: ideological and narratological. What I am calling the "ideological" explanation for the neglect of Bathsheba has to do with her gender and role. Ideology is a term that can itself be defined in a number of ways; its Marxist roots emphasize how cultures are structured in such a way that a group holding power is enabled to maintain power and control with a minimal amount of conflict. These dominant groups work through values and worldviews, including the social adoption of ideas about the way things are and the way things work, to promote, legitimize, and normalize their dominance.[8] Other definitions of ideology see it as basically synonymous with worldview or a perceptual grid.[9] But both of these

---

6. Chatman, *Story and Discourse*, 105.

7. For example, Hausl's *Abischag und Batscheba* gives equal weight to both of the two women in 1 Kings. Besançon's *L'Affaire de David et Bethsabee* considers the different accounts of Jesus' genealogy in Matthew and Luke.

8. Cf. Eagleton, *Ideology*, 1–31. Eagleton admits that the word *ideology* cannot be defined in a simple way, but instead carries with it a wealth of meaning. He discusses its political and epistemological definitions, its cognitive and affective dimensions, and the way it may use or utilize distortion and falsehood in promoting its perspective.

9. Bell, *Ritual Theory*, 188.

definitions would explain why Bathsheba has been ignored. Men have occupied the center of power in Western society as a whole for millennia, and interpretation of the Bible has correspondingly been biased towards a male-focused worldview. Mieke Bal writes, "It is my contention that, in spite of major differences in the innumerable readings of the Bible, there has been in Christian, Western culture a continuous line toward what I refer to as 'the dominant reading': a monolithic misogynist view of those biblical stories wherein female characters play a role, and a denial of the importance of women in the Bible as a whole."[10] From that perspective, it is not surprising that the female character Bathsheba has been considered less important and of less interest than the male characters in the narrative.

Analogous to the way that Chatman's comment has become anachronistic, though, Bal's statement may today be challenged by the many recent publications within Christian Western culture that highlight the role and importance of the women in the Bible, and happily, there is no sign that such attention will abate. Moreover, if Terry Eagleton reminds us that ideology is specifically related to power-structure and power-relations, Michel Foucault expands our understanding of power by demonstrating how power is multidirectional, and domination is not the essence of power.[11] That is, a Foucauldian perspective on power allows us to see that Bathsheba, and other female biblical characters, may have more power than we originally thought. For although certain female biblical characters do not occupy traditional positions of power, they actually affect the outcome of events more than the male characters in a story.[12] Bathsheba clearly plays a powerful role in establishing her son Solomon on the throne in 1 Kings; we will see that she is by no means powerless in 2 Sam 11. But even with the increased emphasis on female biblical characters in general and a more expansive view of power, Bathsheba's unique role and importance has not been adequately considered.

Ideological bias may also be seen under a more specific "David" umbrella. Alice Bach comments, "Critics consistently define women as foils for David's development. As we have noted, female characters tend to have their identity stolen. Traditional commentary has failed to fill

10. Bal, *Lethal Love*, 2.

11. See Foucault, "The Subject and Power," 126–44.

12. Cf. Sarai and Hagar vis-à-vis Abram in Gen 16; Rebekah and Isaac in Gen 27; Deborah and Jael vis-à-vis Barak in Judges 4, etc.

out the identity of Abigail, Michal and Bathsheba, binding them by their gender to the overpowering portrait of David."[13]

Even allowing that David gets more attention than the women in his life, Bathsheba in particular threatens a specific theological picture of David as the supreme human ruler of Israel. That is, God's promise to David in 2 Sam 7 and its development into royal theology and messianism are all connected to an understanding of David as God's chosen, beloved king. When David's clay feet are exposed when he commits adultery with Bathsheba (and subsequently kills her husband), it has, in some cases, been important to devalue Bathsheba in order to maintain a high view of David. Such an interpretive move, however, is hardly theologically necessary, as the Bible is replete with examples of God choosing and using very flawed people through whom to work in the world. In fact, the text itself is often unrelenting in its exposition of the weaknesses of those people. Still, an ideology that insists on a morally superior David might need to ignore the story of Bathsheba. Perhaps the most salient example of this is found in Chronicles, which simply excises the story of Bathsheba from its history of David.

Second, and perhaps more significantly, Bathsheba may have been ignored for "narratological" reasons. Narratology, or "narrative criticism," can be defined as the systematic study of the typical features of literary narratives.[14] From a narratological perspective, Bathsheba is undeniably a minor character. She appears in only four chapters in Samuel-Kings, and speaks just a few lines. The few verses she occupies stand in stark contrast to those many where David and Solomon (or even Nathan, Joab, or Adonijah) are located. There are more words and space given in the text to David and Solomon, so there is more to work with regarding

13. Bach, *Pleasure*, 34.

14. Narratology is a diverse field, as can be seen in Rimmon-Kenan's introduction to her *Narrative Fiction*, where she describes her approach as drawing on Russian Formalism, Anglo-American New Criticism, French Structuralism, the Tel-Aviv School of Poetics, and the Phenomenology of Reading. *Narrative Fiction*, 5. Most narratological scholars, however, agree that narratology is related to structuralism, both "high structuralism" as exemplified by Levi-Strauss and Greimas, and "low structuralism," which corresponds more closely with the work of Genette. Low and High Structuralism (or surface and deep structures) need not be mutually exclusive categories, though, and in fact are often combined; cf. Bal, *Narratology*. Harshav critiques structural narratology for choosing the event as its key unit, and argues instead that the richest unit in a literary world is a character—an assertion that has implications for this work's focus on character and characterization. *Explorations in Poetics*, 14.

their characters, and so correspondingly, more work has been done on their characters. In comparison with the characters in the narratives of Samuel and Kings, Bathsheba says and does very little, and so those who might be interested in her character have very little to go on.

Although the neglect of Bathsheba is explicable, it is not excusable. Indeed, just as there were ideological and narratological reasons for not paying attention to her, there are both ideological and narratological reasons why we should not ignore Bathsheba. First, in terms of ideology, we must be aware of what Martha Nussbaum says when she quotes Dickens, that "we read as if for life."[15] That is, what we read and even the way we read affects our life. If we only pay attention to certain characters in literature, it can similarly condition our response to the human "characters" we meet in the world. While it is easier to see and pay attention to those who are in the spotlight, those in the background or on the outside are still present and ought to be watched for. Certainly it can be tempting to focus on those characters about whom we have the most information, perhaps because we can more easily understand or identify with them. Gina Hens-Piazza, however, warns that to ignore the minor character, the one who is more mysterious, or with whom we cannot so easily identify, is ultimately destructive to us.

> Our sense of ourselves and who we can become does not occur in a vacuum. It is mediated by others, and those "others" are made up not only of persons in life and characters in stories that we are quick to identify with or who seem most like us. Some of the most compelling insights about ourselves and what is possible for our lives will be prompted by those least like ourselves and by those individuals we might be trained or encouraged to ignore. Whether in life or in literature, identification with only the important figures, those with power or those crafted as the tragic or comic protagonists, breeds a fallacious understanding of ourselves. Self-understanding demands an enormous range of characters to learn from and identify with. Only then can we begin to achieve an honest assessment of our strengths and vulnerabilities, our virtues and vices, our talents and shortcomings, and our potentials and limitations. At the same time grappling

---

15. In *David Copperfield*, that phrase describes David reading frantically, as if his life depends on it. Nussbaum uses the quote as a *double entendre* to say that reading is done for life, to answer the question asked by the fifth-century Greeks: how should we live? Because life itself does not provide us with enough experiences and examples for a full answer to the question, literature may fill in those gaps. *Love's Knowledge*, 10–29.

with the broadest range of characters grants us urgently needed insights into the many and different "others" who make up our world and whose importance we might otherwise ignore.[16]

This monograph, therefore, takes an extended and sustained look at Bathsheba. By focusing on this mysterious and often maligned female character, we will not only learn more about her, but we may also discover insights about the minor characters in our lives, and even insights about ourselves.

But if it makes sense to pay attention to Bathsheba for ideological and ethical reasons, the narratological warrant for focusing on her may need more explanation. Paradoxically, the narratological reality that there is not much information about Bathsheba is also an important reason to study her. Hens-Piazza points out that the less information we are given about a character, the more closely and carefully we must examine those bits of information we do have. Such focused work with the small details in a text has the added advantage of drawing us as readers deeper into the text.[17] We ought not to "make mountains out of molehills," but examining the molehills carefully may help us read the entire narrative more attentively. Richard Bowman contends that one of the advantages of narrative criticism is that it guards against overinterpretation, which he defines as "the practice of assigning meanings to a story that exceed the possibilities generated by the data in the story itself. Since narrative criticism emphasizes textual data, it prevents the inclusion of extratextual information that alters the focus of the text in favor of the extraneous material."[18]

Additionally, from a narratological perspective, minor characters are important for the narrative. Though Mary Doyle Springer defines minor characters as secondary to major characters, she explains that they have a function that "is nevertheless necessary or highly desirable to the affective power of the work as a whole."[19] Her caveat is important; while Bathsheba is undeniably a minor character in the story of David (and the story of the Old Testament), she still functions to make this narrative more emotionally powerful. We know from David's story that even one chosen, beloved, and blessed by God (2 Sam 7; 12:7–8) can and does

16. Hens-Piazza, *Nameless, Blameless, and Without Shame*, 20–21.

17. Ibid., 22.

18. Bowman, "Narrative Criticism," 19.

19. Springer, *Rhetoric of Literary Character*, 14.

fall into sin, but the presence of Bathsheba in the story helps this knowledge become more than an abstracted truism. When we read about her mourning her husband Uriah, or needing comfort after the death of her child, we can enter into the pain caused by David's actions, we are made more aware of the consequences his decisions have for others, and we may even feel a more personal connection to the story.

Bathsheba Distorted

Even though there has not been a sustained study of Bathsheba before now, she has not been completely ignored; certain people have shone the spotlight on her. Yet, therein lies another rub, for some of the spotlights that have been turned on Bathsheba have presented a distorted picture of Bathsheba. These distortions have occurred in three main ways. First, she is seen by some as a character lacking complexity. Adele Berlin exemplifies this when she describes Bathsheba in 2 Samuel as only serving a functionary role in the story, without any depth or nuance to her character whatsoever. Berlin writes that Bathsheba is "a complete non-person. She is not even a minor character, but simply part of the plot . . . she is not a full-fledged character. She cannot even be viewed as a type . . . I will call her an 'agent,' an Aristotelian term which describes the performer of an action necessary to the plot . . . The plot in 2 Sam 11 calls for adultery, and adultery requires a married woman. Bathsheba fills that function. Nothing about her which does not pertain to that function is allowed to intrude into the story."[20]

The second way Bathsheba's character is distorted is that she is viewed negatively: either she is blamed for seducing David, or she is seen as stupid. An example of the seductive Bathsheba can be seen in the medieval book of hours of Louis XII, where court painter Jean Bourdichon depicts Bathsheba bathing in a provocative manner. Not only is she explicitly and graphically naked and in full view of King David (who occupies the upper right of the painting), but she coyly watches him watching her. While this portrait of Bathsheba is notable because it is

---

20. Berlin, "Characterization," 224. Admittedly, Berlin classifies Bathsheba as an "agent" only in 2 Sam 11, and allows for more complexity to her character in 1 Kings. However, I argue that Berlin is not paying attention to the way Bathsheba is described in 2 Sam 11, and that Bathsheba is more than functionary in that chapter, as well as in subsequent ones.

so overtly seductive,[21] there are other pictures of Bathsheba that display her in similar seductive ways.[22] Contemporary scholar Robert Whybray describes Bathsheba as "a good-natured, rather stupid woman who was a natural prey both to more passionate and to cleverer men."[23] While he does allow for her to be "good natured," which is a positive assessment, his use of the words "rather stupid" tip his view of her over to the negative side. A third way that Bathsheba's character is distorted is when her development from Samuel to Kings is not recognized. Whybray provides an example of this. He describes her as he does based on his argument that Bathsheba was naïve and unaware of the way others used her in 2 Samuel, and she remained that way in 1 Kings, explaining, "On each occasion someone makes use of her: David for his lust (II Sam. 11), Nathan in order to defeat Adonijah's plot to seize the throne (I Kings 1) and Adonijah to further his romantic designs (I Kings 2) . . . After this we are not surprised to find her good-naturedly helping Adonijah in his romantic affairs (2.13ff.) without pausing to consider either whether there was some more sinister scheme behind them, or whether the whole plan was not more likely to send Adonijah to his funeral than his wedding."[24]

George Nicol has a different perspective on Bathsheba's character than Whybray, but he also assumes that Bathsheba does not change; Nicol sees Bathsheba as clever and resourceful throughout the text.[25] Nehama Aschkenasy takes a position similar to Nicol's, explaining that if we work backwards from the end of the story to construct Bathsheba's character, we see that the woman who acted cunningly in 1 Kings in order to get Solomon on the throne was likewise cunning in 2 Samuel when David first saw her bathing.[26] None of these three interpreters see any change or

21. Kren, "Looking at Louis XII's Bathsheba," 45.

22. Many of these do occur in visual art, either as paintings or in film. Exum describes several in *Plotted, Shot, and Painted*, 47–73, as does Gunn in "Bathsheba Goes Bathing in Hollywood," 75–101. Walker-Vadillo considered visual depictions of Bathsheba in late medieval French manuscripts, and concluded that the choice to present her as naked and outdoors "imbues Bathsheba with the evil seductive character for which she is known." *Bathsheba in Late Medieval French Manuscript Illumination*, 90.

23. Whybray, *Succession Narrative*, 40.

24. Ibid.

25. Nicol, "Bathsheba," 360–63. In his "The Alleged Rape," Nicol writes that Bathsheba is a "clever and resourceful woman who in marrying David evidently achieves her goal," 53.

26. Aschkenasy, *Woman at the Window*, 117.

development in Bathsheba's character from Samuel to Kings. These three distortions (Bathsheba lacks complexity, is characterized negatively, and does not develop from Samuel to Kings) are not mutually exclusive, but overlap.

In the same way that the lack of focus on Bathsheba is explicable, so, too, these characterizations of Bathsheba can be explained. One reason is the nature of the text itself as heavily gapped. Bal describes gaps as "spots in the text where the information is insufficient, which provokes questions for the reader."[27] As mentioned above, the four chapters that contain the story of Bathsheba are especially sparse in their description of feelings or motives. The lack of information about Bathsheba may be what leads Berlin to conclude that she is not a full character.

Ideally, all readings of the text would pay close attention to what is actually said in the text, but this is especially true for gapped texts. However, another explanation for the distortions about Bathsheba is that the readers have either not seen what is in the text, or have seen something that is not in the text. Thomas Kren admits as much about the picture of Bathsheba in the book of hours of Louis XII, writing, "In relation to the biblical narrative, this depiction takes liberties."[28] Neither does Joseph Heller's novel *God Knows*, which portrays Bathsheba as idiotic and wanton, purport to reflect the biblical story, but there is no disclaimer to that effect anywhere in his writing. While those who know the biblical story well are able to recognize ways that some interpretations depart from the text, many others are not aware of the liberties taken in interpretation. Those distorted reflections of the text about Bathsheba may end up shaping people's views of Bathsheba more than the actual text does. Katharine Sakenfeld suggests as much: "Popular accounts in movies, historic artwork, and even children's Bible stories (if children's books dare tell this story at all) have filled in the gaps in information to such an extent that it is difficult for us to let go of our preconceptions and recognize what the text actually tells us and what it does not say. Therefore, we must read attentively to overcome our own assumptions about the relationship between David and Bathsheba."[29]

27. Bal, *Lethal Love*, 18.
28. Kren, "Looking at Louis XII's Bathsheba," 44.
29. Sakenfeld, *Just Wives*, 71.

The view of Bathsheba as unchanging is explained by Nicol when he writes that the total reading of a text must be consistent and coherent.[30] For him, that includes his desire to read Bathsheba as a consistent character throughout Samuel and Kings. In fact, the question of whether or not a character can change is philosophical as well as methodological,[31] and it seems that Nicol decides they do not. It also would appear that Nicol, as well as Whybray and Aschkenasy, are borrowing from E. M. Forster's well-known classification of characters as "flat" or "round," and all three see Bathsheba's character as flat—or unchanging—instead of being round. In fact, Forster explains that a character is round if that character "is capable of surprising in a convincing way."[32] Other ways to describe character would allow for seeing a greater change in Bathsheba.

Even though these distortions regarding Bathsheba can be explained, there is a way to view her that more accurately reflects the character presented in and by the text. In the pages to follow I will demonstrate that the minor character Bathsheba is presented in the text as a complex and generally positive character who shows development from Samuel to Kings. These aspects to her character are interrelated, yielding a character who is deep and rich. Each of the elements to this description of Bathsheba (minor, presented by the text, complex, generally positive, and showing development) deserve some further comment.

Bathsheba: A Complex Character

First, that Bathsheba is a minor character is fairly self-evident. As mentioned above, she does and says very little in the text, especially when contrasted with other characters. Her status as a minor character is connected with her complexity. It is not that she is complex *in spite* of being a minor character,[33] but *because* she is a minor character in this narrative,

30. Nicol, "The Alleged Rape," 51.

31. Anyone who has dealt with a recalcitrant person might be pessimistic on the answer to that question. Often, a complete character change comes only after a major experience or event, like a health scare or accident. Cf. Loder, *Transforming Moment*. But while most people have a consistency to their character, they also grow and develop over time. So, too, with Bathsheba—there are certain consistencies in her character that are evident in her entire story, but she does also demonstrate growth and development over the course of the text.

32. Forster, *Aspects of the Novel*, 118.

33. Though that is certainly true: Forster explained that a small character could be a "round" character (and ostensibly that a main character could be one-dimensional or

she is complex. Her complexity is connected with the gaps in this narrative; again, this set of texts is particularly full of gaps. I will highlight the gaps I notice in the narrative as I proceed to work through it. But gaps are present in any narrative. Shlomith Rimmon-Kenan suggests that the way to create a narrative is to begin with a hole,[34] and points out that not even an extended narrative like *War and Peace* will render every detail of the story, but will leave certain events, motives, or thoughts untold and undramatized.[35] In addition to being present in all narratives, gaps can also be positive, allowing for a level of richness and depth that would not be present if every question were answered.[36]

The places where details are left untold also encourage the reader's own participation in constructing meaning of the text. Wolfgang Iser explains that it is the omissions in a story that make it dynamic, and give the reader the opportunity to demonstrate her or his faculty for establishing connections and filling in the gaps.[37] Iser also suggests that texts with more possibilities and potentials for meaning encourage a greater level of reader participation and interest than those that allow for fewer interpretive possibilities.

> [E]very literary text invites some participation on the part of the reader. A text which lays things out before the reader in such a way that he can either accept or reject them will lessen the degree of participation as it allows him nothing but a yes or no. Texts with such minimal indeterminacy tend to be tedious, for it is only when the reader is given the chance to participate actively that he will regard the text, whose intention he himself has helped to compose, as real. For we generally tend to regard things that we have made ourselves as being real. And so it can be said that indeterminacy is the fundamental precondition for reader participation.[38]

"flat"), and he uses Jane Austen as an example of an author who creates characters that are small, but round. Forster, *Aspects of the Novel*, 113.

34. Rimmon-Kenan, *Narrative Fiction*, 128.

35. Rimmon-Kenan, *Concept of Ambiguity*, 46.

36. Cf. Fokkelman, *Narrative Art*, 427–29.

37. Iser, "The Reading Process," 285. Rimmon-Kenan similarly notes that the gap "always enhances interest and curiosity, prolongs the reading process, and contributes to the reader's dynamic participation in making the text signify." *Narrative Fiction*, 130.

38. Iser, "Indeterminacy," 13–14.

Yet, while the indeterminacy of this narrative regarding Bathsheba is positive, insofar as it invites a reader's participation, it can also be problematic. It becomes difficult to know how to adjudicate among the dizzying array of possibilities for understanding Bathsheba, especially when many of the readings of her seem mutually exclusive; for example, while Whybray describes her as stupid, George Nicol sees her as clever and calculating.[39] Are both views correct? How are we to decide?

First, we must acknowledge that not all gaps are equal—in size, or in import for the text. Sternberg explains, "This gap-filling ranges from simple linkages of elements, which the reader performs automatically, to intricate networks that are figured out consciously, laboriously, hesitantly, and with constant modifications in the light of additional information disclosed in later stages of the reading."[40]

In other words, some gaps we fill in almost without thinking, but many of the gaps in the Bathsheba story take more deliberate work. Some of the gaps regarding Bathsheba can be filled in by using background knowledge. For example, there are several gaps about the timing of events in 2 Sam 11–12. How long did David wait between seeing Bathsheba (2 Sam 11:2) and sending for her (2 Sam 11:3)? How long did she remain in the palace before she returned to her home (2 Sam 11:4)? When did she send the announcement of her pregnancy to David (2 Sam 11:5)? How old was the child when he died (2 Sam 12:18)? We know, however, that the gestational period is nine months, so that provides a *terminus ad quem* for the events between 2 Sam 11:5 and 2 Sam 11:27. And, we might assume that Bathsheba waited at least a month after David slept with her before she told him she was pregnant. Other background knowledge may come from the comparative ancient Near Eastern world. We might also fill in gaps by using linguistic evidence, considering the semantic range of a given word,[41] or looking carefully at the syntax. Other linguistic connections might be made to other places

39. Nicol, "Clever" and "The Alleged Rape." Cf. n. 25.

40. Sternberg, *Poetics*, 186.

41. For example, if we wonder about the age of the child, we might consider the Hebrew words used to describe the child. They are son (בֵּן, 2 Sam 11:27, 12:14), and child (יֶלֶד, 2 Sam 12:15 and 12:18, and נַעַר, 12:16). None of those specify exactly the age. Isaiah 49:15 and 65:20 use עוּל to refer to a suckling child, a word that corresponds to the modern Hebrew word עוֹלָל for baby or infant. Modern Hebrew also refers to an infant with תִּינוֹק. The words in our text refer to a child of varying ages, and therefore the semantic range itself does not help us fill in the gap.

in the biblical narrative, when words or phrases that occur in our text are used elsewhere. As Sternberg said, another way to fill in gaps will be to continue to read, and to see how the end of the story helps us understand the beginning or middle. For example, when David first sees Bathsheba, she is bathing, but nothing more is said at that point. It is not until later in the chapter that we are told that it was a bath of purification after her menstrual period, which helps us understand that when she conceives, David must be the father.

Second, we must recognize that no matter how we as readers work with gaps, certain gaps may not be completely filled, but only narrowed. In general, biblical texts are more interested in answering certain questions than others,[42] and the gaps that remain tell us that the text is not as interested in answering those questions. As we attempt to focus on and understand Bathsheba's character—which includes filling in gaps—we must respect those gaps that ultimately remain in the text. While we would like to have answers, the questions about her that cannot be answered create a character who is mysterious and complex. To use language borrowed from Russian literary scholar Mikhail Bakhtin, Bathsheba is an unfinalizable[43] character. That is, there are aspects of Bathsheba that will neither be fully known nor apprehended, and that makes her more rich and compelling.

Another way to respect Bathsheba's complexity is in the way we understand the texts themselves. Sometimes indeterminate texts are described as "ambiguous texts." Rimmon-Kenan, however, makes a distinction between texts that are ambiguous and texts that are open, vague, or indeterminate. As she defines it, an ambiguous text is a highly determined form in which there is equal evidence for the truth and falsity of two options. But the component alternatives in an ambiguous text cannot both be true; they are mutually exclusive. She explains,

42. In his essay, "The Strange New World within the Bible," Barth makes the point that when we come to the Bible with our own questions, they may not be answered, but there are answers to the questions of the text, 28–50.

43. For Bakhtin, to "finalize" a character is akin to closing off that character; indeed, Bakhtin refers to finalizing in parallel with "deadening." *Problems of Dostoevsky's Poetics,* 59. Obviously, a character that is unfinalized is opposite: it is alive, free, and complex—to use another one of Bakhtin's terms, *dialogic.* Cf. Newsom, "Bakhtin, the Bible, and Dialogic Truth," 294–96 and "The Book of Job as Polyphonic Text," 87–108; Green, *Mikhail Bakhtin and Biblical Scholarship*; Tull, "Bakhtin's Confessional Self-Accounting and Psalms of Lament," 41–55; Claassens, "Biblical Theology as Dialogue," 127–44; Olson, "Biblical Theology as Provisional Monologization," 162–80.

> Narrative ambiguity . . . is constructed around a central infor-
> mational gap, in relation to which all the narrative units can be
> defined. The reader relates the units to each other with a view to
> forming a hypothesis that will fill in the gap. But the logic of the
> story is such that two, rather than one, hypotheses emerge, and
> the two are mutually exclusive. The links among the units are
> thus conditioned by their relation to the mutually exclusive hy-
> potheses, the units assuming the role of hermeneutic clues which
> confirm or refute each of the conflicting possibilities.[44]

An open, vague, or indeterminate work, by contrast, may have more than one possible meaning. Rimmon-Kenan discusses the difference between an "ambiguous" work and an "open" work specifically in regards to characters. "All too often, a narrative is labeled 'ambiguous' because its characters or its represented world are neither wholly good nor wholly bad but a mixture of both."[45] An author like Henry James, she argues, does not say that people are complex and difficult to judge, but he presents two separate, complete, contrasted but equally credible possibilities simultaneously.[46]

Although the biblical text about Bathsheba is gapped, it is not ambiguous as Rimmon-Kenan defines ambiguity, where there are two mutually exclusive ways of looking at Bathsheba. If it were, then Bathsheba would either be wholly innocent or wholly culpable (and many have tended to characterize her in those terms). Instead of being a strictly ambiguous text, then, the biblical text is open, in which we see a combination of different elements in Bathsheba's character. Although she is the victim of certain circumstances out of her control, such as when David takes her or when her husband and child die, she is not entirely victimized. Although she uses her persuasive powers with David to help Solomon take the throne, she did not persuade David to sleep with her.

44. Rimmon-Kenan, *Concept of Ambiguity*, 51.

45. Ibid., 14. Several biblical scholars do refer to 2 Sam 11, in particular, as "ambiguous." For example, Yee subtitles her article, "Fraught with Background: *Literary Ambiguity in 2 Sam 11*," emphasis mine. Nicol identifies five examples of ambiguity in 2 Sam 11 in "The Alleged Rape," 51. Sternberg also uses 2 Sam 11 as the exemplary of biblical ambiguity in his chapter titled, "Gaps, Ambiguity, and the Reading Process," in *Poetics*. But those scholars do not see the same level of "ambiguity" in 2 Sam 12, or 1 Kgs 1 and 2. In fact, it is hard to sustain an argument that the text remains ambiguous after the statement in 2 Sam 11:27: "The thing that David did was evil in YHWH's eyes." This will be discussed in more detail in the following chapter.

46. Rimmon-Kenan, *Concept of Ambiguity*, 15.

Instead, like the "characters" we meet in real life, Bathsheba is a complicated and complex character. Another term which can accurately describe Bathsheba is that she is "hybrid."[47] This "open" text yields a hybrid—or complex—character.

But even with more precise terminology to describe characters or texts, two hermeneutical dangers remain when we fill those gaps or answer those indeterminacies. One is to say that the text means anything one wants. Perhaps this tendency is especially dangerous for the Bible, a text given such ideological power. The history of interpretation is full of examples of people who have abused and twisted the Bible to make it say what they want it to say. But the other danger in dealing with an indeterminate text is to do violence to the text itself, and assert that the text only means one thing. Iser explains, "The interpreter's task should be to elucidate the potential meanings of a text, and not restrict himself to just one."[48] His exhortation holds especially true for the biblical narratives, marked as they are by gaps and meaning potentials. And Bathsheba's character, similarly, is more than one-dimensional, and has different potentials.[49]

A way to navigate between this hermeneutical Scylla and Charybdis is to recognize that a gapped text does invite different potential meanings, but the text itself will also provide constraints on meanings. Roland Boer notes, "in giving out its own instructions as how to read, the text allows certain possibilities while closing off others."[50] Brian Blount suggests that "the text language has a potential of meaning whose boundaries are limited by textual and ideational data. A text cannot be made to mean anything a community desires. Meaningful conclusions must respect established textual and ideational parameters."[51] While readers may discover that a text means different things to each one of them, it cannot mean anything or everything. Even Iser, who emphasizes the role of the reader in making meaning out of indeterminate texts, still asserts that it is important for the reader to respect the text.[52]

47. In "Davidmachine," Britt describes David as "hybrid."

48. Iser, *Act of Reading*, 22.

49. In particular, Jewish midrashic readings of the Hebrew Bible seem to delight in the different possibilities for meaning, and some of those will be noted in chapter 5.

50. Boer, "National Allegory," 102.

51. Blount, *Cultural Interpretation*, 28.

52. In fact, Iser has been described as determined "to hold in tension the twin poles

In other words, a gapped text does have different possibilities for meaning, but it cannot mean anything. Specifically, there are different possibilities for understanding Bathsheba's character, but her character cannot be anything a reader wants. Because we are not told what Bathsheba thought, or felt, there are a number of possible legitimate interpretations of her that could be supported by the text. But, simultaneously, some of the interpretations that have been done regarding her cannot be supported by the text. For example, it is difficult to sustain the interpretation that Bathsheba is wholly passive based on 2 Sam 11:5, which explains that "she came to him." Even if she may not have had much ability to refuse the king's summons, she still is the subject of that verb. Thus, the best interpretations of Bathsheba will be the ones that best account for the details of the text itself—its language, its indicators, its images, and its gaps. I will closely and carefully attend to those details by pointing them out as I proceed. I will articulate the different possibilities for Bathsheba's character, and will argue for the characterization best supported by the text as I see it.

Bathsheba: A Predominantly Positive Character

The description of Bathsheba as a predominantly positive character needs some explanation and qualifications. First, I must admit more of my own predispositions. I like Bathsheba, and am inclined to be a generous reader of her. Because certain misreadings of her have been negative—those that see her as stupid, scheming, seductive—I would like to rehabilitate her. In many ways, I do not want to use the word *positive* as a blanket term, but to counter specific negative characterizations of her. That is, what I mean by describing Bathsheba as "positive" is that she is not stupid. She is not to blame for seducing David. She is not sinister or conniving. But my own proclivities do not give me warrant to ignore the textual evidence. The problem with those "negative" readings is not just that they are negative, but that they do not do justice to the text: they neither pay attention to what the text says, nor the way that the text says it. Because of my desire to respect the text, I also have added "generally" or "predominantly" as a modifier to "positive." That is, if Bathsheba is not stupid, scheming, or seductive, neither is she a simplistic examplar

---

of the textual object and the real reader's subjectivity, so that one is not effaced by the other." *Postmodern Bible*, 41.

of virtue. In fact, this description of Bathsheba as "generally positive" at times will conflict with the description of her as "complex," for as certain gaps remain open so the possibility genuinely remains that she does not have pure, noble, or positive motives.

Describing Bathsheba as "positive" also has moral connotations, and it is important not to be anachronistic; my sense of morality is not necessarily relevant for the ancient context. In fact, while I tend to equate "seductive" with "negative," Fokkelein Van Dijk-Hemmes views Tamar's seduction of Judah (Gen 38) as something positive insofar as it exemplifies the way Tamar takes power and shows initiative.[53] However, the cases of Tamar and Bathsheba are different in three ways. First, their contexts are quite different: Tamar's husbands have died, and her father-in-law was unwilling to give his third son to her in marriage, but Bathsheba was married to a husband who was still quite alive when she and David slept together. Second, the text itself valorizes Tamar, when Judah says that Tamar is more righteous than he (צדקה ממני, Gen 38:26). We do not read that Bathsheba was righteous for sleeping with David. But that leads to the third and perhaps most important difference: the text does not support that Bathsheba seduced David, while Tamar's dressing up demonstrates intent on her part.

One way to measure "positive" is in legal terms, but here, too, we see complexity. For, clearly, adultery is wrong (cf. Exod 20:14; Lev 20:10; Num 5:11–28;[54] Deut 5:18), but when Nathan comes to confront David about his sinfulness, he does not also confront Bathsheba. In fact, the punishments are put on David, not her, and God (through Nathan) does not declare her to be in the wrong. Therefore, another element to this description of Bathsheba as "positive" will be in comparison to David, for the text makes it evident that he has done what is wrong; the text is less obvious that Bathsheba has broken laws. If Bathsheba is seen as

---

53. Van Dijk-Hemmes, "Tamar and the Limits of Patriarchy," 135–56. Foucault's insights on the productive aspect of power in sexuality ("Body/Power," 56–57) would support the view that by taking charge of her body, her sexuality, Tamar increases her power; in van Dijk-Hemmes' words, she "reverses her position of powerlessness to one of power," 150.

54. The *Soṭah* treatise in the Mishnah, Tosefta, and Babylonian and Palestinian Talmuds expands the definition of the rules of procedure in Numbers regarding a wife who is either actually or supposedly unfaithful. Bach asserts that the ritual is constructed around suspicion of adultery rather than proof of crime. Bach, "Good to the Last Drop," 31.

more positive than David, however, her evaluation as positive will not be limited to David as the only standard of comparison.

Not only is there a legal dimension to what is positive, but the word *positive* can be connected with honor and shame. Here, examples from scholars working with honor and shame in other stories are helpful. First, Hens-Piazza discusses the cannibalistic mothers in 2 Kgs 6:24–33. She does not attempt to whitewash their actions, but refers to their cannibalism as "a repugnant and desperate act," "difficult to deal with," and "reprehensible."[55] However, she also urges readers to pay attention to issues of power, and the larger structural issues of injustice, to see that the women themselves are victims.[56] The title of her work, *Nameless, Blameless, and Without Shame*, ultimately conveys that even a negative action must not be automatically connected to shame.

A second place where honor and shame are dealt with is in the book of Esther. Timothy Laniak deals with the structural themes of honor and shame in the book, considers the semantics of the terms within biblical lexicography, and also engages the insights of psychology and anthropology.[57] Laniak asserts that there are two literary patterns in the biblical text: the first is a sin > alienation > reconciliation pattern, in which the shame is based on guilt and the goal of the movement is a return to an original state of grace or favor with God and with the community.[58] The second plot he calls a "pattern of challenge and honor," where the protagonist is a victim of injustice who enters a stage of abandonment and alienation, after which divine intervention leads to vindication and reemergence into a new status, often with increased prosperity and/or prominence.[59] It is interesting to consider Bathsheba based on Laniak's two patterns: should she be shamed based on her guilt, or has she been a victim whose honor has been challenged? Is she a sinner in need of reconciliation, or someone who has experienced suffering only to emerge with increased status and prosperity? It would appear that Bathsheba fits into the second pattern more than the first, for any act that may be

55. Hens-Piazza, *Nameless, Blameless, and Without Shame*, 82.

56. Ibid.

57. Laniak, *Shame and Honor*.

58. Ibid., 8. He notes that examples of this pattern are found in ritual laws, but are also common in historiography, the prophets, and especially in reference to exile.

59. Ibid., 8–15. Examples of this type of pattern for Laniak include Job, the laments, and the court stories of Joseph, Daniel, and Esther.

considered shameful is not entirely of her own doing, and she emerges in an exalted situation. It is important to note, however, that Laniak's classification of the narratives in the Hebrew Bible into one of two patterns is somewhat reductionistic. Even when we utilize his taxonomy, we see Bathsheba's complexity, for her fit into one of the two patterns is not quite as obvious or neat as some of his other examples. Overall, though, the work of Hens-Piazza and Laniak demonstrates how the dimensions of honor and shame give greater precision to the word *positive*. Ultimately, then, to describe Bathsheba as "positive" is not simple, as this is a term that has different dimensions and nuances to it. Again, it must be qualified by an understanding of her complexity. Bathsheba's positive characterization carries moral and legal connotations, and it often (though not always) is comparative vis-à-vis David.

Bathsheba: A Character Who Develops from Samuel to Kings

One of the contributions of this study is that it considers Bathsheba in both Samuel and Kings in order to see how her character develops throughout the narrative. Often, she has been considered only in Samuel *or* Kings, and not both sets of texts together.[60] While there are many good and practical reasons to focus on a smaller textual pericope, such a view only provides an incomplete picture of her character. One of the first steps in exegetical work is to define the limits of a pericope: Bathsheba's story begins in 2 Sam 11 and ends in 1 Kgs 2. And an important piece of characterization is to observe the character throughout the narrative, gleaning all the possible information that is given. David Gunn and Danna Fewell explain: "We shape our understanding of a character as the narrative unfolds over time, offering further clues and, frequently, complexity. Longer stories require more patience and a higher tolerance for ambiguity on the part of the reader. Rather than assessing a character on the basis of only one set of circumstances, readers of longer stories see

---

60. Cf. Leneman, "Portrayals of Power," 139–55; Garsiel, "The Story of David and Bathsheba," 244–62; Kim and Nyengele, "Murder S/He Wrote?" 95–116; Ostertag, "La Veuve dans le Plan Messianique de Dieu," 5–26; Rosenberg, "The Institutional Matrix of Treachery in 2 Samuel 11," 103–16; Lawlor, "Theology and Art," 193–205. Most of these focus on the narrative in Samuel, not Kings.

characters in several situations, engaging in different relationships, and changing over the passing of time."[61]

Indeed, when Bathsheba first appears in 2 Sam 11, there is very little information about her. It is only as we move through that chapter and the following one that we start to construct an understanding of her character. Even that construction is incomplete until we read about her in 1 Kings. Again, one way that textual gaps are filled is as the text itself proceeds. Therefore, we will look at the entire story of Bathsheba from Samuel to Kings in order to see how she develops throughout the narrative.

In characterizing Bathsheba, I will borrow from a number of different methodologies for characterization in order to have a full measure of her as a character,[62] and in particular, I will consider the qualities Bal

61. Gunn and Fewell, *Narrative in the Hebrew Bible*, 79.

62. Berlin affirms an eclectic process, saying, "In most cases the slavish application of one particular method or approach to a text produces mechanical, lifeless criticism." "Characterization," 281. Perhaps the most detailed taxonomy for classifying character comes from Hochman, who evaluates character in terms of a sequence of eight categories and their opposites: (1) stylization/naturalism, which posits a scale from naturalistic portraiture to maximal stylization; (2) coherence/incoherence, which has to do with the underlying unity or dissonance within a character; (3) wholeness/fragmentariness, where the former is when the character's qualities appear to cohere in such a way as to convince us that what we are given of the character is representative of the whole of that character; (4) literalness/symbolism. Although all elements or signs in literature are ultimately symbolic and no sign is able to capture with precise literalness that which it signifies, some characters are presented as more literal than those who symbolize a class or type; (5) complexity/simplicity; (6) transparency/opacity, which deals with perceptions of the inward life of the character and is interested in such questions as, How accessible are the character's thoughts, and how clear or opaque are her motives?; (7) dynamism/staticism. Hochman believes that all characters are implicitly dynamic, for conflict and the dynamism that it generates is, for him, the ground of character. Yet, from the way that they are presented and perceived, there are static characters who seem not to change throughout the narrative; and (8) closure/openness. If a character is closed, there are no further questions about the character. If a character is open, then questions about the character which were raised by the presentation of that character still remain. *Character in Literature*, 91–139.

Within Hochman's categories, Bathsheba would be a relatively "natural" and unstylized character because she is complex. She would fall somewhere in the middle in the spectrum between coherency/incoherency and wholeness/fragmentariness. She is not wholly (and coherently) a seductress or a naïf, but there does seem to be a consistency to her character that would belie a lack of any unifying principle. Also, in a text where there are so many gaps, it is hard to describe Bathsheba as completely whole, but there are enough similarities in the way she acts to caution us from seeing her as entirely fragmentary. In terms of literalness/symbolism, Bathsheba is more individualized and literal

highlights as important for characterization: gender, personal name, physical description, actions, speech, and a character's development or change throughout the narrative.[63] As mentioned, many have not considered the way Bathsheba develops throughout the narrative. But my desire to recognize her development comes from the text itself, and not from some ideal outside the text. That is, I will take a qualified "purist" approach to her character, and not a "realist" approach. Those terms—purist and realist—come from a long debate in the field of characterization: the relationship between characters in a text and people in the real world. In the 1960s, Marvin Mudrick explained,

> One of the recurring anxieties of literary critics concerns the way in which a character in drama or fiction may be said to exist. The "purist" argument—in the ascendancy now among critics—points out that characters do not exist at all insofar as they are a part of the images and events which bear and move them, that any effort to extract them from their context and to discuss them as if they are real human beings is a sentimental misunderstanding of the nature of literature. The 'realistic' argument—on the defensive nowadays—insists that characters acquire, in the course of an action, a kind of independence from the events in which they live, and that they can be usefully discussed at some distance from their context.[64]

Bal explains that one of the problems with believing the characters are real is that it causes readers to ask questions that the text cannot answer, such as, how many children did Lady Macbeth have? Instead, she advocates that "we must restrict our investigation to only those facts that are presented to us in the actual words of the text."[65] Joel Weinsheimer, a "purist," believes that characters are so "textualized" that they disappear. "As segments of a closed text, characters at most are patterns of recurrence, motifs which are continually retextualized in other motifs.

---

than she is a symbolic type. It bears repeating that Bathsheba is a complex character, not a simple one, although again that has something to do with the gaps in the text. That same gapped text presents an opaque rather than a transparent character, especially in reference to her feelings and motives. Bathsheba is more dynamic than she is static, despite some commentators who argue that she does not change at all. Finally, Bathsheba is definitely an "open" character, as may be demonstrated by all the questions and different responses to her that remain.

63. Bal, *Narratology*, 122–27.
64. Mudrick, "Character and Event in Fiction," 211.
65. Bal, *Narratology*, 116.

In semiotic criticism, characters dissolve."[66] Springer similarly explains, "The 'life' of a literary character thus comes to a close when his or her part in the work is complete."[67] Martin Price suggests that the objective of a scholar should be to "recover more clearly the inevitable artifice in the conception of character. The character we admire as the result of long attention is something constructed by conventions as arbitrary as any other, and we can only hope to recover an art by recognizing it as an art."[68] Like Price, Beverly Gaventa emphasizes the relationship between art and artifice. Though she acknowledges that literary characters are "imitative of 'real' people," ultimately she concludes that they are artificial, a product or invention of the author's understanding.[69]

Describing a character as imitating a "real person," however, would support the idea that a strict purist approach might need to be mitigated by a sense of seeing a character in somewhat realistic terms. Doyle Springer explains that by their very artificiality, literary characters "bring us closer to life than life itself can do."[70] Chatman admits that while Hamlet and Macbeth are not living people, "that does not mean that as constructed imitations they are in any way limited to the words on the printed page."[71]

It seems as if the connection between literary characters and real people cannot be completely severed—Bal acknowledges that a literary character's resemblance to a human person is one of the major attractions of narrative.[72] Hochman calls for a balance between seeing them as constructs and envisioning them as real.

66. Weinsheimer, "Theory of Character," 195. As Weinsheimer analyzes Jane Austen's *Emma*, he concludes, "Emma Woodhouse is not a woman nor need be described as if it were," 187.

67. Springer, *Rhetoric of Literary Character*, 14. The "afterlife" of some biblical characters in the history of interpretation, however, challenges Doyle Springer's statement. An example can be found in the appeal of a book like Diamant's *The Red Tent*, which follows the biblical character Dinah in her life after she disappears in Genesis 34:31 (she is mentioned by name in 46:15, but her children are not; she is not included in the blessing Jacob gives his sons in Gen 49).

68. Price, "Other Self," 292–93. Wilson, who responds to Price, says that "the distinction between characters and real persons is absolute" so that we must ask different questions about characters in fiction than about people in life. "On Character," 194.

69. Gaventa, *Mary*, 21.

70. Springer, *Rhetoric of Literary Character*, 202.

71. Chatman, *Story and Discourse*, 177.

72. Bal, *Narratology*, 115.

[T]he substance of literature is dissipated if we pretend that characters have nothing to do with people . . . I believe that characters in literature have more in common with people in life than contemporary critical discourse suggests. What they have in common is the model, which we carry in our heads, of what a person is. Both characters and people are apprehended in someone's consciousness, and they are apprehended in approximately the same terms. Yet they are clearly not identical. To equate them is to overlook the peculiarities of their habitation—which for characters in literature is the world of language—and to erode the salient qualities of both characters themselves and the texts that generate them. In the pages that follow I tread a delicate line between the view that readers must apprehend a character in their own terms and the view that readers must honor the terms laid down by the text. I hope I can keep a reasonable balance as I move along that line.[73]

This study will not quite provide an equal balance between a realistic and a purist approach, but will instead weigh more heavily what the text says about Bathsheba, within the terms and confines of the text. In taking a predominantly purist approach to her character, I mean to affirm the piece of the thesis that states that Bathsheba is "presented in the text." That is, there is not some idealized composite Bathsheba who exists outside the text. Any realism that will occur will be in the way that we fill in the gaps. Harshav writes,

In a real-life situation, one assumes that, ideally, there are ways of finding evidence and ascertaining what the real state of affairs was . . . since the referents supposedly do exist "out there." In a literary text, for referents which are unique to its Internal [Field of Reference] . . . there are no such ways outside of the given text because those referents do not exist outside of it. We learn about them, however, in much the same way as we learn about any absent [fields of reference] in the real world: by means of further verbal and non-verbal evidence about them, subsuming them under known categories and models and judging the reliability of the informants. Thus in Gore Vidal's historical novel *Lincoln*, Lincoln and many characters were historical figures, they existed in External Fields of Reverence, in the real world, but their food at breakfast and their dialogues as presented in the novel are fic-

---

73. Hochman, *Character in Literature*, 7–8.

tional. Still, we can try to compare those internal [fields of reference] to what we know about the mores of breakfast of that time.[74]

We will learn about the absences surrounding Bathsheba in the same way we learn about absent fields of reference in the world, but we will also attempt to respect the internal field of reference of the text. While Bal advocates that we restrict ourselves to only those facts presented to us in the actual words of a text as we characterize, she is not naïve about the way we as readers bring ourselves and our knowledge to a text. She identifies what she calls "referential characters," saying that they "act according to the pattern that we are familiar with from other sources. Or not. In both cases, the image we receive of them is determined to a large extent by the confrontation between, on the one hand, our previous knowledge and the expectations it produces, and on the other, the realization of the character in the narrative."[75]

Bal's insight is helpful because Bathsheba could be considered a referential character: if we have seen Bathsheba through the distorted spotlights identified above, we may expect her to act accordingly. This is why we must pay careful attention to the realization of the character of Bathsheba in the narrative, the way the text itself presents Bathsheba. The overall picture of Bathsheba will emerge as someone who is complex, characterized in a generally positive manner, and develops from Samuel to Kings.

The following two chapters (chapters 2 and 3) will take a close look at Bathsheba as she is presented in the MT of Samuel and Kings. Chapter 4 will consider other early versions of the text: the LXX, Syriac Peshitta, and Aramaic Targums. Even as these translations change the text, their changes will support the aforementioned way of characterizing Bathsheba. My examination of the versions will be done more from the perspective of literary criticism than textual criticism, although the two are not unrelated, as I will discuss in more detail in chapter 4. Chapter 5 will look at Jewish interpretations of Bathsheba, specifically those found in Josephus' *Antiquities*, the Talmud, and the Midrash. These texts will provide examples of interpretive trajectories of Bathsheba's story. In some ways, they will provide resolution to the questions and gaps of the text, but even as they give their answers, they respect the complexity of

74. Harshav, *Explorations in Poetics*, 9.
75. Bal, *Narratology*, 121.

this open text. The Jewish interpretations will support the characterization of Bathsheba as complex, generally positive and developing from Samuel to Kings, but they also signal the start of some change in the view of her—a change that has its end in a characterization of Bathsheba as flattened and negative. In the concluding chapter, I will briefly review the argument of the whole, but then will highlight implications, as well as areas for further study.

This monograph will take the minor character, Bathsheba, and shine a fine light on her. My spotlight on Bathsheba will not be a fixed spot, but will move with her as she moves and changes in the text. It will neither be so bright that I see things that are not in the text, nor so dim that I cannot see things that are in the text. This spotlight will be one that shifts the focus away from the main character on the stage, David, and moves its light onto Bathsheba, who has not been looked at in this way before.

2

Bathsheba in the Masoretic Text of 2 Samuel

IN THIS CHAPTER I WILL LOOK AT BATHSHEBA IN 2 SAMUEL OF THE Tiberian Massoretic Text (hereafter abbreviated as MT). The MT developed from certain Tiberian families during the sixth to the tenth centuries CE, and therefore can be understood as a medieval representative of an ancient text.[1] Its name derives from their Massorah, or collection of notes on the text and transmission. Starting in the second century CE, the consonantal version of the MT was accepted as the authoritative text within Judaism, and still is the central text of the Hebrew Bible, often referred to as the received Hebrew text. Additionally, the MT is important because it is the only Hebrew text preserved in its entirety.

The MT of Samuel is defective, suffering from numerous instances of haplography. McCarter explains, "On the positive side, it should be noted that the MT, however riddled with holes in its present form, harks back to a legitimately short textual tradition that was generally free of the kinds of expansion displayed by some of the versions."[2] For McCarter, a text that is "free of expansion" is often preferred because it is thought to be more original than those that have explanatory expansions added.[3] However, as chapter 4 will demonstrate, none of the versions are expansive regarding Bathsheba; she will remain a minor character in LXX, the Peshitta, and the Targums. Additionally, none of the versions has many

---

1. Tov, *Textual Criticism*, 19. The earlier forms of the MT are called "proto-Massoretic."

2. McCarter, *1 Samuel*, 8–9. As I asserted in chapter 1, my interest in the different versions is not for the final result of finding an original text, but to understand the effects of their differences for Bathsheba's character.

3. Yet, McCarter does not uncritically prefer less expansive texts; he makes it clear elsewhere that he prefers the more distinctive or suitable, sensible, or elegant reading. *Textual Criticism*, 21. McCarter also eschews dogged application of such rules, as he encourages the text critic to "treat each case as if it were unique." Ibid., 24.

explanations about Bathsheba, so in every text we are required to pay close attention to the details that we are given.

While McCarter may appreciate a brief text because it appears to be more original, we can appreciate the brevity of the MT for the way it involves readers in the hermeneutical process. The typically laconic nature of Hebrew narrative[4] requires its readers to be careful and attentive to each word, and as discussed in the previous chapter, the gaps mean that the readers are drawn into the process of making meaning by filling those gaps. Additionally, the gaps in the Bathsheba story are theologically important for the lens they provide on life, and on God. Yee explains, "The ambiguity of biblical narrative, the fictive world, reflects the ambiguity of the so-called 'real' world. The readers encounter the same equivocal, ambivalent state of affairs in real life that they do in the realm of the story."[5] Brueggemann goes on to assert that the literary ambiguity often found in the text is not marginal or incidental, but instead makes up "the very stuff of the Old Testament."[6] Indeed, as we read about the choices made by David and Bathsheba, we might imagine other ways that the story could have happened, ways that it would not be so fraught with problems and pain, and we are reminded that our choices do matter. This is a cautionary story in which God judges and punishes. But the God who strikes (2 Sam 12:15) is also the God who loves (2 Sam 12:24). There is a complexity to the characters and the outcomes of the choices they make, but this narrative also reminds us of the complexity of God.

Even with (and in many cases because of) all the brevity in this narrative, we will see Bathsheba as a complex character who is presented in a largely positive manner, and develops as a character from Samuel

---

4. This has been discussed with great detail elsewhere. Auerbach contrasted the story of the Akedah with the story of Odysseus' return to home, and concluded that biblical narrative is "fraught with background" in comparison with the Homeric style that tells so much more. *Mimesis*, 1–20. Alter encourages us to remember that "Biblical narrative is laconic but by no means in a uniform or mechanical fashion." *Art of Biblical Narrative*, 20. Amit describes the stories as "minimalist" (*Reading Biblical Narratives*, 148), while Fokkelman explains that the apparent simplicity of a story "proves to be the result of a total and flexible mastery of form, and much more is going on in the text than the simple message to be read on the surface"; *Reading Biblical Narrative*, 18.

5. Yee, "'Fraught with Background,'" 252.

6. Brueggemann, *Theology of the Old Testament*, 111. He includes metaphor, hyperbole, irony, incongruity and contradiction to the list of rhetorical strategies, ultimately affirming, "We have no Old Testament text without them, for they form the way this textual community gives voice to its reality, its life, and its life with God." Ibid.

to Kings. The following chapter on the MT of Kings will say more about her development; this chapter will focus on Bathsheba's complexity and her generally positive characterization, as it can be seen in the passages within Samuel. The structure of this chapter will follow the plot outline of the text, but will concentrate on only those verses that directly deal with Bathsheba, or at least, those that affect our understanding of Bathsheba. Those verses include 2 Sam 11:1–5, 8–11, 19–21, 26–27, and 2 Sam 12:1–4, 5–6, 7–15, and 24.

2 Samuel 11:1: The Setting

From the very start of this narrative, before Bathsheba enters the picture, we are confronted with two gaps. The first is what Bodner calls a "textual ambiguity"[7] in the *Kethib/Qere*: 2 Sam 11:1 tells us that the time is "the turning of the year" (לִתְשׁוּבַת הַשָּׁנָה), when either the kings or the messengers are going forth. The MT has as the *Kethib* הַמַּלְאָכִים, "the messengers," but tells us to read הַמְּלָכִים, "the kings." The *Qere* is supported by LXX, Targ., Vulg., and multiple Hebrew manuscripts, which demonstrates how we need the different versions to help us understand the MT.[8]

This K/Q also demonstrates how what might be understood within text criticism as a simple scribal error[9] also has interesting hermeneutical implications. Bodner suggests that to read "kings" could be what textual criticism refers to as the *lectio facilior*, the smoother or easier reading.[10] But if "kings" is the *lectio facilior*, then the *Kethib*, "messengers," becomes the *lectio difficilior* or the harder reading, and one of the text-critical principles is that the more difficult reading is to be preferred.[11] Therefore,

---

7. Bodner, *David Observed*, 79.

8. Most English translations follow the *Qere*; YLT (1862/1898) is one of the only ones that reads "messengers."

9. The difference between הַמַּלְאָכִים, "the messengers," and הַמְּלָכִים, "the kings," is only one letter, the consonantal *aleph*. The addition could have to do with the fuller orthography that includes *matres lectionis*, which developed from the tenth through the sixth centuries. Cf. Gogel, *A Grammar of Epigraphic Hebrew*, 49–74, and Zevit, *Matres Lectionis in Ancient Hebrew Epigraphs*. Cross and Freedman, however, note that the use of *aleph* as a *mater lectionis* in Hebrew was always more limited than it was in Aramaic. *Studies in Ancient Yahwistic Poetry*, 29 n. 82.

10. Bodner, *David Observed*, 82.

11. Ibid., 83. Metzger explains the principle as "based on the recognition that a scribe is more likely to make a difficult construction easier, than make more difficult what was

"messengers" might also be taken seriously as an option. In fact, in the verses to follow (2 Sam 11:4, 19, 22, 23, and 25), the messengers are the ones who go forth in all the "sending" that will take place.[12]

The textual ambiguity of the *Kethib/Qere* is related to the second gap in v. 1, which can be stated as the following question: why does David send out Joab and the army, while he himself remains in Jerusalem?[13] For several reasons, we must take notice of David's location. First, the syntax signals that something is different here in this verse. In 2 Sam 11:1, the first four verbs are *wayyiqtols*,[14] but the verb in the final clause is a participle. Additionally, the rest of the verse follows typical Hebrew word order where the verb precedes the subject, but in the final clause, the subject, David, precedes the verb. The second reason to take notice of David's setting is because of semantics. If ישׁב is translated as "to sit," instead of "to remain,"[15] then the contrast in the type of action is heightened: David is *sitting* in Jerusalem, while all the others who go out ויצרו וישׁחתו, "do violence to . . . and besiege" Ammon and Rabbah. The contrast is also seen in the subjects of the verbs: all the other people (Joab, and his servants,[16] and all of Israel) go to fight against the Ammonites, and David (alone?) is "remaining in Jerusalem" (וישׁב בירושׁלם).

---

already easy." *Text of the New Testament*, 112. McCarter further describes *lectio difficilior* as the "one great rule" for evaluating readings. *Textual Criticism*, 21. But Albrektson is more cautious, pointing out that there are cases where a *lectio difficilior* may be more difficult simply because it is wrong, and that some of those difficulties themselves might arise from scribal errors that were preserved in a text. Albrektson, "Difficilior Lectio Probabilior," 5–18.

12. Polzin writes, "the chapter's subsequent emphasis on messengers as the means by which things get done is a plausible argument for the going forth of messengers in its opening verse." *David and the Deuteronomist*, 111. Fokkelmann prefers "messengers" to "kings" because "it provides the advantage of integration by establishing a temporal relationship between the action in 11.1 and 10.1–5. Simultaneously, the motif of the campaign, 11.1b–d, is kept alive for us. In this way, an individual adjunct of time follows a general one: 'And it happened with the coming (literally: return) of the new year, at the (same) time as the envoys (i.e., the diplomats, consolers) had marched out, that David sent out Joab, etc.'—which creates the implication of the revenge for the envoys' humiliation having been aptly timed." *Narrative Art*, 1:51.

13. Bodner refers to this as "motivational ambiguity." *David Observed*, 79.

14. "And it was," ויהי; "and he sent," וישׁלח; "and they ravaged," וישׁחתו; "and they besieged," ויצרו.

15. Cf. *HALOT*, 444, BDB, 442.

16. The way that we must read through the text to understand what is happening is seen even in this small clause, for at this point in the narrative, it is not entirely clear

It is possible to read this as genuinely ambiguous, where David's location in Jerusalem could be understood as either positive or negative. Moshe Garsiel points out that while a king's presence on the battlefield raises morale, it also gives the enemy an opportunity to win the battle outright by killing him (1 Kgs 22:31–36).[17] Other generals are sent out in the Bible; Sisera is sent out by King Jabin in Judges 4, and Nebuchadnezzer sends Holofernes to fight in Judith 2. There is precedence for David himself to send out generals—in the previous chapter, David also sent out Joab and the whole army against the Ammonites and Arameans (2 Sam 10:7). Only when David was informed that the Arameans had come to Helam did he come out and join the battle (2 Sam 10:17). Moreover, McCarter interprets המלכים to refer not to kings in general, but to the specific kings of Syria whom David defeated at the end of the preceding chapter (2 Sam 10:15–19),[18] and therefore it is not a time when all kings should go forth, just these Syrian kings.

But it could also be read that there is something amiss in David's location at this time. One of the criteria for kingship in Samuel is that the king provides leadership in battle (1 Sam 8:20), and David has certainly filled that role up to this point in his story. After being anointed by Samuel, David's first public act was to kill Goliath in battle (1 Sam 17). Saul's jealousy of David is connected with David's abilities to lead in battle, especially when the people recognized in song that David "killed his tens of thousands" while Saul only "killed thousands" (1 Sam 18:7). Bodner points out that the reason the people of Israel were enamored with David is that he did "go out before them" (1 Sam 18:16), and suggests that his military leadership is "vital in his rise to power."[19] Later in David's story, the text will make it a point to justify when he does *not* go forth to battle, emphasizing that he refrains from active participation when he is counseled to do so.[20] Active leadership in battle was not

---

to whom the servants belong: is it David, or Joab? In 2 Sam 11:11, Uriah will refer to Joab as "my lord," so the best sense is that these servants referred to here are Joab's own servants—his soldiers, over whom he is the commander.

17. Garsiel, "Story of David and Bathsheba," 249.

18. McCarter, *2 Samuel*, 284–85. The definite article affixed to מלכים in 2 Sam 11:1 indicates that these are specific kings, possibly המלכים to which 2 Sam 10:19 refers.

19. Bodner, *David Observed*, 84.

20. During Absalom's rebellion, David tells the people that he will go forth with them, but they persuade him to remain at home in the city (2 Sam 18:2–4). When he narrowly escapes being killed by the Philistine Ishbibenob, David's men swear to him,

only an Israelite virtue; Ashurnasirpal and Shalmaneser brag about their wartime victories, as do Pharoahs Thut-mose III, Seti I, and Rameses III, to name a few.[21]

These gaps in v. 1, though, can be filled. I prefer to follow the *Qere* and read "kings," not only because it is a *lectio facilior* and is attested to in so many other ancient versions, but also because by filling in the textual gap as "kings," the motivational gap is emphasized. That is, while kings should be going out, it is the messengers who come out; King David does *not* go out, but remains in Jerusalem.[22] Even that motivational gap can, to some extent, be filled. In Uriah's words in 2 Sam 11:11, the narrator repeats that David is "sitting/remaining in Jerusalem" when everyone else is in booths. Neither Uriah nor the narrator is so obvious as to say that it is wrong for David to do so, but the critique that was heavily veiled in 2 Sam 11:1 becomes a bit less oblique in 2 Sam 11:11. Moreover, as 2 Sam 12 ends, David does go forth to Rabbah to capture the city, and his presence there provides a resolving ending to the battle that began in 2 Sam 10.[23] Thus, as the narrative proceeds, it becomes clearer than it is at the start that something is amiss in David's decision to stay in Jerusalem.

"do not go out again with us to battle, so that you do not quench the lamp of Israel" (2 Sam 21:17). Cf. Polzin, *David and the Deuteronomist*, 110.

21. *ANET*, 234–38, 253–54, 262–63, 275–81.

22. Polzin explains, "In terms of the immediate story, the reference to kings going forth (to battle) sets up an ironic contrast between the beginning and end of the verse, that is, between what normally takes place at this time of the year on one hand, and this particular instance on the other, when 'David was remaining in Jerusalem' (v. 1). This verse signifies that David, who has been a hands-on king, now becomes a stay-at-home, one who conducts military affairs at a distance." *David and the Deuteronomist*, 109. Fox translates the K/Q as "kings" and notes, "Either meaning is attractive given the story; I lean toward 'kings' as an indictment of David's being at the palace and not with the troops." *Give Us a King!* 197.

23. The description of the Ammonites "hiring" a coalition which includes the Arameans of Zobah (2 Sam 10:6) raises the question about the connection between this campaign and David's campaign against the Arameans described in 2 Sam 8:3–8. Eissfeldt suggests that these are the same campaign (review of *The History of Israel*, 371), but Bright is not convinced. *The History of Israel*, 202 n. 38. McCarter notes how the historical nature of this account of David's war is made more complex when its place and literary function in the text are considered. *2 Samuel*, 273–76. Lawlor, however, focuses on the literary nature of 2 Sam 10–12, and demonstrates that there is a concentricity and chiastic symmetry to the text. "Theology and Art," 193–205. He describes 2 Sam 10:1–19 as the "revolt by Ammon, only partial victory by Israel," and 2 Sam 12:26–31 as "Israel's complete victory over Ammon," 205.

But even as we fill in the gaps, the text is neither heavy-handed nor obvious about this position. In fact, these ambiguities at the very beginning of the narrative let us know that we are reading a text that allows its implications to build in a subtle and nuanced way. We must wait to see what will transpire—with David, with the battle, and with Bathsheba. The style of the writing from the first verse therefore cautions us not to make conclusions too quickly but to continue to build our understanding and construct the characters throughout the process. Of course, the information about setting in v. 1 not only prepares us for the ambiguities to follow,[24] but it also becomes important for the plot of the rest of the story. Had David gone out, had he been with everyone else in Rabbah and not in Jerusalem, he never would have seen Bathsheba when and where he did.

Obviously, all this information in v. 1 primarily has to do with David's character, location, and the way that that will affect the plot. But this information is still important for understanding Bathsheba's character in two ways. First, our suspicions that David is not where he should be will mitigate any explanation that it is entirely Bathsheba's fault that he sees her. Second, as the very beginning signals us that this is a text that deals in gaps and ambiguities, we become prepared to expect gaps and ambiguities in Bathsheba's character and motivations.

2 Samuel 11:2–5: Initial Encounters between Bathsheba and David

Second Sam 11:2 gives us more information on setting with respect to David, as we read that it is "evening time" (לְעֵת הָעֶרֶב) when he got up from his bed. Here is another gap: what does it mean that David rises in the evening? Once again, there is no clear indictment of David, but this information about timing suggests a level of indolence on David's part.[25] We may also fill in this gap by reviewing other places in the text

24. Bodner writes, "After this *overture of uncertainty* in the opening verse of 2 Sam 11 . . . the reader is prepared to encounter a host of more elaborate ambiguities that will be unfolded in the ensuing incidents: whether Uriah knows or suspects what David has done, if Bathsheba is in any degree complicit in the matter, whether Joab is suspicious about events in Jerusalem, and so forth." *David Observed*, 87.

25. Certain interpreters, though, fill in this gap by understanding that David was simply taking a siesta, not sleeping in until the evening. So Garsiel, "Story of David and Bathsheba," 253. Cohen takes the idea of the siesta further, reasoning that it must have been a particularly hot day and David was unable to get up from his bed until evening

where characters rise in the evening. Many biblical characters rise in the morning or at night for a number of reasons,[26] but only four other times besides this one is the word "to arise" (קוּם) connected with a word for evening, and three of those references are negative.[27] The four lepers arise in the twilight (נֶשֶׁף) to desert to the Arameans in 2 Kings 7:5, only to find that the Arameans have already risen up in the twilight to flee (2 Kgs 7:7)—both instances of treachery and defeat. In Judg 19:9–10, the Levite rises in the evening[28] to begin his journey home—a foolish time to undertake a journey, one that ends in horrific tragedy. Therefore, based on the way that the MT uses rising in the evening, we begin to wonder about David's rising at that time.

When David does arise from his bed, he is "walking back and forth on the roof of the house of the king." Bailey observes that when the hithpael of הלך is used by David in Samuel, it is when David is having problems with the local inhabitants (1 Sam 23:13; 25:15; 30:31).[29] The verb, however, is used in positive ways closer to our pericope (2 Sam 7:6–7), so the word itself is not necessarily an indicator that something questionable must happen. Similarly, there is nothing within the MT that suggests David's location on the roof in 2 Sam 11:2 is an inherently negative place to be; for example, the pious Daniel is seen "on the roof of the house of the king" in Daniel 4:26 (ET 4:29). Still, the location proves

----

because it was too hot. Cohen goes on to explain that the heat heightened David's susceptibility to sexual temptation, writing, "a sirocco-type heat wave must have imprisoned David in his room that entire afternoon and greatly weakened his self-control." "David and Bathsheba," 144. The Bible, however, says nothing about the heat.

26. Those who rise in the morning include Abraham in Gen 22:3, Abraham's anonymous servant in Gen 24:54, Balaam in Num 22:13 and 22:21, the Levite and his concubine in Judg 19:5 (and the Levite alone in Judg 19:27), the Israelites in Judg 20:19, Ruth in Ruth 3:14, Saul and Samuel in 1 Sam 9:26, David himself in 2 Sam 24:11, the anonymous attendant of the man of God (אִישׁ הָאֱלֹהִים) in 2 Kgs 6:15, and those who have not learned that the Lord provides, in Ps 127:2. Those who rise at night include Jacob in Gen 32:23, Pharoah in Ex 12:30, Gideon in Judg 7:9, Abimelech in Judg 9:34, Samson in Judg 16:3, Samuel in 1 Sam 3, Saul and his attendants in 1 Sam 28:25, the men of valor (אִישׁ חיל) in 1 Sam 31:12, one of the prostitutes in 1 Kings 3:20, the king of Israel in 2 Kgs 7:12, King Joram of Judah in 1 Kgs 8:21, Nehemiah in Neh 2:12, the psalmist in Ps 119:62, the industrious wife in Prov 31:15, Judah's attackers in Jer 6:5, and those lamenting the destruction of Jerusalem in Lam 2:19.

27. The only positive reference to rising in the evening is when Ezra rises up at the time of the evening sacrifice in Ezra 9:5.

28. Literally, "when the day declines to the evening," רפה היום לערב.

29. Bailey, *David in Love and War*, 86.

problematic for David, for it is from "the roof of the house of the king" that David sees Bathsheba bathing.

The text makes clear that David is on the roof, but Bathsheba's location is less obvious—another potential gap. Joel Rosenberg refers to the preposition מעל in this passage as "ambiguous," explaining that it "can mean both 'atop' and 'from atop.'"[30] Unlike nouns and verbs, prepositions do not have the kind of independent meanings that could be ambiguous. Instead, ambiguity for prepositions is either structural or grammatical, "a property of the phrase or clause rather than the preposition itself."[31] But Rosenberg's larger point remains: it might be possible to understand this as a description of David's position, "he saw a woman bathing from atop the roof," or Bathsheba's position, "he saw a woman bathing atop the roof." In other words, is the preposition describing David's position, on top of his roof, or Bathsheba's position, bathing atop her roof?

A comparison with some of the Greek versions is illustrative. Instead of "he saw a woman bathing from atop the roof," the Lucianic, Armenian, Sahidic, Syro-hex-j, and Theodotian say, "and he saw from the roof a woman bathing."[32] McCarter also points out that many textual witnesses have the phrase "from atop the roof" in varying positions in their versions.[33] If the MT had placed the phrase at the beginning of the clause as the Greek versions do, it would be much clearer that it was referring to David, not Bathsheba. In that way, we can see that the MT is, indeed, more ambiguous than some of the other versions because of the syntax.

But this gap, too, can be filled. The preposition מעל is used later on in the same chapter (2 Sam 11:20, 21, 24), referring to the messenger's report that the Ammonite archers shot at the Israelites from on top of (מעל) the wall. Clearly, in that case, the "from atop" refers to the subject, the archers, and not the object, the Israelites. In other places in the text

---

30. Rosenberg, "Institutional Matrix of Treachery in 2 Samuel 11," 107.

31. Waltke and O'Connor, *Introduction to Biblical Hebrew Syntax*, 224.

32. See chapter 4 for further discussion. The NAB, NASB, NIV, TNK, KJV, and JPS all read, "from the roof he saw a woman bathing," while the NRSV reads, "he saw from the roof a woman bathing." None of these English translations, therefore, indicates that she was "on" the roof.

33. The Syriac omits the phrase completely, and McCarter believes that "represents the primitive situation," and the textual variations mean this phrase was added secondarily. McCarter, *2 Samuel*, 279.

where we see מֵעַל, the emphasis is on "from," not "atop."[34] Bathsheba has often been the subject of censure among commentators who assume she was bathing in the open, where she could be seen.[35] Yet upon closer look, we see that David and not Bathsheba is the one who was on the roof; indeed, the verse has already made it clear that David is walking on top of the roof of the house of the king.

Another way to narrow the gap about Bathsheba's position vis-à-vis David is to consider how archaeology lends insight to ancient architecture. While specific information about David's palace is scanty,[36] connections have been made between the palaces of David and Solomon and the building types known as *bit hilani* excavated at Tel Halaf (Gozan), Zinjirli (Sham'al), and Megiddo.[37] By analogy, a possible layout for

34. E.g., Gen 4:14; 6:7; 7:4; 13:11; 23:3; 25:6; 41:42; Exod 32:12; Lev 2:13; Num 16:26; 25:8, 11; Deut 9:17; 13:11; Josh 10:27; Judg 3:21; 15:14; 1 Sam 17:15, 26; 20:15; 2 Sam 10:14; 20:21, 22; 24:21, 25; 1 Kgs 20:41; 2 Kgs 10:31; 12:19; 13:23; 15:18; 17:21; 1 Chr 21:22; 2 Chr 33:8; 35:15; Isa 7:17; 25:8; 56:3; Jer 7:15; 15:1; 23:39; 32:31; 52:3; Ezek 8:6; 11:15; 13:20; 14:6; 23:18; 32:13; 45:9; Hos 9:1; Joel 4:6; Mic 2:9; Mal 1:5.

35. Calvin said, "She should have exercised discretion, so as not to be seen. For a chaste and upright woman will not show herself in such a way as to allure men, nor be like a net of the devil to 'start a fire.'" *Sermons on 2 Samuel*, 481. Cohen writes, "[Bathsheba's] house was so suffocatingly hot that she was forced to bathe outside. Had she remained indoors, David could hardly have observed her at all behind her narrow slit windows." "David and Bathsheba," 144. As mentioned previously, some medieval books of hours depict Bathsheba bathing naked in the open, with David looking on. Cf. Gunn, "Bathsheba Goes Bathing in Hollywood," 78–79, and Walker-Vadillo, *Bathsheba in Late Medieval French Manuscript Illumination*. James Tissot's painting, *David Sees Bathsheba Bathing*, portrays David sitting on one part of the roof and Bathsheba lounging naked on another part of the same roof, mere feet away from where David sits. While Tissot has seriously misread the textual information about the roof and presents Bathsheba as an exhibitionist, the way he poses David captures significant insight. Tissot's David has his forehead resting on his hand as if he is trying to avoid seeing the naked woman, which illustrates that even if she were flaunting herself (something not supported by the text), David could still try not to look.

36. 2 Sam 5:11 and 2 Chr 2:2 tell us that David's palace was built with the assistance and building materials of the Phoenicians, but the Bible does not provide any details about David's palace, nor have its remains been recovered in excavations. The Bible does give more information about Solomon's palace (1 Kings 7:1–12), built under similar influence from Hiram of Tyre, but no remains of his palace in Jerusalem have been found to this point, and very few early Phoenician remains have survived. Reich, "Palaces and Residencies in the Iron Age," 202.

37 . Galling, "Archäologischer Jahresbericht," 243; Watzinger, *Denkmäler Palästinas 1*, 95; Ussishkin, "Solomon's Palace and Megiddo 1723," 176–86, and "King Solomon's Palaces," 84–105. There is some debate about how strictly to apply the analogy; Fritz, for example, challenges the identification of Meggido building 1723 as a *bit hilani* because it

David's palace may have had an entrance with pillars leading to a large room adjacent to a large courtyard, surrounded by residential rooms. The *bit hilani* palace at Megiddo had two staircases that led to an upper story.[38] Additionally, we can hypothesize about the location of David's palace in Jerusalem by comparing the location of palaces found at other sites. Frequently in the Iron Age, palaces in the southern Levant were located on the highest point of a tel.[39] If David's palace was built on a similar high place in Jerusalem, it would have been possible for David to look down from the roof into a room of an adjacent building, and it would have been much less likely that Bathsheba needed to be out in the open for him to see her. When Absalom slept with his father's concubines on the roof, the detail that all Israel was able to see him doing so (2 Sam 16:22) suggests a height of the palace roof that is above the other buildings. Obviously, I am not intending—nor am I able—to provide an actual historical setting for David, but with some knowledge of history and culture, our assumptions about David's location are disciplined and specified. That is, although we cannot know for certain about David's location, what we do know about general archaeology and architecture helps us fill in this gap with some logical presumptions. And again, this information will help us understand Bathsheba better. With more lexical and historical perspective we understand that David was on his roof, and she was not out on her roof.

Even if it plausible that David could have seen into Bathsheba's home, at this point we do not know why Bathsheba was bathing. Was she bathing to seduce or with the hopes of being seen? This is another temporal gap, and it will be closed in v. 4 when it is explained that her bathing was done as purification. At this stage in the story, before we are told the reason for Bathsheba's bath, it is helpful to compare her with

---

included an inner courtyard, an architectural feature not present in the northern Syrian *hilani* palaces. Fritz, "Die Syrische Bauform," 55–58.

38. Ussishkin, "Solomon's Palace," 183.

39. For example, the Omride palace was on the highest rock platform in Samaria. *Harvard Excavations at Samaria,* 69. The citadel from the Late Iron Age, found in Strata V at Ramat Rahel, was located at the center of the tel. Aharoni, *Excavations at Ramat Rahel,* 1–51. Reich argues that the building found at Hazor is not a palace because it was located at the side of the mound. Reich, "Palaces and Residencies," 208. Aharoni also explains that during the entire Israelite period, the central palace at Lachish stood on an elevated platform overlooking the rest of the buildings and the city gate. *Investigations at Lachish,* 34.

other literary characters that are seen bathing. We will see some marked differences between Bathsheba's bathing scene in this narrative and the bathing done by Gilgamesh, Susannah, and Bilhah.

First, in Gilgamesh, the title character is seen by the goddess Ishtar when he is washing himself after his battle with Humbaba. After seeing him, Ishtar calls to him to be her lover, but he refuses her call.[40] Second, Susannah desires to bathe in her garden on a hot day, but is careful to ask her maids to shut the garden doors so she can bathe in privacy. When the lustful elders who were hiding in the garden attempt to seduce her, she chooses to face their lies rather than sleep with them, and is eventually vindicated with Daniel's help. Third, the book of *Jubilees* has an extended account of how Reuben saw his father's wife Bilhah when she was bathing "in a secret place" (*Jub.* 33:2). The *Testament of Reuben* within the *Testaments of the Twelve Patriarchs* explains that Reuben saw Bilhah bathing "in a covered place" (*T. Reub.* 3:11), but still suggests that her bath was intended to be private.

But the comparative lack of details in our narrative about Bathsheba lends to the complexity and the possibilities for her. Susannah, we are told, was careful only to bathe in her garden behind shut doors, but the narrator does not explain anything like that about Bathsheba. Bilhah likewise bathes in either a secret or a covered place, and we are not given any location for Bathsheba's bath. James Kugel contrasts Bilhah with Bathsheba when he explains that the words describing where Bilhah bathed "seem clearly designed to rule out the possibility that Bilhah had consciously sought to arouse Reuben's passions: unlike Bathsheba, this text seems to be saying, Bilhah had bathed in a *covered* place and thus bore no responsibility whatever for Reuben seeing her nakedness."[41]

The author of *Jubilees* goes on to clarify Bilhah's innocence by saying that Reuben tricked her (33:3), and Bilhah herself expresses her grief and shame over what Reuben had done to her (33:5–7). By contrast, we have no such explicit description of Bathsheba's innocence, which requires us to pay attention to the much more subtle ways the narrative explains her character. I do not disagree with Kugel that the texts about Bilhah make it crystal clear that she did not intend to be seen. But, while the MT of 2 Samuel simply does not say anything about Bathsheba's location, Kugel seems to have assumed that Bathsheba did bathe in an open, vis-

---

40. *Gilgamesh*, Tablet 6, columns 1–2.
41. Kugel, "Reuben's Sin with Bilhah," 533.

ible place, and therefore bears some responsibility for David having seen her. As discussed, the MT has suggested that David ought not be where he is when he is, and even if Bathsheba's bathing location is problematic, so, too, is David's location.

When we compare Bathsheba with Gilgamesh, we can see the rather obvious point that not all bathing witnessed by others is done for the purpose of seduction. On the other hand, we see that even though there are serious consequences for Gilgamesh's refusal of Ishtar, he does refuse, as Susannah refuses the elders' request to sleep with them. By contrast, our text does not have Bathsheba refusing David. Perhaps she tried, but we simply have no record of it, which leaves her situation more enigmatic than that of Bilhah, Susannah, or Gilgamesh.

If we compare Bathsheba with other scenes of seduction, though, her story reads quite differently. For example, Judith 10:3–4 tells about Judith's elaborate preparations before she encounters the general Holofernes: "She removed the sackcloth she had been wearing, took off her widow's garments, bathed her body with water, and anointed herself with precious ointment. She combed her hair, put on a tiara, and dressed herself in the festive attire that she used to wear while her husband Manasseh was living. She put sandals on her feet, and put on her anklets, bracelets, rings, earrings, and all her other jewelry. Thus she made herself very beautiful, to entice the eyes of all the men who might see her." Both Bathsheba and Judith bathe, but after that, the amount of detail explaining Judith's subsequent actions provides a stark contrast with the laconic text of 2 Sam 11:2. Judith intends "to entice the eyes" of the men who see her. Our text does not say anything about Bathsheba's intent after her bath.

Another contrast can be made between the way the text depicts Bathsheba, and some of the images of the "seductress" found in Mesopotamian iconography, described by Zainab Bahrani: "The figure is presented in a frontal position to the viewer, holding up her breasts with her hands, or holding joint hands under her chest. An alternative version of the frontal nude has one hand pointing to one breast and the other to her genitals . . . The frontal display of the body and the gestures of pointing at the explicitly portrayed genitals and breasts place the viewer's focus on these sexual attributes. The main purpose of these images appears to be the display of the sexual attributes in a way that seems to say, 'desire me.'"[42]

Although Bathsheba has been characterized as being a seductress,[43] such characterization hardly does justice to the subtlety of the text. Even though I agree with J. Cheryl Exum's point that the biblical narrator puts us into the position of voyeurs when we see Bathsheba bathing through David's eyes,[44] this says as much about the narrator and the viewers as it does about Bathsheba. The text itself does not focalize Bathsheba in a sexualized manner, but leaves such focalization to our imaginations. In fact, the text says nothing about Bathsheba's state of dress or undress. It is another gap, which we tend to fill in by assuming that she is either naked or partially clad. John Kessler writes, "There is no reason to assume that Bathsheba was naked . . . Public nudity was viewed as abhorrent and humiliating (cf. Hos 2:10). It seems unlikely that we are to envisage a naked woman in public view on the slopes of Jerusalem's eastern hill."[45]

The other piece of information we are given about Bathsheba in 2 Sam 11:2 is that she is טובת מראה מאד, "very beautiful in appearance." Though such a description is an example of direct characterization, we still must attempt to understand what it means for her character. Biblical narrative does not often give details about a character's visage, so it is worth noting that Bathsheba's beauty is mentioned. Most often, these descriptors connect with what will happen in the story; for example, Absalom's abundant hair (2 Sam 14:26) will become a trap for him (2 Sam 18:9).[46] One could argue that the same is true for Bathsheba's beauty: because she is beautiful, David will look at her, which will lead to other things. In fact, Bar-Efrat believes that Bathsheba's beauty "is mentioned solely because it plays the central role in the course of events, providing the motivation for David's . . . licentious behavior." [47] While I agree

---

42. Bahrani, *Women of Babylon*, 83.

43. Again, cf. Heller's *God Knows*, Bourdichon's Bathsheba in *The Hours of Louis XII* (which looks like Bahrani's description of the seductress with a frontal display of her breasts, and her genitals explicitly visible), the 1951 film *David and Bathsheba*, and the 1985 film *King David*.

44. Exum, *Fragmented Women*, 174–75, 194–95; Exum, *Plotted, Shot, and Painted*, 25.

45. Kessler, "Sexuality and Politics," 418. Kessler is correct to point out that Bathsheba's nakedness is an assumption. Yet, he also makes his own assumption that Bathsheba is bathing "in public view," which is another gap, discussed above.

46. Bar-Efrat, *Narrative Art*, 48–50.

47. Ibid., 49.

with Bar-Efrat's assessment that Bathsheba's beauty will be significant for the narrative, it seems unlikely that it is the (only) motivation for David's behavior. That her beauty is connected with David's gaze would be supported by Elaine Scarry, who notes that the first response to beauty is to stare.[48] Indeed, in the Old Testament, beauty is a neutral description, neither immediately positive nor negative. It is the way that people respond to beauty that differs. Amnon's response to Tamar's beauty (2 Sam 13) is to rape her, while it is Abigail's beauty—and wisdom—that is praised by David and the text (1 Sam 25:3, 33).

It is not surprising, then, that with Bathsheba, we are not given any more details than the description of her appearance; there is no indication as to whether her beauty will lead to something positive for her or not. Therefore, it is illustrative to see the places where other characters are described in ways similar to Bathsheba. The phrase מראה טובת, "beautiful of appearance," is used to describe Vashti in Esther 1:11,[49] and Vashti is another enigmatic but strong character.[50] The only other woman described by the exact phrase that describes Bathsheba is Rebekah, in Gen 24:16.[51] Rebekah is a complex biblical woman; she is also a strong character, who plots with her son Jacob to deceive Isaac (and Esau). There is, however, no explicit condemnation of Rebekah for her complicity in the deception. In fact, what Rebekah does is in line with God's earlier predestining oracle about Jacob ruling over Esau (Gen 25:23), so in a sense, Rebekah acts to fulfill God's will. Like Bathsheba, Rebekah has been seen as both positive and negative; like Bathsheba, she is a complex character.

48. Scarry, *On Beauty,* 5.

49. The young women in Artaxerxes' harem are also described as מראה טובת in Esth 2:3.

50. Fox describes Vashti as "a woman of dignity, too proud to allow herself to be put on display alongside other pieces of royal property before a bunch of bibulous males. She consequently loses her queenship. Her independence and dignity are worth respect." *Character and Ideology,* 164. So, too, Berlin: "The biblical Vashti can be interpreted as a character with an independent spirit and a desire to maintain her dignity in the face of her husband's loss of his own dignity." *Esther,* 14.

51. Sarah (Gen 12:11), Rachel (Gen 29:17), and Tamar the daughter of Absalom (2 Sam 14:27) are each described as יפת־מראה, as is Joseph (Gen 39:6). When David first appears in 1 Sam 16:12, the narrator describes David using similar terms: טוב ראי, such that there is a linguistic connection between the physical appearance of David and Bathsheba.

The gap in v. 3 is the identity of the person who answers David's inquiry about Bathsheba. It could be an anonymous source, as the JPS and NASB translations reflect: "And one said." The NRSV also leaves the subject of the report unknown, translating ויאמר ("and he said") with the passive statement "it was reported." Randall Bailey, however, argues that the referent of ויאמר is David himself, and his identification of Bathsheba is an example of inner direct speech.[52] Bodner points out that no matter who identifies Bathsheba, the information that is shared accentuates the "drama of conscience" for David.[53] For not only is Bathsheba's name revealed, but also revealed are her connections to Eliam and Uriah. If David wants to pursue Bathsheba, he must do so with the knowledge that this woman is married; she is אשת אוריה החתי, "the wife of Uriah the Hittite."

In fact, 2 Sam 11:3 is the only place in the chapter where Bathsheba is called by name. Elsewhere, she is referred to as a woman (אשה, vv. 2, 5), or, more frequently, the wife of Uriah (אשתו and אשת אוריה, vv. 11, 26). Even after Bathsheba becomes David's wife (11:27), the narrator evocatively continues to refer to her as Uriah's wife (12:15). Only after the death of the child is she described as David's wife, and only then is she again referred to by her proper name (12:24). This continual reference to her relationship with Uriah is significant for her character, as well as for the narrative as a whole. By using such terminology, the narrator reminds us that within the drama of this narrative, what is important about Bathsheba is that she was the wife of another, and when David slept with her, he knowingly committed adultery. Again, she is a minor character, and this drama is ultimately about him. It would seem that the New Testament wants to emphasize David's adultery over Bathsheba's

---

52. Bailey, *David in Love and War*, 85. He explains that there is no other subject in the verse, and there is no use of ל to indicate that David has become the indirect object of the verb. Bodner supports such an interpretation, pointing out that another reason that this could be understood as inner direct speech is semantic: the verb אמר can be translated as "to think." Bodner, *David Observed*, 94. Cf. BDB, 56, *HALOT*, 66. Also cf. 1 Sam 18:11 and 2 Kgs 20:19.

53. Bodner, *David Observed*, 97. Wesselius, who believes David to be the source of the information, points out the implications for David's ensuing action. "It seems likely that David's unusual words in 2 Sam. xi 3, 'Is not she Bathsheba, daughter of Eliam, the wife of Uriah the Hittite?' indicate some consideration on the part of David, apparently leading to the conclusion that he could do what he wanted without fear of the consequences." "Joab's Death," 347 n. 15.

personal identity as well; Matthew's genealogy does not give her a name, but refers to her as "the wife of Uriah" (Matt 1:6).

But we can glean some insight into the character of Bathsheba in the way she is identified in 2 Sam 11:3. There are a few personal names in the MT that begin with the preface בֶּן, "son of,"[54] but the only two personal names in Biblical Hebrew that begin with בַּת, "daughter of," are Bathsheba and Bathshua.[55] Martin Noth suggests Bathsheba's name is a *Wortname*, one that signifies a connection between her identity and her characterization.[56] If the patronym for her name is analyzed as שֶׁבַע, she is either "the daughter of abundance," which may point to her fertility,[57] or "the daughter of an oath," which may foreshadow her reminder to David in 1 Kings that he had sworn to her an oath.[58] First Chronicles 3:5, however, refers to her as Bathshua, "the daughter of error," (שׁוּעַ).[59] The Chronicler tends to whitewash David, far more than Samuel-Kings does.[60] Perhaps it is therefore not surprising if the Chronicler subtly

54. E.g., Ben-Ammi in Gen 19:38; Ben-Oni and Benjamin in Gen 35:18; Solomon's prefects named in 1 Kgs 4:8–13: Ben-Hur, Ben-Deker, Ben-Hesed, Ben-Abinadib, and Ben-Geber; and Ben Hadad in 1 Kgs 15, 20; 2 Kgs 13; and Jer 49:27.

55. Women in the biblical text are regularly referred to as "daughter of," but "daughter of" is absent from their personal names. E.g., Gen 11:29; 24:24; 25:20; 26:34; 28:9; 29:10; 34:1; 36:2, 3; 41:45; 46:20; Exod 2:5; 6:23; Lev 24:11; Num 25:15; 26:46; 1 Sam 14:50; 18:19; 2 Sam 3:3; 6:16; 17:25; 21:8; 1 Kgs 4:11, 15; 9:24; 11:1; 15:2; 16:31; 22:42; 2 Kgs 8:26; 11:2; 15:33; 18:2; 21:19; 22:1; 23:31, 36; 24:8, 18; 1 Chr 1:50; 2:21; 3:2, 5; 4:18; 15:29; 2 Chr 11:18, 20f; 13:2; 20:31; 21:6; 22:2, 11; 27:1; 29:1; Neh 6:18; Esth 9:29; Jer 52:1; Hos 1:3. In the Aramaic Palmyrene Inscriptions, though, feminine names formed with בַּת as their first element are well attested. Cf. Stark, *Personal Names in Palmyrene Inscriptions*, 80.

56. "Nun für den Namen בַּת־שֶׁבַע sheint mir seine Deutung: Die Üppige, Vollkommene annehmbar zu sein. Der Name hat dann also profane Bedeutung und kann als Wortname sehr wohl von den oben behandelten Satznamen trotz der äußerlichen Ähnlichkeit getrennt werden." Noth, *Die Israelitischen Personnamen*, 147 n. 2.

57. Bathsheba does get pregnant right away, and Noth equates בַּת־שֶׁבַע with the physical characteristic "üppig." *Die Israelitischen Personnamen*, 226.

58. Bodner, "Nathan," 52.

59. Harvey, "Bathsheba," 1:366.

60. Japhet notes Pseudo-Rashi's comment on 1 Chr 10:1: "And when he recounts the story of David, he does not mention anything demeaning: he only speaks of David's heroism and greatness, for the book is really in honour of David and the kings of Judah." *Ideology*, 469 n. 64. Klein explains that in Chronicles, David is presented in an idealized fashion, with a greater emphasis on his public actions than on his private life. For example, the Chronicler omits David's struggles with Saul, his adultery with Bathsheba, the murder of Uriah, and Absalom's revolt, and nothing is said of

denigrated Bathsheba by changing her name to Bathshua. Then again, Noth believes שׁוּע to be synonymous with עֲזֻר, "help, assistance,"[61] in which case she would be "daughter of help," although he does not specify if that would mean that she is someone in need of help, or someone who gives help. Clearly, even in her name there are different possibilities for understanding Bathsheba's character.

Bathsheba's identification as "the daughter of Eliam," also gives us insight into her character. David Clines observes that the name formula "X *ben* Y" may be used for reasons of narrative form: to introduce a new character into a narrative; or when a speaker mentions a character for a first time; or for contextual significance, when the relationship of X to Y is meaningful in the context; or where the name Y has some significance for the narrative.[62] These reasons are helpful for understanding Bathsheba's name formula in v. 3. It is the first time she is introduced (although not the first appearance in the text; she was seen bathing when she was yet unnamed), and it is the first time her name is spoken. The relationship between Bathsheba (X) and Eliam (Y) is meaningful in the context on two levels: first, since a woman who had no relational connections to others was likely to be relatively powerless and unprotected,[63] by making it clear that Bathsheba was not only someone's wife, but also someone's daughter, the writer signals that she was known and cared for. Second, the identity of Eliam has significance for the narrative, as

---

David's weakness in his final days. "It is an overstatement, however, to say that David is presented as perfect. His sins are noted in 1 Chr 15:13 (improper care for the ark) and in 21:1, 3, 8 (the census), and he was barred from building the temple because he was a shedder of blood (22:8) and a man of war (28:3)." *1 Chronicles*, 44. Petersen also explains, "It would be wrong to suggest that the Chronicler's portrait is a simple or one-sided view. We are rather given a different canonical slant." "Portraits of David," 141. The name *Bathshua* also appears in 1 Chr 2:3, where she is identified as Judah's first wife. Japhet notes how the Chronicler also includes Tamar in the list of David's children (1 Chr 3:9), whereas she is not present in the corresponding genealogy of 2 Sam 3:2–5. She identifies "a general inclination to parallelism between David's household and that of Judah." *1 Chronicles*, 96. Japhet also writes, "it may be that the references to these woman in David's life purposely echo the references to Judah's wives (and daughter in law) in 1 Chronicles 2." *1 Chronicles*, 348 n. 286.

61. Noth, *Die Israelitischen Personnamen*, 154. *HALOT* translates שׁוּע as "cry for help," 1444.

62. Clines, "X, X *ben* Y, *ben* Y," 266–67.

63. The orphan and widow are often mentioned in tandem, along with the encouragement to care for them. Cf. Exod 22:22; Deut 10:18; 24:17, 19ff.; 27:19; Ps 94:6; 146:9; Isa 1:17, 23; Jer 7:6; 22:3; Ezek 22:7; Zech 7:10; Mal 3:5.

he is one of David's thirty elite bodyguards mentioned in 2 Sam 23:34. Bathsheba's father Eliam is further identified as the son of Ahithophel the Gilonite, one of David's key advisors, who will play a significant role in Absalom's revolt against David (2 Sam 15:12ff.). Bathsheba, therefore, is not an unknown, unimportant woman, but belongs to a powerful family. David does not commit adultery with an unknown, unimportant woman. Obviously, David's act of adultery is committed with someone's wife, but the narrator reminds us that she is also someone's daughter.

Bathsheba's husband, Uriah the Hittite, is identified as another one of David's fighting men in 2 Sam 23:39—one who serves the king along with Eliam and Ahithophel. In this text his ethnic identity is also revealed; Uriah is not an Israelite, but a Hittite.[64] There is speculation about whether this detail means that Bathsheba herself is of Hittite descent,[65] but the text does not identify Bathsheba as a foreigner, nor does it refer to her father Eliam or her grandfather Ahithophel as Hittites. There is nothing about Bathsheba's marriage to a Hittite that ought to be seen as negative for her character.[66] Moreover, Uriah's name has a good

64. Uriah's ethnic identity as a Hittite is not always emphasized in Samuel. He is referred to as Uriah *the Hittite* in 2 Sam 11:3, 6, 17, 21, 24; 12:9, 10; 23:39, but sixteen times he is named without being identified as the Hittite. In the texts of 1 Kgs 15:5 and 1 Chr 11:41, he is "Uriah the Hittite," with his name and ethnicity included. Kim discusses how, despite Uriah's faithfulness to torah, he remained an outsider because of his ethnic identity as a Hittite. Bathsheba, by contrast, is an insider, an Israelite who will be the "right" wife of David and mother of Solomon. "Uriah the Hittite," 78. Because Uriah is not an Israelite, some assume that he is nothing better than a mercenary soldier or a hired gun. But Wesselius refers to Deut 10:18 and Ps 146:9 to point out that as a resident foreigner, a גר, Uriah should have been protected. "Joab's Death and the Central Theme," 344.

65. Luther refers to Bathsheba, as well as the three other women mentioned in Jesus' Matthean genealogy, when he discusses the inclusion of the Gentiles into the chosen of Israel. *Luther's Works: Lectures on Genesis, Chapters 38–44*, 14. Johnson writes, "it is highly probable that, at the time of the composition of Matthew, each of the four [women], in Jewish tradition, was considered to be of Gentile stock ... indirect reference to the 'wife of Uriah' in Matt. 1:6 probably serves as a reminder that Bathsheba's husband was a Hittite, hence that she herself was not a full Israelite from the later Rabbinic point of view." *Biblical Genealogies*, 153. Wyatt also thinks Bathsheba is a Hittite, but argues for that because of Ezek 16:3, 45, where God addresses Jerusalem, saying, "your father was an Amorite and your mother a Hittite." Wyatt writes, "it is quite likely that Ezekiel looks upon Bathsheba as 'Hittite' by virtue of her marriage to Uriah, if not in her own right, as the personification of the city, with perhaps more than a hint at her adultery." "'Araunah the Jebusite,'" 42. However, the identification of David as an Amorite is strained, and thus it is not convincing that Ezekiel's phrase provides any evidence that Bathsheba was considered a Hittite.

66. Hittites are both positive and negative characters in the text, but the problem seems largely to be with Israelite men who marry Hittite women. For example, Ephron

theophoric Yahwistic element, and his actions will stand in stark contrast with David: David the Israelite is the one who breaks the laws, while Uriah the Hittite is the one who follows them.

After Bathsheba has been given a name and a context, David sends messengers to take her in 2 Sam 11:4. If the story about Bathsheba is gapped, this verse is especially so. Its brevity has been well noted by others, notably Sternberg. He explains that the rapid sequence of verbs to describe the external actions ("he sent, he took, she came, he lay, and she returned") gives rise to what he calls a "clash between matter and manner in the discourse."[67] There is no information given at all about the motives and emotions of the characters involved. Much happens, but much is left unsaid. We are not told if this is a romantic encounter. No speech is recorded. We do not know how much time all of the action took, or even how much time transpired between the individual events. These are major gaps, especially about Bathsheba's motivations or feelings. Moreover, these are not merely temporal gaps that will be filled in at the end of the narrative. We simply do not know these certain things about her.

But even as 2 Sam 11:4 remains riddled with gaps like a minefield, there is some safe ground for Bathsheba's characterization. The verbs associated with her actions tell us a bit about her—even as the reasons for her actions remain unsaid. Because there are third person feminine singular verbs in this verse, she is not wholly passive. She came to him (וַתָּבוֹא אֵלָיו), and she returned to her house (וַתָּשָׁב אֶל־בֵּיתָהּ). While these actions by themselves are inconclusive as to what kind of a woman Bathsheba is, they do tell us that she is the subject of some verbs and hence not only the object who is acted upon. In fact, in 2 Sam 11:4, the role of the subject alternates between David and Bathsheba, and if the clause about Bathsheba's purification is included, Bathsheba is the

---

the Hittite is the one from whom Abraham buys the cave in which to bury Sarah (Gen 23 and 25). The wives of Esau are described as "a source of bitterness" to Isaac and Rebekah (Gen 26:34–35; 27:46). Hittites are among the nations that fall under the חֵרֶם in Deut 20:16–18, but Judg 3:5–6 explains the Israelite failure to completely destroy them and adds that the Israelites intermarried with them. Ahimelech the Hittite is a companion of David whom David trusts enough to ask him if he will accompany him into Saul's cave (1 Sam 26:6). In Ezra 9, the Hittites are included in the list of the foreign wives that are sent away, but there is not any mention of Hittite husbands.

67. Sternberg, *Poetics*, 197.

subject as often as David. She is, however, objectified—messengers took her—while David is not the object of any verb at all in this verse.

It would be more logical to locate the clause about Bathsheba's purification (והיא מתקדשת מטמאתה, "and she was purifying herself from her uncleanness") in v. 2 as an explanation for Bathsheba's bathing than in 2 Sam 11:4 where it interrupts, in a number of ways, the rest of the information given. It is a linguistic interruption, as it includes a participle in the midst of *waw*-consecutive third person verbs; it is a syntactical interruption, as it begins with the emphatic personal pronoun היא; and it is a chronological interruption, for it happened before the encounter in 2 Sam 11:4.[68]

But the clause also lends some insight into her character. When the verb "to purify" (קדש) is used elsewhere in the hithpael form in the biblical text, it has positive connotations of consecration through purification.[69] The verb קדש is a *hapax legomena* in this form; only in this passage does it occur in the feminine singular hithpael participle. In fact, Lev 15:19–24 commands such ritual bathing after a woman's menstrual cycle. Thus, this information contributes to Bathsheba's generally positive characterization.

Of course, it also increases the intrigue in the plot, for if Bathsheba was purifying herself after her menstrual cycle when David saw her bathing, there can be no doubt that David is the father of the child. Elna Solvang suggests that by delaying the information about Bathsheba's purification until after the sexual encounter has been described, the author demonstrates that adultery is the primary issue in this text, and David's fathering the child because of the timing is only secondary.[70]

The other verbs also give us some insight into both David and Bathsheba. First, David sends messengers. Bal draws on Algirdas Julien Greimas when she distinguishes between actors in a narrative as "power" and "receiver." Greimas uses the French terms *destinateur* and *destinataire*—literally, "sender and receiver."[71] This terminology is illuminating in light of the repeated use of the verb שלח, "to send." David often has

---

68. Driver explains that to express anything subsequent to the clause "he lay with her," a finite verb and not a participle would have been used. *Notes on the Hebrew Text*, 223.

69. Cf. Exod 19:22; Num 11:18; Josh 3:5, 7:13; 1 Sam 16:5; 1 Chr 15:12, 14; 2 Chr 5:11; 29:5, 15, 34; 30:3, 15, 17, 24; 31:18; 35:6; Isa 66:17.

70. Solvang, *A Woman's Place*, 178.

71. Bal, *Narratology*, 198.

the position of power, as he sends a number of times in the narrative (cf. 2 Sam 11:1, 3, 4, 6, 14, 27).[72] But although David sends messengers for Bathsheba, they do not take her; with the third person masculine singular verb, it is clear that David takes her. It is hardly uncommon for the Hebrew to use the verb לקח, "to take," where wives are the object. But, the combination of the verbs "to send" and "to take" where one man acquires another's wife is limited to four texts in the Old Testament: Gen 20, 1 Sam 25, 2 Sam 3, and 2 Sam 11. Bathsheba is the third woman to be "sent for" and "taken" by David, after Abigail and Michal. Rudman concludes that on each of these three occasions when David acquires a wife, he is portrayed more negatively than the last, and his claim to each woman "becomes increasingly doubtful."[73]

As was mentioned previously, Bathsheba was not only taken, but she also "came to him."[74] The verb בוא is exceedingly common, but this detail informs the reader that she is not wholly passive in this encounter. Even though it may be debated how much choice Bathsheba had to refuse, especially when she was "taken," she still has some volition. David is

72. As discussed in chapter 1, though, Bathsheba also has power in the narrative, which is seen among other ways in her "sending" to David in v. 5. For that matter, this narrative does not neatly fit Greimas' actantial model because there is some shifting in terms of who sends and who receives. For Greimas, the actants of a narration fell into one of six roles: a *sender* transfers an *object* to a *receiver* by agency of a *subject* who is helped or opposed by a *helper* or *opposer*. *Sémiotique* [3].

73. Rudman writes that in 1 Sam 25, "with Abigail's husband dead, there is nothing wrong with the marriage *per se* . . . In the next example (II Sam iii), one may feel that David is justified in reclaiming the wife taken from him by Saul. . . . When David's calculating attitude is set alongside the behavior of Paltiel, the reader senses that though David may be legally in the right, his actions are morally ambiguous. In II Samuel xi, the benefit of any doubt the reader may have hitherto given David is dispelled when he takes Uriah's wife Bathsheba, and has his servant killed." "Patriarchal Narratives in the Books of Samuel," 245.

74. Regarding Esth 2:12, when the time comes for the women in the harem "to go to the king" (לבוא אל־המלך), Berlin writes that "this expression has sexual overtones. Compare 2 Sam 11:4; Ruth 4:13." *Esther*, 27. Mazor similarly argues, "When she is brought to the king, the text says, 'And she came in unto him' (11,4) as if she took an active part in the illicit affair. The verb used here [Y.B.A.] has a connotation of sexual intercourse, as in Genesis 16,4: 'And he [Abraham] came unto Hagar and she conceived.' Bathsheba is thus presented as a loose woman unfaithful to her husband." "Cherchez la femme," 47. But even though both Berlin and Mazor reference specifically the text about Bathsheba, it is hard to sustain such semantics for the context of our text. The word בוא is used so often that only in particular contexts could the sexual overtones be clear, and with all the gaps of our text, it is not clear that Bathsheba's action is an obviously sexual one.

the recipient in this clause, not the object. Then, the text explains that he lay with her, which is another common verb, and here she is the object.[75] In chapter 4, I will show how, according to the LXX, Bathsheba is far more objectified, most notably in the sexual interaction. If, as the LXX tells it, the only thing Bathsheba did as the subject of verbs was to return to her home, then she becomes an unwilling victim of David's advances. The MT keeps the reader uncertain about Bathsheba's role and position in their interaction (why did she come to him?), and makes us wait to understand her character until 2 Sam 12. Then, when we read about the punishments meted out, we understand that it was David who abused power, and not Bathsheba who is to blame.

A comparison with the Genesis Apocryphon is helpful in considering the verbs connected with both David and Bathsheba. Column 20 recounts in detail when the Pharaoh takes Sarai from Abram (cf. Gen 12:10–20). We are told that after the Pharaoh heard about Sarai's beauty, his feelings for her were aroused,[76] and "he sent" (וישלח), "had her brought" (דרבהא), and "took her to himself as a wife" (ונסבהא לה לאנתא).[77] Like David, then, the Pharaoh sent and took. Unlike Bathsheba, who *came* to David, Sarai is *brought* to the Pharaoh. Twice in the Genesis Apocryphon, Abram explains that Sarai was taken from him forcefully,[78] but no explicit words about power or force are used in the MT. Lot advises the Pharaoh to send (שלח) Sarai back to Abram, and another advisor urges, "Let them return Sarai to Abram" (יתיבון נה לשרי לאברם).[79] By contrast, the last clause of 2 Sam 11:4 explains that Bathsheba returned to her house.[80] We presume that she returned of her own volition, unlike Sarai.

---

75. Women do lie with men in the Old Testament: in Gen 19, the daughters of Lot lie with him, and Ruth lies down at Boaz' "feet" in Ruth 3:7. So, the fact that it specifies that David lie with her suggests that he is the initiator in their sexual encounter.

76. The Aramaic is, literally, "he loved her," רחמה, but Fitzmeyer translates it as "he coveted her," explaining that it has the nuance of desire. *The Genesis Apocryphon of Qumran Cave 1*, 127.

77. Column 20, lines 8–9.

78. In line 11, Abram says, "Sarai was taken from me by force" (מני שרי באונס דבירת), and in line 14, "she has been taken from me in strength" (אנתתי מני בתוקף דברת).

79. Column 20, lines 23 and 25.

80. There are few places in the Old Testament where a house is referred to with a third person feminine possessive pronoun, so Bathsheba is in select company. Other women who have a "house" include Potiphar's wife (Gen 39:14), the women of Exod

There are fewer gaps in 2 Sam 11:5 than in the previous verse, which has Bathsheba as the subject of all four verbs in the verse: וַתַּהַר, "and she conceived," וַתִּשְׁלַח, "and she sent," וַתַּגֵּד, "and she declared," and וַתֹּאמֶר, "and she said." However, despite what these verbs tell us about her, we are still not privy to Bathsheba's motivations. The first verb הרר, "to conceive," lets us know that Bathsheba is not barren, but conceives readily.[81] Jeremy Schipper points out how there is evidence in biblical, ancient Near Eastern, and rabbinic material "that infertility was viewed as a disability or illness in antiquity."[82] Bathsheba's fertility, then, is part of her generally positive characterization, as it affirms there is nothing wrong with her. Of course, her conception also drives the plot, as it makes David's act of sleeping with her more obvious, with greater consequences.

The second verb שׁלח, "to send" has already been identified as a powerful word, connected with authority. Not only does David "send" a number of times in 2 Sam 11, but Joab does as well, and God will also "send" Nathan in 2 Sam 12. Therefore, Bathsheba's sending illustrates that she is not without power or authority in this story.[83] Lillian Klein sees a connection between power and procreation in the sequence of verbs: first Bathsheba conceived, and that conception gave her the power to send.[84]

3:22, Rahab (Josh 2:15), Pharaoh's daughter/Solomon's wife (1 Kgs 9:24), the anonymous woman in 2 Kgs 8:3, 8:5, and both the wise and foolish woman in Proverbs. Later, though, that location will be referred to as Uriah's house (2 Sam 11:8–11, 13), so it would appear that the main reason the home is referred to as Bathsheba's is for purposes of contrast. The palace was where she was *taken*, her own home is where she *returns*.

81. Several biblical women must pray—or be prayed for—because they are barren, including Sarah, Rebekah, Rachel, and Hannah. Bathsheba is like Eve, Hagar, Lot's daughters, Leah, Judah's wife, Tamar, Moses' mother, Isaiah's prophetess wife, and Gomer, who conceive without any mention of barrenness. Klein wonders if Uriah is sterile, because there is no mention of Bathsheba's other children. "Bathsheba Revealed," 52.

82. Schipper, *Disability Studies*, 93–95.

83. Brueggemann refers to שׁלח as a "sovereign verb." Brueggemann, *David's Truth*, 57. Other biblical women who "send" are strong characters, including Rebekah (Gen 27:42), Pharaoh's daughter (Exod 2:5), Deborah (Judg 4:6), Delilah (Judg 16:18), Jezebel (1 Kgs 19:2; 21:8), Esther (Esth 4:4), and Oholibah (Ezek 23:16). Bailey specifically connects Bathsheba with Rahab, Deborah, and Delilah, as he contends that this verb indicates use of authority. Bailey, *David in Love and War*, 86. Again, we can contrast Bathsheba here with Sarai in the Genesis Apocryphon. The latter never "sent," but instead was sent and sent for by Pharaoh.

84. Lillian Klein believes that Bathsheba's ability to "send" shows her power, but that power came from her pregnancy. "This sequence suggests that conception gives woman

The third and fourth verbs are related, and at first glance may seem somewhat redundant. Yet, the verb נָגַד, "to declare, to tell," is used for indirect discourse, and only when it is combined with אָמַר, "to say," is there a direct quotation. The two verbs used together underscore that Bathsheba does not keep the information about her pregnancy to herself. She does not ask David what he is going to do, nor does she ask him for help, but she does share the information with him. Additionally, it is important that Bathsheba does speak in direct discourse, for it shows us that she has a voice in this narrative.[85] Speech is an important aspect of defining a character, even though it is under the category of indirect characterization, as it can give a great deal of insight into the character.[86] And for all characters, their voice is part of their characterization. What Bathsheba says is simple, only taking two words in the Hebrew to convey: הָרָה אָנֹכִי, "I am pregnant." The very directness of what Bathsheba says tells us that she is unwilling to keep silent about her pregnancy. But still the gap remains as to why she breaks the silence. We have no record of anything else she said; perhaps it was not necessary to convey any other information to David, or perhaps more words passed between them than the ones recorded. The brevity of Bathsheba's speech is part of her complexity.

---

power, perhaps power beyond that of a male." "Bathsheba Revealed," 51. Cf. Foucault, *History of Sexuality.*

85. Certain translations do not reflect both verbs in the Hebrew, and make Bathsheba's direct quotation into reported speech. For example, the BBE reads, "and she sent word to David that she was with child"; the REB says, "she sent word to David that she was pregnant"; and the NLT translates the verse as, "Later, when Bathsheba discovered that she was pregnant, she sent a message to inform David." Hammond believes that the switch from direct to reported speech effectively silences Bathsheba and removes some of the clues the narratives give us as to her character. "Michal, Tamar, Abigail and What Bathsheba Said," Gilligan's psychological work points to the importance of "voice" for a woman's development. *In a Different Voice.*

86. Springer explains, "we have only to think about how much a character suggests himself by what he says, and how much light comes even from between the lines of what he says . . . There are several kinds of partial light on character that speech, especially in dialogue, can cast. It can argue a case so that we can see where the character's choices are tending, it can produce an emotional penumbra in which we make some part of our decision for or against him as a character, and it can indicate the relative importance of things . . ." *A Rhetoric of Literary Character,* 27–28. Bal also explains that speech gives insight into the character especially when it is direct discourse, and not mediated through the narrator. *Narratology,* 45–51.

2 Samuel 11:8–11: David's First Attempt at a Cover-Up

After Bathsheba sends her message to David, she recedes into the background, and the characters of David, Joab, and Uriah move to the center of the stage. But although she is not physically present, we still continue to build her character, especially as the others discuss her. Second Samuel 11:8–11 is where David makes his first, unsuccessful attempt at a cover-up. Pinsky writes,

> Contrary to the notion of David passionately in love with Bathsheba, so caught up in his passion that he does evil, the king's interview with Uriah . . . suggests that David wants an alibi more than he wants Bathsheba: if Uriah violates his soldierly vow of celibacy in time of battle, if he sleeps with his wife Bathsheba as the king practically urges him to do, then David will be relieved of responsibility for the pregnancy. This is not Paolo swept up in the hurricane of his sinful love for Francesca of Rimini; David satisfies his desire and then calculates ways to avoid the unlooked-for consequences.[87]

David's interaction with Uriah will provide some interesting information about Bathsheba, even as other gaps are opened. The gap in 2 Sam 11:8 has to do with what David means when he commands Uriah to go to his house and wash his feet, for we can read it in one of two ways: either straightforwardly, or with a wink and a nod. First, to wash one's feet is a common custom after a long journey before entering a house for the night. Most people went either barefoot or in sandals, and several other Old Testament narratives record people washing their feet after their journey.[88] But the second way we could read this command is on a euphemistic level, with the word רגליו, "feet," as a euphemism for genitals,[89] so that although David does not explicitly command, "Go home and sleep with your wife," it was what he meant. This openness is not missed by the different interpreters of this text. Nicol explains, "Behind the surface meaning that he should go home and wash his feet, there is another *barely hidden* meaning that his 'feet' (sexual organ) should be 'washed' by the act of sexual intercourse."[90] By contrast, Garsiel

---

87. Pinsky, *Life of David*, 104–5.

88. E.g., Gen 18:4; 19:2; 24:32; 43:24; Judg 19:21.

89. Cf. Exod 4:25; Isa 6:2; 7:20; Ruth 3:4, 8, 14. The verb רחץ also recalls Bathsheba's washing in v. 2, which was followed by David's sleeping with her.

90. Nicol, "David, Abigail and Bathsheba, Nabal and Uriah," 138 n. 28.

explains that the phrase "cannot be a euphemism for sexual intercourse, as David cannot bring suspicion on himself by a direct order, although it is what he is hoping for."[91] As readers we are already prepared to read the command in the second way because we know what has taken place. Later, Uriah reveals that he, too, understood David's underlying meaning.

Second Samuel 11:8 ends with the description of a "gift from the king" (מַשְׂאַת הַמֶּלֶךְ) that follows Uriah as he leaves. This phrase is also found in Gen 43:34, and based on that parallel, Driver suggests that it is probably a gift from the king's table.[92] Jonas Greenfield believes that the gift was a covenant meal of the sort that would seal a pact.[93] If that is true, then David would have assumed that Uriah would go and sleep with Bathsheba, although the text does not specify any agreement on their part.

But Uriah does not go down to his house, but goes down and sleeps at the "door of the house of the king." The repeated use of the verb יָרַד and the location בֵּיתְךָ/בֵּיתוֹ highlights Uriah's disobedience to David's command—he was commanded to go down, and he went down, but not to his house. Although Uriah and Bathsheba do share some of the same verbs and actions, as mentioned above, here we see an important difference: they both obeyed the king in coming to him (2 Sam 11:4, 7), but Uriah does not obey the king's command. This is another piece of the puzzle in Bathsheba's complexity. The contrast may be mustered as evidence that Bathsheba was complicit in the adultery, for she did not disobey David. Then again, her status as a woman might account for why Uriah as a man, and a member of David's elite troop, could disobey the king, but she could not. The MT here does not give any answers, but preserves the gap, so we must continue to wait to build Bathsheba's character.

When David hears that Uriah did not go down to his house, David questions Uriah why. In response to David's questions, Uriah says, "Are not the Ark, and Israel, and Judah remaining in Succoth, and my lord Joab, and the servants of my lord on the face of the field camping? And I, I will go down to my house to eat and to drink, and to lay with my wife? As you live, and as your soul lives, I will not do this thing."

91. Garsiel, "Story of David and Bathsheba," 257.
92. Driver, *Notes*, 223.
93. "An Ancient Treaty Ritual," 396.

Several things about Uriah's response help us fill in some gaps. As discussed earlier, Uriah's words may include an implicit critique of David, affirming that David was not where he should have been at the beginning of this narrative. With the close association between David and the Ark, David and Israel, and David and Judah, it is strange that David was יושב, "remaining" (2 Sam 11:1), at Jerusalem while the other three were ישבים, "remaining" (2 Sam 11:10), at Succoth. However, it may not be that Uriah *himself* is criticizing David, but rather that the critique arises from the writer's choice of Uriah's words. The language play throughout this narrative does not always mean that a particular character knows what happened earlier, but instead that the author is encouraging the readers to be aware of the specific language used. Second, this is where Uriah makes explicit what may have been merely suggestive in David's command from v. 8. David commanded him to wash his feet, but Uriah understood that as a command to sleep with Bathsheba, לשכב עמ־אשתי, "to lay with my wife." Third, the language that Uriah uses is important, as he uses the same phrase that the MT used in v. 4, describing David's adultery וישכב עמה, "he lay with her." But the difference between v. 4 and v. 11 is the identity of the woman. Whereas v. 4 merely reported, "he lay with her," v. 11 specifies the identity of the woman, "my wife" אשתי, underscoring that David lay with another man's wife. Fourth, Uriah's oath that he will not do "this thing," highlights a contrast between David and Uriah.[94] Uriah refuses to act for his own enjoyment when his comrades were out fighting in battle. Of course, this frustrates David's plans, and continues to increase the intrigue in the plot. But it also shows that Uriah the Hittite is an upright and righteous man, while it is becoming increasingly difficult to characterize David using similarly positive terms.

Even as the text reveals details about the characters of Uriah and David, who are the main characters at this point in the story, there are still

---

94. It is typical of an oath formula to begin with "by the life of PN," and the fact that Uriah is making an oath signals that his words carry force and determination. What is unusual is the form of the oath, "by your life and the life of your soul." In the rest of Samuel, oaths are made "by the life of YHWH" (cf. 1 Sam 20:3; 25:26; etc.), and on the basis of this, Driver suggests that the text should be emended to more closely resemble the other oaths in Samuel, or at least "omit וחי נפשך as an explanatory gloss on the uncommon חיך." Driver, *Notes*, 223. Perhaps, though, the unusual form is significant, and by repetition, serves to highlight and emphasize David's life. Because Uriah will not do this thing, his own life will be cut off.

implications for the character of Bathsheba. We see Uriah in a positive light—he is a moral man, and he also understands David's "command" to him (2 Sam 11:8, 11), which raises his esteem in our eyes as readers. He is not just a dupe. This challenges the interpretive traditions that suggest Uriah is somehow morally deficient, and Bathsheba is better off without him.[95] These verses also are important for Bathsheba's character in that they highlight how Uriah chose not to sleep with her, while David chose adultery.[96] In other words, Bathsheba is not so sexual that men cannot refuse her. Then again, I do not believe that there are any circumstances in which men are rendered helpless in the face of female sexuality; even if Bathsheba were explicitly seducing David (an idea not supported by the text), it would still be his choice.

2 Samuel 11:19–21: Joab Connects Death to a Woman

Another male character who lends some insight into Bathsheba's character is Joab. He is present throughout 2 Sam 11: in v. 1, Joab went out to battle while David remained in Jerusalem; in v. 6, he is the intermediary between David and Uriah; and in v. 11, Uriah identifies Joab as his lord. It is in vv. 14–21, though, that Joab takes the stage as a main character. Several scholars point to vv. 14 and 15 as the pivotal point of the chapter,[97] when David sends a letter to Joab by the hand of Uriah, carrying Uriah's death warrant. The content of the letter is chilling. David does not simply command Uriah's death, which would have been bad enough, but commands Joab to have the troops withdraw from Uriah, so that he will die alone. Joab, however, does not completely obey David's reprehensible command. Instead of withdrawing from Uriah at the front, he places

95. The most notable expression of this is found in the 1985 movie *King David*—directed by Bruce Beresford and starring Richard Gere in the title role—which portrays Uriah as an abusive husband. Herbert Rand characterizes Uriah as "intensely loyal to David and to his comrades-in-arms, he put duty first and was insensitive to the needs of his wife, who had to cope with the life of an army wife with an absentee husband." "David and Ahab," 91. Rand's characterization is interesting: while positively describing Uriah's loyalty as a soldier, he assumes that this means Uriah did not make a good husband.

96. That still tells us more about Uriah and David than it does about Bathsheba, but it does have implications for her character. Solvang asks, "How is it that [Bathsheba's] beauty leads David to commit adultery but does not draw her own husband home?" *A Woman's Place*, 133.

97. Bal, *Lethal Love*, 23; Fischer, "David und Batseba," 51. By their very location, these verses are the center of the chapter.

Uriah among the men of valor (אנשי־חיל),[98] and others die along with Uriah (2 Sam 11:17, 24).

What is of special interest for Bathsheba's character is the conversation between Joab and the messenger who is to report the news of Uriah's death to David.

> [Joab] commanded the messenger, saying, "As you finish telling all the things of the battle to the king, it will be that the anger of the king rises up, and he will say to you, 'Why did you draw near to the city to attack? Did not you know that they would shoot from upon the wall? Who struck Abimelech, son of Jerubbesheth? Wasn't it a woman who dropped a millstone upon him from upon the wall, and he died in Thebez? Why did you draw near to the wall?' And you will say, 'Also your servant Uriah the Hittite died.'" 2 Sam 11:19–21

But even as this conversation lends insight into Bathsheba, another gap is opened as to what extent Bathsheba should be connected with Uriah's death. For in Joab's imagined conversation with David, there are several strange things,[99] but the reference to Abimelech (cf. Judg 9:50–55) is especially so. Joab does not openly compare Uriah and Abimelech because a direct comparison would fall flat. Uriah is innocent, whereas Abimelech is a usurper who gets his "just deserts." Abimelech chooses a stupid position, whereas Uriah is betrayed. Abimelech is killed *by* an anonymous woman, whereas Uriah is murdered *for* Bathsheba, his wife. And yet, the connection to Abimelech is not completely random. First, it illustrates why Joab's strategy was so bad. Yigael Yadin explains that Abimelech's end served for a long time as a classic warning to the armies of Israel to take careful heed when approaching the fortifications of a city.[100] Second, figuratively, Joab's recollection of Abimelech's death at the hand of a woman implies things for the knowing reader.

98. It is not entirely clear who these men of valor are. If they are Ammonite soldiers, Joab is to some extent obeying David, and placing Uriah where the battle is certain to be fierce. This seems a less likely option from the context. But if the אנשי־חיל are Joab's own soldiers, which seems more likely, then Joab may be allowing some of his other soldiers to be endangered along with Uriah in order to cover up the fact that Uriah alone is the intended victim of this fatal military "mistake." Such a reading would be consistent with Joab's character elsewhere in the David cycle. See n. 103 below.

99. For example, why does Joab assume that David will be angry? Is it because Joab disobeyed David's direct order? Or, why does Joab ascribe these specific words to David?

100. Yadin, *Art of Warfare*, 261. Yadin illustrates the biblical passages with several reliefs that depict archers firing down from city walls, such as one from Ashurnasirpal II's

Fokkelman explains that the comparison between the deaths of Abimelech and Uriah rests on six motifs: death-woman-wall-battle-shame-folly.[101] Bal says that Fokkelman's six motifs may be interpreted within the framework of psychoanalysis, expressing the unconscious complex of the fear of woman. They imply "one dies a shameful death as soon as one is so foolish as to fight woman when she is defending her wall/entrance from her mighty position as the feared other."[102] This unconscious fear of a woman may extend to the three main men in this narrative: David, Uriah, and Joab.

> The metaphorical evocation of Abimelech has two compared objects: David and Uriah. Literally, Uriah is the victim compared to Abimelech. He died in the circumstances listed by Fokkelman: being too near the wall, he got shot from the wall. Figuratively, too, he is the compared object in one sense: he had to die because of a woman. Metonymically, the compared object is, however, displaced onto David. Like Abimelech, he is a usurper of what does not belong to him. And he, too, is in danger because of a woman: stuck with child, covered with shame. Again, two men are interchanged.
>
> Joab may feel angry with David and guilty about Uriah, as Fokkelman puts it. But he speaks here "in David's name," imagining David's obsession to an unnamed messenger. His anger is displaced in its turn: let us not forget that in his evocation, the woman is the killer. It is possible that his anger with David about the bad strategy and the death of an innocent man imposed on him, an anger that, as a subordinate "servant of the king," he cannot afford, is directed against the intuitively appropriate scapegoat, woman in general.[103]

palace in Nimrud and another from the palace of Sargon at Khorsabad. *Art of Warfare*, 392–93, 422–23.

101. Fokkelman, *Narrative Art*, 1:69. Fokkelman believes that Joab is reprimanding David (through the speech of the messenger) in v. 21, and that the undertones of the response should read, "if you draw too near to a fortress wall, you not only expose yourself to a shower of arrows but also give a woman the chance to put you out of commission in a very stupid manner! Haven't you made the same kind of blunder as Abimelech?" Ibid., 1:67.

102. Bal, *Lethal Love*, 33.

103. Ibid., 34–35. Bal and Fokkelman both assume that Joab is angry, but the text itself does not define the tone associated with Joab's words. Throughout the story of David, Joab is portrayed as a fiercely loyal man whose actions are crucial for David to hold onto his power. It could be argued that Joab followed David's ultimate order to have Uriah killed, and his disobedience ended up protecting David. That is, by allowing other

Bal warns, however, that 2 Sam 11:21 is so complex that even so-phisticated readers may be trapped into reading too much into it. She advocates, instead, an interpretation that accounts for both the structural details of the test, as well as "the mistakes it provokes," demonstrating the need to connect interpretation with its ethical implications.[104] In other words, using surface structuralism, there are comparisons between Bathsheba and the woman in Judges and between Uriah and Abimelech in Joab's words. But, using deep structuralism, we see that the comparisons cannot ultimately be sustained: the direct comparison between Uriah and Abimelech falls flat, and so too does a direct comparison between Bathsheba and the "certain woman" in Judg 10:53. Even if the two women are connected figurally, or intertextually, there is nothing in 2 Samuel to suggest that Bathsheba deliberately killed Uriah in the same way that the woman in Judges dropped a millstone on Abimelech's head. Moreover, the ethical implications of the assumption that Bathsheba is the one who is responsible for Uriah's death (or for David's downfall, or for Joab's anger) are seriously detrimental for women, who are often blamed or scapegoated in other areas.

2 Samuel 11:25–27: Bathsheba Mourns and Gives Birth

After the messenger recounts the news of Uriah's death to David, David's response is not what Joab had anticipated. Instead of being angry, David told the messenger to tell Joab, "Let not this thing be evil in your eyes. For the sword consumes this one as that one. Strengthen your battle on the city and destroy it" (v. 25).[105] Immediately after David says this, Bathsheba returns as the main character in the next verses. Again, there

---

troops to be killed along with Uriah, Joab prevented David's plot from being quite as obvious as it might have been.

104. Bal, *Lethal Love*, 34.

105. In v. 11, the phrase הדבר הזה, "this thing," referred to sleeping with Uriah's wife. In this verse, its meaning is left unclear. If Joab knows about David's adultery, David could be urging Joab not to condemn him for his action—"this thing". Or, David could simply be commanding Joab not to be bothered by the series of events that resulted in the deaths of his soldiers, including Uriah. Fokkelman points out that Uriah has literally been replaced with the platitude כי־כזה וכזה תאכל החרב, "the sword just happens to consume this one, then that one." *Narrative Art*, 1:63. Joab has heard before that the sword consumes (תאכל חרב); in 2 Sam 2:26, Abner asks Joab if the sword will consume for eternity, and Joab stops his pursuit of Abner. However, Joab later stabs and kills Abner, and David places the blood-guilt for Abner's death on Joab (2 Sam 3:26–30), so David's words may be to remind Joab of his own crimes.

are aspects to her character that are revealed, even as other gaps are opened. In 2 Sam 11:26 she is once again identified not by her name, but in relationship to Uriah. Within this single verse, her relationship with Uriah is repeated three times: "And *the wife of Uriah* heard that *Uriah her husband* was dead, and she mourned for *her master.*"[106] Fokkelman explains, "v. 26a is a posthumous homage to this marriage and its close, mutual bonds by taking up both man and woman together in one line for the last time . . ."[107] This repetition has the rhetorical function of emphasizing this relationship, and we are meant to take notice.[108]

Bathsheba's action in 2 Sam 11:26 is noteworthy, if still somewhat enigmatic. Her response to the news of her husband's death is to lament (ספד) for him. Some have wondered if Bathsheba's time of mourning is merely perfunctory or performatory.[109] And certainly, there are other passages in the MT that describe grief much more explicitly and dramatically.[110] Then again, this is a text that is devoid of emotions, so a verb that is connected with an emotion is worth noting. Within the immediate context of a verse that repeats her relationship to her husband so

---

106. The text refers to Uriah one time as Bathsheba's husband (איש), and a second time as her master (בעל). The word *master* (בעל) is only used to refer to a husband in Deut 22:22; 24:4; and in Prov 12:4; 31:11, 23, 28. But the different terminology is not as important as the repetition of their relationship.

107. Fokkelman, *Narrative Art*, 1:70; cf. Solvang, *A Woman's Place*, 183. Again, when Bathsheba is recalled in the genealogy of Jesus in Matt 1:6, she remains "the wife of Uriah the Hittite."

108. We might compare Song 6:3, אני לדודי ודודי לי, "I am my beloved's and my beloved is mine," although in that passage we only have the relationship mentioned twice, and in our text it is spoken of three times.

109. For example, Kirsch writes, "Bathsheba observed the customary period of ritual mourning—but when the formal display of grief was done, David and Bathsheba wasted no more time on appearances." *King David*, 192. Calvin explains, "she exposed herself to shame when she returned to the house of her adulterous partner. This shows us that it was not a true affection, but rather feigned, when she mourned over her husband . . . she readily went with David to live in his house, forgot the death of her husband, and paid no attention to the villainous and detestable outrage which had been done to him." *Sermons on 2 Samuel*, 516–17. The time of mourning is not specified in the text. In Gen 50:10, we read that Joseph mourned (אבל) for seven days for his father; in Deut 34:8, the Israelites mourn for thirty days for Moses. In other passages where the Bible refers to mourning, the time is not specified; 2 Sam 14:2 and 1 Chr 7:22 discuss mourning "for many days" (ימים רבים). The two time periods recorded follow the Jewish mourning practices of sitting *shiva* for seven days, and then observing *shloshim* for thirty days following the burial.

110. Cf. David's grief over Absalom (2 Sam 19:4); Jer 8:18—9:1; Ps 6:6–7; Lam 1.

many times, we could suppose that the word סָפַד does suggest genuine sorrow.[111]

The full verse that ends 2 Sam 11 reads: "And the time of mourning passed, and David sent and gathered her to his house, and she was to him for a wife, and she bore to him a son. And the thing that David had done was evil in the eyes of YHWH." As David acted in 2 Sam 11:4, so he again acts here—in both verses, David sent for (שָׁלַח) Bathsheba. But unlike the earlier text, here Bathsheba does not "come" to him. Instead, he gathers her to his house,[112] which makes her even less participatory at this point than she was previously. She is the subject of two verbs in 2 Sam 11:27: she was/became (וַתְּהִי) a wife, she bore (וַתֵּלֶד) a son. But each of these verbs is followed by the prepositional phrase לוֹ. Bathsheba is a wife *to* David and bears a son *to* him.

The final, concluding clause of 2 Sam 11 is pointed.[113] Fokkelman writes, "David's behavior literally provokes heaven, and God himself

---

111. In Mic 1:8, the term is used in reference to the sound that is made by jackals. Yet, earlier in that verse, the prophet explains that he will mourn because of the destruction of Jerusalem. In fact, each place where the word סָפַד is used in the text is a situation of genuine sorrow. For example, Abraham laments over Sarah in Gen 23:2, Jacob's children lament over him in Gen 50:10, all Israel mourns for Samuel in 1 Sam 25:1 and 28:3, David mourns for Saul and Jonathan 2 Sam 1:12, etc. The prophetic texts sometimes include commands not to mourn in situations of genuine sadness; for example, Jeremiah 16 explains that because YHWH has withdrawn favor from the people, they are not to be mourned, even when they die. In Ezek 24, YHWH tells Ezekiel that he is not to mourn even when אֶת־מַחְמַד עֵינֶיךָ (the delight of his eyes) dies. In Zech 12:10, the word סָפַד is connected with מָרַר, "bitter grief." In Eccl 3:5, the word is contrasted with רָקַד, "to dance," so that it is clear that mourning is not a time of celebration. Cf. Seow, *Ecclesiastes*, 161. Interestingly, the word סָפַד is not used in 2 Sam 12 to describe David's response to the child's death. Of course, he fasts and pleads with God when the child is still alive, trying to change God's mind, but once the child is dead, he does not seem to grieve much.

112. BDB refers to this verse and explains that when the object is a person, the verb אָסַף implies responsibility and protection, and may even be translated as "take up, care for." BDB, 62. This is, however, an idealistic reading of David, and in many other places where this verb is used with people as objects (e.g., Gen 29:22; 42:17; Exod 3:16; Num 11:16; Josh 24:1; 1 Sam 5:8; 2 Kgs 23:1; etc.), BDB translates it as "to gather, collect"; Ibid. *HALOT* translates the occurrence of the word in this verse as "to take home a woman," 74.

113. Some editions of the Bible will separate out 2 Sam 11:27 into two clauses, and put the final clause about God's displeasure at David's action in the same paragraph as 2 Sam 12:1. For example, the Harper Collins Study Bible, NRSV; The Oxford Annotated Bible, NRSV; and the JPS Hebrew English Tanakh all do this. While 2 Sam 11 and 12 are a continuous story, it is important to respect that even before Nathan speaks God's word of condemnation to David in 2 Sam 12, the final word in 2 Sam 11 is that David's action was evil in YHWH's eyes.

intervenes."[114] To some extent, this definitive and divine judgment acts as a finalizing statement. YHWH, who has not been present as a character throughout the narrative, shows up at the end as a "focalizing character," and David's actions are focalized negatively "in the eyes of YHWH."[115] Several scholars agree that the main point of the narrative is the moral condemnation of David's actions, and therefore the reason that so many other things in the narrative are left ambiguous is that they are not important when compared with the unambiguous moral claim that David has done wrong.[116] Certainly, the conclusion does clear up some things. It contributes to Bathsheba's generally positive characterization when only David's name is mentioned. That is, we read, "the thing that David had done," not, "the thing that David and Bathsheba had done." In many ways that is not surprising, for again, this is a narrative primarily about him, and she continues to be a minor character. Yet in other places in the OT, both a man and a woman are condemned if they are both responsible. For example, both Eve and Adam are punished in Gen 3, and both Jezebel and Ahab are punished in 1 Kgs 21. So singling out David here makes it clear that he has done wrong. But the conclusion is not finalizing in terms of Bathsheba's character. She remains an enigmatic and complex character, and continues to be so throughout the rest of the narrative in 2 Samuel.

2 Samuel 12:1–4: Bathsheba in Parables

As the greater narrative about David and Bathsheba continues in 2 Sam 12, Bathsheba remains a minor character. She is not even physically present as an actor until v. 24. Yet, there are references to her in the parable (vv. 1–4), in God's condemnation (vv. 9–10), and in the child's identifica-

114. Fokkelman, *Narrative Art*, 1:71.

115. Stone, *Sex, Honor, and Power*, 101.

116. Cf. chapter 1, n. 45. Arpali believes that the author refrains from describing the inner world of the characters because that world is irrelevant to the moral claim that David did wrong. "Caution: A Biblical Story!" 685–84. Garsiel points out that by not explaining the psychological motivation(s) of David, we as readers are not tempted to sympathize with David and thereby miss the point that he was in the wrong. "The Story of David and Bathsheba," 261–62. Sternberg and Perry explain that it is because the moral evaluation about David is so clear at the end that the rest of the narrative has been so ambiguous. "The narrator is well aware that he can perfectly rely on the reader to arrive at the desired normative conclusions even without explicit guidance." "Caution: A Literary Text!" 680.

tion (v. 15). These references, though subtle, will further help us understand her character. As with 2 Sam 11, however, plenty of gaps remain. In 2 Sam 12:1–4, God sends (שׁלח) Nathan the prophet to David.[117] Nathan tells David a story that may be summarized as follows: There are two men in one city; one is rich and the other is poor. The rich man has an abundance of flocks and herds of animals, while the poor man has only one little ewe lamb[118] that he had paid for. This lamb is much more than mere property—it is like a child to the poor man. The poor man shares his food with the lamb; she eats from his morsel, drinks from his cup, and lies in his bosom.[119] One day a traveler comes to the rich man, and standards of hospitality require that the rich man provide a meal for his guest. But the rich man is loath to feast on one of his own animals, so he takes the poor man's ewe lamb to kill, and then feeds it to the man who comes to visit.

There has been no lack of scholarly discussion about how to classify 2 Sam 12:1–4. Hermann Gunkel refers to this story as one of the *Märchen* of the Old Testament.[120] George Coats and Gerhard von Rad classify it as a fable.[121] Others agree that it is a parable, emphasizing

117. It is not clear how much, if any, "gap" in time exists between when God sent Nathan to David and when he came. Were there any hesitations about his call to confront the powerful king? The way it is presented in the text, it seems as if when Nathan arrived at the palace, he immediately launched into the parable, without any niceties of introduction or announcements. But the fact that the text does not tell us if there were any of those things signals the text's lack of interest in such matters. Most likely, there was some sort of announcement, and a formal reception (cf. 1 Kgs 1–2). However, court protocol is not the primary interest of this text. Its focus is on God's displeasure about David's actions, and what God said through Nathan about those actions.

118. The word used for "ewe lamb" is the Hebrew כבשׂה. In two out of the three other places where this word occurs, this animal is sacrificed; in Lev 14:10, the ewe lamb is sanctioned as a sacrifice for purification, and in Num 6:14, the ewe lamb is to be a sacrifice for sin. The other place this word is found is Gen 21:28–30, where Abraham gives Abimelech seven ewe lambs as a witness that he dug the well at Beer-Sheba. There are some interesting resonances with Bathsheba's story: in Lev 14:8, one of the steps for purification is "to bathe" (רחץ), which is what Bathsheba is doing when David spies her in 2 Sam 11:4. The same word for "sin" (החטאת) that is used in Num 6:14 is also used in 2 Sam 12:13, when Nathan tells David that the Lord has passed over his sin.

119. The same expression will be used in 1 Kgs 1:2, when David's servants seek a woman to "lie in his bosom" (ושכבה בחיקך). Abishag the Shunnamite is the woman who does that, to keep David warm. She will be discussed in more detail in the following chapter.

120. Gunkel, *Das Märchen*, 35–36.

121. Coats defines a fable as that which "paints a picture of relationships in the human world in exaggerated form with characters from the subhuman world . . . does not

that a parable involves a sort of comparison.[122] Uriel Simon argues for more specific terminology when he calls Nathan's story a juridical parable, a genre that "constitutes a realistic story about a violation of the law, related to someone who had committed a similar offence with the purpose of leading the unsuspecting hero to pass judgment on himself."[123] Yee outlines the structure of a juridical parable as follows: (*a*) parable, (*b*) judgment by the addressee, (*c*) interpretation by the prophet, (*d*) recital of the benevolent actions of God, (*e*) indictment, and (*f*) sentence.[124]

Clearly, there are similarities between Nathan's account and the textual account of what happened in 2 Samuel 11. There are similarities in the characters: two men play an important role in both, and those men are divided by different status.[125] There are also linguistic similarities between the two chapters. The network of verbs—eat, drink, and lie with—are what Uriah says he will not do with Bathsheba in 2 Sam 11:11, but in 2 Sam 12:3 those same verbs are used to illustrate the closeness of the relationship between the man and his lamb.[126] The lamb is described as a daughter to the poor man, and the Hebrew בת recalls Bathsheba.[127] Moreover, as Bathsheba was taken (לקח) in 2 Sam 11:4, so the lamb is taken (לקח) by the rich man in 2 Sam 12:4. Nathan makes the similari-

focus on a sequence of events, each with its own significance in the overarching plan of the story, but rather it focuses on one or two events that describe the relationships at the center of the picture." "Parable, Fable and Anecdote," 368–82. Von Rad also refers to Nathan's story as a fable, but does not go into details about what defines the genre as a fable. *Wisdom in Israel*, 43.

122. Cf. Seebass, "Nathan und David in 2 Sam 12," 203–11. Boadt explains that parables have four different criteria: they are narrative in some fashion, they appeal to experience, they propose some sort of lesson for the hearer, and they are artfully crafted in the language of simile or metaphor. "Understanding the Mashal," 161. Ricoeur defines a parable as "a fiction capable of describing life." "Biblical Hermeneutics," 89.

123. Simon, "Poor Man's Ewe-Lamb," 220–21.

124. Yee, "Form-Critical Study of Isaiah 5:1–7," 33–36.

125. Stone writes, "The parable indicates . . . that the difference between David and Uriah, a difference signified by the opposition 'rich man/poor man,' was a crucial component of YHWH's displeasure." *Sex and Power*, 105.

126. Schipper notes that these three roots are also connected with Uriah in 2 Sam 11:13: "David summoned Uriah. Uriah ate (אכל) before him and drank (שתה) and David made him drunk. Yet when it was evening, Uriah went to lie (שכב) on his bed among the servants of his lord, but he did not go down to his own house." "Did David Overinterpret?" 388.

127. Fokkelman, *Narrative Art*, 1:79. The simile works for the readers to make the connection between this female lamb and the woman last discussed in 2 Sam 11.

ties explicit when he pointedly proclaims to David in 2 Sam 12:7, "You are the man!" If David is the rich man, then Uriah might be understood as the poor one and Bathsheba might be understood as the lamb.

The differences between Nathan's parable and what has happened, however, must not be ignored, and four are worth noting. The first and immediate difference is that Bathsheba is not "like a daughter" to Uriah— she is his wife, as the text continually reiterates (2 Sam 11:3, 11, 26; 2 Sam 12: 9, 10, 15).[128] Second, there is no guest in 2 Sam 11 who precipitated the "sacrifice" of Bathsheba.[129] Third, while Nathan explains the rich man's reason for taking the lamb, David's reason for taking Bathsheba is not specified in the text but instead remains an unfilled gap, for it can hardly be explained as the same as the rich man's reason. Fourth, and perhaps most obvious, is the death of the ewe lamb. In the parable, the rich man (David) sanctions the death of the ewe lamb (Bathsheba), and the poor man (Uriah) is physically unharmed. In 2 Sam 11, it is Uriah's death that David sanctions.[130]

Indeed, these differences are an important reminder that Nathan's story is not intended to be a one-to-one correspondence with what happened. If the similarities between the offense in the story and the one that David committed were too obvious, David would not pass judgment on himself.[131] Pyper explains, "The story can only work because an effect of distanciation is introduced. David can only be led to identify

---

128. Stone warns against anachronism in our own mental associations and assumptions about the relationship between a father and a daughter. "Daughters are significant in some cultural contexts not only because one might have affection for them, but also because they are thought to contain within themselves a feature which comes to serve as a sort of symbolic capital for their male kinsmen: their sexual purity. In this regard, the taking of a lamb who is 'like a daughter' and the taking of a wife for sexual purposes can be seen as not altogether different actions, particularly from the perspective of the male subjects involved, that is, the man who takes and the man from whom the female objects are taken." *Sex, Honor, and Power*, 103.

129. Simon discusses a practice of the Bedouin tribes in the district of Beersheba, who allowed for the legitimate filching of a sheep or goat from the flock of a neighbor to make a feast for a guest, a practice called *Adayieh*. Certain conditions and restrictions governed this practice, however: it was allowed only for an unexpected guest, and the animal must not be a "sheep that had once been the pet lamb of the family." He therefore notes that the emphasis of the parable was not just on the theft, but on the emotional attachment the poor man had to his lamb. Simon, "Poor Man's Ewe-Lamb," 227–31.

130. For this reason, Delekat and Wesselius suggest that the ewe lamb represents Uriah. Delekat, "Tendenz und Theologie," 33; Wesselius, "Joab's Death," 346–47 n. 15.

131. Simon, "Poor Man's Ewe-Lamb," 221.

himself as 'the man' because he has initially not identified himself as the man."[132] Therefore, we as the readers must be careful not to stretch the connection too far. As mentioned above, what happens to Bathsheba is not exactly what happens to the ewe lamb. Yet, the text itself does invite a comparison with the ewe lamb, especially when the language used around Bathsheba and the ewe lamb is the same. So, while we take care not to make too much of the characterization of Bathsheba as the ewe lamb, we ought not to ignore the suggestions that such characterization opens up for Bathsheba.

The first thing to notice about the ewe lamb is that she herself is described using the simile of a daughter.[133] This comparison is made to stress how beloved the lamb was to the poor man. Not only is their relationship described in familial terms, but the parable illustrates it with examples. She is raised as one of the children, she eats from his mouth, drinks from his cup, and sleeps at his breast (2 Sam 12:3). The MT explains that he nourishes her, וַיְחַיֶּהָ. The Piel of חיה occurs in Ezek 16:6, the passage where God intimately and personally cares for Jerusalem. It also occurs in Neh 9:6, as descriptive of God's act in preserving or keeping alive all the heavens and the earth and all that is in them. Based on the way this verb is used in Nehemiah, then, the lamb might not exist without the care of the poor man. Obviously, it is a stretch to assume that Bathsheba would not exist without the care of Uriah, but at the very least, this description of the relationship between the lamb and the poor man suggests that Bathsheba was loved by Uriah. Of course, such information was nowhere specified in 2 Sam 11, and even here the feelings of Uriah towards Bathsheba can only be extrapolated. Yet as we continue to build our understanding of what had happened previously, this close connection between the lamb and the poor man might invite us to consider a similar closeness between Bathsheba and Uriah.

The specific analogy of Bathsheba to a sheep, like the parable as a whole, is an analogy that must not be stretched too far.[134] However, it

---

132. Pyper, *David as Reader*, 90.

133. 2 Sam 12:3 reads, "and she was to him like a daughter" (וַתְּהִי־לוֹ כְּבַת).

134. Boer notes that in Nathan's story, "there is the comparison of Bathsheba to an animal in the possession of a human male." "National Allegory," 103. Boer wants to demonstrate the ethical problems when a woman is dehumanized by being considered the property of a man. In fact, the language of the MT would support that the lamb is owned by the man: it explains that he "bought" her, using the transitive verb קנה. When this verb is used elsewhere in the text, the object is rarely a person or being, and more often

is interesting that Nathan would choose to use a lamb in his parable, because David, the shepherd, was one who ought to know how to care for the sheep. [135] When David is crowned king in Hebron (2 Sam 5:2), the Israelites remind him of God's call that he would shepherd the people. And when God previously told Nathan to speak to David, one of the things Nathan was to say was that God "took you from the pasture, from following the sheep" (2 Sam 7:8). Therefore, the reference to a lamb in the parable highlights the disjunction between how David the shepherd should act toward the lamb and how he did act. That disjunction parallels and illustrates the problem with how David, the chosen of the Lord, should act towards Bathsheba, and how he did act.

2 Samuel 12:5–6: David's Judgment

In 2 Sam 12:5–6, David responds to Nathan's story with outrage. Such a response is appropriate considering his position as king, for it is his responsibility to uphold the cause of the powerless and prevent such abuse (cf. Ps 72:2, 4, 12–14).[136] Of course, it is all the more outrageous that the king has been the one to exploit and abuse, something that Nathan will point out to David in subsequent verses. But though David's emotions are clear, what is not quite clear is exactly why he is angry.[137] The text gives us two reasons for David's anger; first, the action is described: the man "had done this thing" (הָאִישׁ הָעֹשֶׂה זֹאת v. 5; also הַדָּבָר הַזֶּה in v. 6); and second, the attitude is explained: he "had no pity"(לֹא־חָמַל).[138]

---

refers to land or other objects. If a person is acquired, she or he is a slave. Cf. Gen 39:1; Exod 21:2; Lev 22:11; 25; Ruth 4; Neh 5:8; Eccl 2:7; Amos 8:6; Zech 11:5; 13:5. Exceptions to this are found in Gen 4:1, with the etymology of Cain's name, as Eve explains that she has acquired a man with God's help. In poetic texts, God acquires the Israelites as a description of redemption (e.g., Exod 15:16; Ps 74:2). Even then, there is a connection with slavery, as the Israelites go from being possessed by the Egyptians to being possessed by God. Levenson, "Exodus and Liberation," 150–53. However, even Boer acknowledges that the connection between Bathsheba and the ewe lamb is a comparison, and to assume that Bathsheba is literally dehumanized by this parable would be an overreading.

135. According to 1 Sam 17:34–36, David does care for his sheep. Brueggemann, *David's Truth*, 24.

136. McCarter, *2 Samuel*, 299.

137. Schipper suggests that David believes the rich man is Joab, with whom he already became angry in the LXX of 2 Sam 11:22. "Did David Overinterpret?" 388–91.

138. The Hebrew word חָמַל was also used in 2 Sam 12:4 to describe the action of the rich man: when the word is followed by a lamed plus a verbal infinitive, it means "to spare oneself from having to do X," so the rich man spared himself from having to take

But in regards to the action, while the demonstrative recalls 2 Sam 11:11, 25, 27b, there is no object that clarifies "this."

Additionally, the sentence that David passes (on himself, as it were) is, if not a gap, at least unclear. David first makes an oath by the life of YHWH, that "the man who did this is a son of death." Often this is interpreted as a death sentence. David goes on to explain that the man must make fourfold[139] compensation for the ewe lamb (Piel of שׁלם; cf. Lev 5:16). Fokkelman points out that David actually passes *two* verdicts: the death sentence and the command of restoration. "The former corresponds with his last and worst crime, the murder of Uriah, and therefore it precedes the other (psycho)logically. The latter corresponds with 11:2–4, 27, the adultery and the marriage with Bathsheba. David may suppress whatever he wishes, but his conscience and sub-conscious preserve the connection between his two crimes and his excitability as judge and even make this relationship apparent to the discrete observer."[140]

The crime the rich man commits does not fit with the punishment of death. Even though the parable gave the animal an almost human status by identifying it as not just a member of a flock, but an individual lamb loved like a child, the rich man is still only guilty of the theft of an animal. The punishment prescribed for such a theft is not death, but restitution.[141]

---

from his flocks. In 2 Sam 12:6, David condemns the rich man because he did not חמל (have compassion). So, within two verses, the same rich man both חמל and does not חמל. Cf. Coats, "2 Samuel 12:1–7a," 170–75. Daube notes that this same verb is connected with Saul's transgression that led to David's anointing; Saul did not follow God's command not "to spare" Amalek (1 Sam 15). Daube, "Nathan's Parable," 282.

139. Where the MT has ארבעתים (fourfold), the LXX has επταπλασιονα (sevenfold). This difference will be discussed further in chapter 4.

140. Fokkelman, *Narrative Art*, 1:77. Derby also discusses David's conscious and subconscious motivation for speaking. He explains that while David's "conscious mind apparently accepts this story as an actual case and he is ready to give the proper ruling," "his subconscious grasps the parable and its meaning." "A Biblical Freudian Slip," 109. Derby also suggests that David's statement "*ben mahvet ha'ish*" is not a sentence, but a Freudian slip. "His deep sense of guilt, hidden in his subconscious, must express itself, and does in this manner." Ibid.

141. For this reason, McCarter translates v. 5 not as "son of death," but as "fiend of hell," saying that David, by using this terminology, "is characterizing the man's behavior, not condemning him to death. We should not, therefore, suppose that David contradicts himself in v. 6 by demanding a sevenfold restitution after he has imposed a death penalty here ('the man who did this is a dead man') or expressed an opinion that the rich man ought to die ('the man who did this deserves to die')." McCarter, *2 Samuel*, 299.

What is clear in this section is that David implicates himself for the crime, something with which Nathan will only agree. Again, we must not be too strict about the connections between the parable and what had happened between David and Bathsheba, but there is no blame ascribed to the lamb for tempting the rich man to take her, or the poor man for not being more vigilant about his lamb. David's own response places the blame squarely on himself, not on Bathsheba or Uriah.

2 Samuel 12:7–15: God's Judgment

Nathan both clarifies and confirms the judgment David had placed on himself. In 2 Sam 12:7, Nathan reveals to David, "You are the man." He then gives David a prophetic speech of God's response to David's actions. David's wrongdoing is serious: 2 Sam 12:9 explains that he "despised the word of YHWH to do evil in YHWH's eyes" (מדוע בזית את־דרב יהוה לעשות הרע בעיני[142]), but 2 Sam 12:10 makes an even stronger statement by removing the buffer "word of YHWH" and explaining that David despised YHWH. Solvang writes, "The victims in the parable are the poor man and his lamb. The victims in the narrative are Bathsheba and Uriah. But Nathan declares another victim in his condemnation of David. That victim is Yahweh." [143] The evil David did is quantified into two specific acts: killing Uriah, and taking Uriah's wife as his own wife. Both of these wrongdoings are repeated twice.[144]

Yet even as the text clarifies that one of David's sins was "taking" Bathsheba, it is not entirely clear if that refers to adultery or to theft. In

---

McCarter's translation attempts to smooth out the contradiction between what David said in vv. 5 and 6. However, I prefer a more wooden translation that would bring to the fore some of the messiness, or openness, of the MT. If there is a contradiction, I prefer to follow Fokkelman's example by considering that contradiction and interpreting its significance.

142. The MT *Kethib* of 2 Sam 12:9 reads, "his eyes," but the MT *Qere* has "my eyes". "Either reading is acceptable," McCarter assures us. "Yahweh himself is speaking, but he has just referred to himself in the third person." McCarter, *2 Samuel*, 295.

143. Solvang, *A Woman's Place*, 135.

144. 2 Sam 12:9 reads, "Uriah the Hittite you have struck with a sword, his wife you took to be a wife for yourself, and him you have killed with the sword of the Ammonites." 2 Sam 12:10 repeats the "taking of Uriah's wife" when explaining the reason for the sword remaining in David's house forever, "because you despised me and you took the wife of Uriah the Hittite to be your wife."

Prov 6:25, the verb refers to seduction done by women,[145] but the legal code of the Bible does not use the word לקח to refer to adultery.

Another gap that is not filled in by Nathan's words is the nature of the intercourse between David and Bathsheba—was it adultery, or rape? One difference between rape and adultery has to do with consent, and the text remains silent on whether or not Bathsheba consented. On the one hand, adultery is a crime for which both partners were to be punished (Deut 22:22), and only David is punished in 2 Sam 12. To be sure, the death of their child still affects Bathsheba, but within the text even that punishment is for David, not for her. But on the other hand, based on the legal material in the Bible, the words used to describe the sexual act, and comparative narratives within the MT, it would seem that in the ancient environment of the biblical text, David's sin was not primarily rape.[146] Horst Seebass inteprets the offense committed by the rich man

145. "Do not let her take you with her eyelids" (אל־תקחך בעפעפיה). "Her" refers to the adulteress.

146. First, in the laws about adultery in Deut 22:23–27, it is explained that if a sexual act took place within the city, the woman is presumed to have consented, for she did not cry for help. If the sexual act occurred in the country, however, she presumably resisted. Location is also important in other ancient Near Eastern laws (*ANET*, 181, 196). Cf. Pressler, *View of Women*, 32. Therefore, because David lay with Bathsheba in Jerusalem, from a strictly legal standpoint this was not rape. Second, Gravett points out that "no Hebrew verb or phrase precisely corresponds to contemporary understandings of rape." "Reading 'Rape' in the Hebrew Bible," 279. But with the three stories most widely associated with rape—the taking of Dinah in Gen 34, the assault on the Levite's concubine in Judg 19, and Amnon's rape of his half-sister Tamar in 2 Sam 13—the piel of ענה occurs. Neither is there the word שגל (cf. Isa 13:16; Zech 14:2), nor the niphal of חמס (cf. Jer 13:22), nor even the verbal root פתה (cf. Jer 20:7). Gravett argues that some of the verbs commonly used to describe sexual intercourse (שכב, "to lay," or ידע, "to know") can be used to depict sexually violent acts of rape, but only when combined with other words such as the piel of ענה, or חזק, "strength, force." Ibid., 281. David did "lay with" Bathsheba, but there are no other words in 2 Sam 11 to indicate force or humiliation. Again, there are simply not many words at all that describe their interaction. Schwartz uses the language of "adultery" to describe David's action in most of her article with the same title, "Adultery in the House of David," 141, 144–46, 148–49, but then concludes with this statement, "Bathsheba, the wife of King David's loyal servant, was raped by the king who then ordered the murder of her husband to cover up the crime (the version in my Bible)," 150. Thus, the question about adultery or rape is not entirely clear for those who have studied it extensively.

Amnon's rape of Tamar is an illustrative comparison. While many scholars see connections between the sexual behavior of David in 2 Sam 11 and Amnon in 2 Sam 13 (Freedman, "Dinah and Shechem," 60; Yamada, "Configurations of Rape," 136), there are some clear differences. Gray writes, "whereas David 'takes' (לקח) Bathsheba (2 Sam 11:4), Amnon 'seizes' (חזק) Tamar. This sense of intensification as we move from David's

not as theft but as an abuse of power, and concludes that David, too, is guilty of abuse of power. Seebass explains that the rich man took the poor man's property because he had little to fear from a lawsuit, for even if he were found guilty, he could easily pay the penalty. The poor man, by contrast, would be reticent to take someone so powerful to court, so his recourse would be to seek the king's protection through a third party. By analogy, Uriah, as David's subject, would not have recourse against the king, except through a divine tribunal.[147] Both Raymond Westbrook and Stone agree with this assessment of David's wrong. Westbrook explains that the rich man in the parable had discretionary power to take a sheep from anyone in the village for the purpose of hospitality, but he abused that power for selfish motives: "David's actions now stand in exact parallel . . . Kings have a perfect right to send their soldiers to death in battle—it is one of the normal prerogatives of a king and cannot be qualified as murder. Nor would there normally be any objection to the king marrying the widow of one of his fallen soldiers—indeed it might be considered a noble gesture. But where the king has deliberately sent the soldier to his death in order to marry the widow—that is an abuse of his authority for a selfish motive."[148]

Of course, Nathan does not describe David's wrong by using language of abuse of power, but this interpretation accounts for the details of both the wrong and the punishment in the text.

If David's wrongdoing is quantified into two things, there are three punishments listed by the text. The first is that the sword will remain in David's house forever, the second is that his wives will be taken by another,[149] and the third is that the child from him and Bathsheba will

---

seduction of Bathsheba to Amnon's rape of Tamar is also apparent in the terms by which, in each case, the moment of consummation is described. With regard to David, we are told, וישכב עמה, but concerning Amnon, וישכב אתה (v. 14). David sleeps with Bathsheba in some sort of relational configuration which, once, admittedly basely, started, persists until the end of his life, whereas Amnon, as is quite literally reflected in the syntax, 'lays' Tamar and then with instantaneous callousness, boots her out." Gray, "Amnon," 48. Another major difference between the stories of Bathsheba and Tamar is the way the text describes Tamar's resistance of Amnon (2 Sam 13:12–14). Again, it could be that Bathsheba did resist David, but the text leaves that as a gap.

147. Seebass, "Nathan und David," 205–6.

148. Westbrook, *Studies in Biblical and Cuneiform Law*, 34. Cf. Stone, *Sex and Power*, 103–6.

149. Linafelt notes how problematic it is that God first admits, or "perhaps even brags" that God gave (נתן) Saul's women to David (2 Sam 12:8), and now God will take

die. The punishment of the sword connects with the sword mentioned in 2 Sam 12:9, and with David's words to Joab in 2 Sam 11:25 that "the sword devours this one as that one" (כי־כזה וכזה תאכל החרב). Just as Bathsheba was taken (לקח), in 2 Sam 11:4, 12:9-10 and the lamb was taken in 2 Sam 12:4, God will take David's wives and give them to someone else.[150] And while the death of their child still affects Bathsheba, the language used in the text suggests that even that punishment is for David, not for her. There are two uses of the infinitive absolute in 2 Sam 12:14: because David "certainly spurned" (נאץ נאצת), the child will "certainly die" (מות ימות).[151] The child's death is therefore connected to David's actions in both juxtaposition and grammatical form.[152]

In response to Nathan's (or God's) words of judgment, David acknowledges his sin in a mere two Hebrew words: חטאתי ל יהוה, "I have sinned before the Lord" (2 Sam 12:13).[153] Bathsheba, however, does not say any such thing. Is this because she is innocent, or because the text does not allow her confession? Again, this text is not focused on Bathsheba; its focus is on David. Gunn comments, "the stunning simplicity of David's response to Nathan . . . functions powerfully to reinstate him in the reader's estimation."[154] Bathsheba has no words, which might mean one of two things. First, her silence might mean that she does not accept

(לקח) David's women and give (נתן) them to his neighbor. He forewarns disappointment for the reader, who expects that now that God has come into the narrative, women will be treated fairly. Linafelt, "Taking Women," 106–7.

150. See n. 147.

151. McCarter notes that the MT מות ימות, "certainly die," is the standard formula in the Priestly legislation of the Pentateuch, found in Exod 21:21; Lev 20:2; and Judg 21:5. *2 Samuel*, 296.

152. It is theologically problematic that God "strikes" (נגף, 2 Sam 12:15) the child so that he dies. Coats, however, explains, "It will not do justice to this text to say that justice demanded a life for a life . . . The text makes no point of saying that now God was satisfied. The death of the child was not appeasement. It was the product of broken intimacy. David and Bathsheba chose a way of life, and the choice carried death as its fruit." "2 Samuel 12:1–7a," 173.

153. The force of this rhetoric is to emphasize that David primarily sinned against God, a point that is made even more explicit in Psalm 51:6 (ET 51:4), "against you alone have I sinned." Yet it is important not to forget that David also sinned against Uriah and Bathsheba, as sins against God and against neighbor are intertwined. McCann writes, "The emphatic 'you, you only' in v. 4 is not meant to indicate that the psalmist's sinful behavior did not have destructive consequences for other people; rather, it suggests that sin has its origin in the failure to honor God." "Psalms," *NIB*, 4:885.

154. Gunn, "David and the Gift of the Kingdom," 20.

responsibility, and thus she is not reinstated in the reader's estimation, in the same way that Gunn points out that David is. On the other hand, her silence and David's confession might suggest that the responsibility lies entirely with him, which again points to rape, not adultery. As we have noted, the openness of the MT does not definitively clarify whether Bathsheba was to any degree culpable. Yet when other biblical texts are quite capable of condemning both a man and a woman when both are culpable for wrongdoing (Gen 3:1-19; Deut 22:22), the absence of any condemnation of Bathsheba is significant and points to a more positive portrait in contrast with David.

Bathsheba is still identified as the wife of Uriah the Hittite in v. 15, when the narrator informs the readers that YHWH strikes the child born to Bathsheba and David. This manner of identification is significant for two reasons. First, it reminds the readers that Bathsheba was still the wife of Uriah when she conceived. Second, Bathsheba is once again identified through her relationships to others. Bathsheba is, however, conspicuously absent in vv. 15–23. The child who dies is not only David's child (v. 14); it is the child she (the wife of Uriah the Hittite) bore to David (v. 15). Yet, it is primarily David of whom we read in these verses. Even when Bathsheba shows up in 2 Sam 12:24, the amount of time and space that is devoted to describing her grief and loss is disproportionate to that of David in 15–23. Clearly, he is the primary character.

2 Samuel 12:24: Bathsheba Is Consoled and Gives Birth

But still, her grief is mentioned. When Bathsheba reappears as a human character in 2 Sam 12:24, she is in need of comfort. Cheryl Kirk-Duggan writes that "the narrator silences her grief by describing only David's pain at the loss of their first child,"[155] but such a statement does not account for the description of Bathsheba being consoled by David. This is the first clear picture of some tenderness David shows toward Bathsheba. Fokkelman writes, "For the first time she is no longer being used but is treated by David as a person."[156]

There are both interesting similarities and differences between this verse and 2 Sam 11:4. Both use the verbs בוֹא ("to go") and שָׁכַב ("to lie"). In fact, the string of words וַיִּשְׁכַּב עִמָּהּ ("and he lay with her") is

155. Kirk-Duggan, "Slingshots," 56.
156. Fokkelman, *Narrative Art*, 1:91.

exactly the same in both 2 Sam 11:4 and 2 Sam 12:24. Yet, the differences between the two verses are important. Whereas 2 Sam 11:4 begins with a description of David sending messengers to take her, 2 Sam 12:24 begins with a description of David consoling "Bathsheba his wife." In the former passage, she is an object to be taken, not even referred to with a separate third person feminine singular pronoun, but in the latter passage, she is referred to by her name and by her relationship to David as his wife. As previously noted, this is the first time, even after 2 Sam 11:27, that Bathsheba is identified as David's wife. Perhaps the echoes from the pre-ceding chapter color the description of their intimacy (lying together) negatively. What should mitigate that negativity is that David consoles her, and she is his wife.

There are two active verbs attributed to Bathsheba in 2 Sam 12:24: the first is וַתֵּלֶד, "and she bore." [157] Part of Bathsheba's character and identity is that she is a mother. While this becomes more central for her identity in 1 Kings, it begins in 2 Samuel. It is not told here whether or not she has other children;[158] Solomon is the one who matters, the one who is important for the story. The second verb for Bathsheba in v. 24 is קָרָא, as she names her son Solomon. However, the verb for the nam-ing involves a *Kethib/Qere* in the MT: what is written is וַיִּקְרָא, "and he called," but what is to be read is וַתִּקְרָא, "and she called." The *Qere* is supported by Syriac, Targum, and Vulgate, while the *Kethib* was possibly influenced by the following verse, where Nathan "called" the name of the child Jedediah. McCarter asserts, "In the time to which our story refers

---

157. One of the gaps that remain in this chapter has to do with any sense of the tim-ing of David's comfort and the conception and birth of Solomon: the text simply lists the events occurring in rapid succession. Viejola argues that the seven-day period of the first child's illness and David's "mourning" corresponds to Bathsheba's time of uncleanness, which would last seven days after the birth of a male child (Lev 12:2). So, when David "went to her and lay with her" (v. 24), Viejola explains that Bathsheba was just at the end of her time of purification and uncleanness, the most propitious time for concep-tion, just as she was when she conceived the first time. "Salomo," 242 n. 47. McCarter, however, notes that there is nothing in the text to support Viejola's first assumption that the seventh day mentioned in 2 Sam 12:18 was the seventh day of the child's life, or his second assumption that the second pregnancy began one week after the death of the first child. McCarter, *2 Samuel*, 303. Viejola himself admits that it is biologically dubi-ous to suppose that Solomon was conceived one week after the birth of his brother, but insists on the legendary character of the story and its emphasis on psychological realism. Viejola, "Salomo," 244.

158. However, according to 1 Chr 3:5, there are four children: Shimea, Shobab, Nathan, and Solomon. In Luke 3:31, Jesus' ancestry traces through Nathan, not Solomon.

it seems to have been the mother's prerogative to name a newborn child
(1 Sam 1:20; 4:21, etc.)."[159]

Even though Bathsheba names the child Solomon, Nathan comes
in during the following verse and names the child Jedidiah, "beloved of
the Lord" (v. 25). Baruch Halpern thinks that the name Jedidiah is given
to imply "not too subtly, that he was the love child of David, *dwd*, 'the
beloved.'"[160] While 1 Chr 22:9 suggests that Solomon is named as he is
because Israel would have peace (שׁלם) during Solomon's (שׁלמן) reign,
Halpern, Timo Viejola, Johann Stamm, and Gillis Gerleman all believe
that the name has a connection to Uriah.[161] Halpern writes that Solomon's
name should be analyzed as meaning "his replacement," and that such an
etymology "indicates that he was presented as Uriah's son in the court."[162]
That is, even if Solomon was really Uriah's son, his other name is given
to him by the prophet to smooth over any doubts that the child belongs
to David.[163] Another possibility for the two names is that the second one

---

159. McCarter, *2 Samuel*, 303. It appears that fathers name their children more in
the Pentateuch, including Adam (Gen 5:3), Abraham (Gen 16:5), Isaac (Gen 21:3),
Judah (Gen 38), Joseph (Gen 41:5), and Moses (Exod 2:22). In addition to Hannah and
Bathsheba, other biblical mothers who name their children include Eve (Gen 4:1), Leah
(Gen 29:32ff), Rachel (Gen 30:5ff), and Samson's mother (Judg 13:24). Pharoah's daugh-
ter names Moses (Exod 2:10), and the women of Bethlehem name Obed (Ruth 4:17).

160. Halpern, *David's Secret Demons*, 401.

161. Viejola, "Salomo" 234–36; Halpern, *David's Secret Demons*, 401; Stamm, "Der
Name des Koenigs Salomo," 296; Gerleman, "Die Wurzel *shlm*," 13.

162. Halpern, *David's Secret Demons*, 403. Despite what the text says about the sexual encounter between David and Bathsheba, Halpern believes that Solomon is really the
son of Uriah. In a correspondence with Halpern, Freedman mentioned the possibility
that Solomon was *Nathan's* son; "citing the detachment of Monica Lewinsky's abortion
from the charges of impeachment against Bill Clinton, he suggests that were the apol-
ogy a contemporary Washington thriller, it would turn out that Nathan was Solomon's
father." *David's Secret Demons*, 403 n. 28. While I do not want to go so far as to think that
the narrator is omniscient, neither do I want to go as far as Halpern does, in the other
direction, to assume that the narrator is untrustworthy. That is, although or even *because*
the text may say one thing (that Solomon is Uriah's son, for example), Halpern argues
that we ought to read the opposite, and I disagree.

163. Noll offers a variation on this theme, arguing that David's marriage to Bathsheba
is eternally condemned as an illegitimate marriage, and any child produced by their
union is a bastard who, according to Deut 23:3, shall not enter YHWH's assembly. Thus,
YHWH's love for Solomon is an act of divine grace that overlooks (but does not excuse)
Solomon's illegitimacy. Noll, *Faces of David*, 70–72. Noll's reading is at best speculative
and, more accurately, incorrect, based on what the text says in 2 Sam 12:24: David comforts *his wife* Bathsheba. After the death of the child she somehow has become his wife.

is Solomon's throne name.[164] When Nathan renames Solomon, though, the relationship between Nathan and Bathsheba may be highlighted. One thought is that Nathan is the leader in this relationship, and a sign of his power over her is that he renames the child. Another thought is that Nathan is aligning himself early on with Solomon, and with Bathsheba—a politically calculated move that will be important for his own status during the succession. Of course, this relationship between Bathsheba and Nathan will become further developed in 1 Kings.

In order to summarize what we have seen so far about Bathsheba in 2 Samuel, I will revisit Bal's particular traits for understanding a character.[165] First, in terms of gender Bathsheba is a female. Bal's example for the way that the gender limited a character was that "a *he* cannot find himself unintentionally pregnant."[166] Bathsheba, a she, does become pregnant, which becomes a crucial dramatic point in this narrative. Second, Bathsheba's personal name, by its very etymology, tells us that there are different possibilities for understanding her: she is voluptuous, fertile, or perfect, and connected with an oath, or help, or even error.[167] She is also clearly someone who is known in relationship to others. As 2 Sam 11–12 refers to her as "the daughter of Eliam," "the wife of Uriah" (or, "the wife of David"), and "the mother of Solomon," we continue to be reminded that her connections with others are significant, and that is another one of Bal's categories. Clearly all of these categories are related—her name reminds us of her role as a female, as daughter, wife, and mother, which point to the variety of her relationships with others. Of course, her identity as Solomon's mother becomes more important in 1 Kings.[168] Alter comments on how biblical narrative will strategically change the relational epithets associated with a character when the context surrounding that character changes: Michal, for example, is referred to as either "daughter of Saul" or "wife of David."[169] Because the circum-

---

164. So Honeyman, "Evidence for Regnal Names," 22–23.

165. Cf. chapter 1.

166. Bal, *Narratology*, 123.

167. Cf. nn. 56–59.

168. Eight times in 1 Kings Bathsheba will either be directly called "the mother of Solomon," or that role will be alluded to when Solomon is called her son. E.g., 1 Kgs 1:12, 13, 17, 21, 30; 2:20.

169. Alter, *Art of Biblical Narrative*, 127.

stances change from Samuel to Kings, the "relational epithets" associated with Bathsheba will change to reflect her primary role in the text.

Bal also encourages us to consider a character's physical description, and we see that Bathsheba is described as beautiful, in the same language that the MT uses to describe Rebekah. We must also be careful not to read Bathsheba's beauty as implying that she is seductive; even though it influences David's subsequent decisions, it is stated as a fact about her. Bathsheba's actions also help to characterize her, and we can understand more about her when we consider her bathing, coming to David, conceiving, announcing her pregnancy, lamenting, becoming David's wife, receiving comfort from David, and conceiving and bearing Solomon. Bathsheba's speech is also significant, though brief. We can only imagine other scenarios where she would keep silent about her pregnancy, but in the text she does not, and the two words she speaks reverberate through the events that follow.

Overall, even as we are told very little about Bathsheba, we are still given much raw material with which to work to build her character. The way she is presented in 2 Samuel requires us as readers to be patient in coming to conclusions about her, for we continue to receive information about her until the end of the narrative. We also are required to be attentive to the small details given to us in the text, which suggest that Bathsheba is portrayed in a predominantly positive light in 2 Samuel. She is never condemned as David is, nor are there are clear indicators in the text that Bathsheba either planned for or desired the events in 2 Samuel to happen to her. On the other hand, Bathsheba also does gain from what happens. These two things are strangely connected: Bathsheba need not be willfully sinister nor seductive in order to profit from the events that transpire. When we see her again in 1 Kings, it will be clear that she has risen to a position of authority and power that she did not have in Samuel. This relates to Bal's final category of transformation, which I will discuss in more detail in the following chapter.

3

Bathsheba in the Masoretic Text of 1 Kings

KINGS CONTINUES THE STORY OF DAVID AND BATHSHEBA THAT HAD BE-
gun in Samuel, and in many ways, Bathsheba's characterization remains
the same. In Kings, as in Samuel, there are enough gaps about her that
she continues to be a minor character and a complex one.[1] She also is
still characterized in a generally positive way. But one of the differences
between Samuel and Kings is that Bathsheba's character has developed in
new ways in the latter texts.

Many people have noticed and commented on the change in David
between the books of Samuel and Kings.[2] He who used to be the virile,

---

1. In contrast with the defective MT of Samuel, the MT of Kings is generally sound.
There are some minor variants in the LXX and other versions, and those that pertain to
Bathsheba's character will be discussed in the following chapter. McCarter explains that
the MT of Kings also has a tendency towards expansion (*Textual Criticism*, 90), but the
Dead Sea Scrolls confirm the overall stability of the MT of Kings in terms of its textual
transmission. Cf. Cogan, *1 Kings*, 85.

2. Keil writes, "This circumstance . . . shows that David had become too weak from
age, and too destitute of energy, to be able to carry on the government any longer . . . As
David was then in his seventieth year, this decrepitude was not the natural result of extreme old age, but the consequence of a sickly constitution, arising out of the hardships
which he had endured in his agitated and restless life." *Books of the Kings*, 16–17. Provan
writes, "The importance of the Abishag incident lies in its indication to the watching
court (and to Adonijah in particular) that David has lost his virility and thus his ability to govern. Here is a very beautiful girl. The David of old had not shown himself to
be impervious to such women's charms (1 Sam 25, especially v. 3; 2 Sam 11, especially
v. 2). He had been known to take great trouble to possess a woman he desired. Yet now,
with Abishag in bed beside him and fully available to him, we are told that the king had
no intimate relations with her. The king is, to coin a phrase, 'past it'; he is impotent, and
Adonijah sees his chance to gain power." *1 and 2 Kings*, 24. Hens-Piazza writes, "Images
of the past when David was powerful, virile, and woefully unrestrained subtly resonate
across the narrative and strain to quell the desperation of those responsible for his care.
Perhaps the king's servants hoped contact with Abishag would heal him . . . Or perhaps
the plan to bring beautiful Abishag to the bedside of the frail king aims to revitalize him.

powerful general and commander has now become a doddering, impotent old man who needs a beautiful young woman to keep him warm.[3] At the beginning of the book of Samuel, Hannah's song describes divinely directed reversals where those who are low will be lifted up, and those who are in high places will be brought down. It would appear that David and Bathsheba fit that pattern: the once exalted David has fallen, and the once lowly Bathsheba has risen to a position of power and authority.[4]

Not everyone sees the change in Bathsheba's character from Samuel to Kings. Again, Whybray, Nicol, and Aschkenasy are examples of those who believe that Bathsheba had not undergone any development.[5] But though the textual evidence is sparse—as it is with everything that we are told about Bathsheba—there is textual evidence that she has developed from Samuel to Kings. Four changes are especially clear. First, she speaks more and does more. In Samuel, she is the subject of thirteen verbs and speaks only two words; in Kings, she is the subject of twenty verbs, and speaks 101 words. Even if we take the purist approach[6] to her characterization, we must acknowledge that she has grown as a character from Samuel to Kings. Second, Bathsheba has an increased level of authority which itself develops throughout Kings. She did exercise a degree of power in Samuel when she sent her message to David, a message that was the catalyst for David's actions, but in 1 Kings 1, Nathan solicits her help, and David listens to her. In 1 Kings 2, Adonijah recognizes her author-

---

Instead, the gesture not only fails, but further underscores the disabled condition of this monarch." *1–2 Kings*, 13. Fretheim notes how Kings begins with the theme of David's failing health and comments, "What a contrast from the David of 1 and 2 Samuel!" *First and Second Kings*, 23. Alter writes, "This extraordinary portrait of a human life working itself out in the gradual passage of time, which began with an agile, daring and charismatic young David, now shows him in the extreme infirmity of old age, shivering in bed beneath his covers." *David Story*, 363.

3. This characterization of David, though, is hard to sustain to its extremes; though he is old and feeble, David seems very aware of what must be done to put Solomon on the throne in 1 Kgs 1:32–35, and he gives Solomon astute, if brutal, advice just before his death in 1 Kings 2. Even if he is influenced by Bathsheba and Nathan, he is not completely helpless.

4. 1 Sam 2: 8 describes God lifting the poor and needy to make them sit with princes and inherit a seat of honor. Bathsheba will be seated with her son in a position of honor in 1 Kings 2.

5. Whybray, *Succession Narrative*, 40; Nicol, "Bathsheba," 360–63; Nicol, "The Alleged Rape," 53; Aschkenasy, *Woman at the Window*, 117. Cf. chapter 1.

6. The purist approach believes a character only exists within the text. Cf. chapter 1.

ity when he goes to her to request Abishag as a wife.[7] Third, Bathsheba lacks any physical descriptors in Kings. While this does not necessarily mean that she is no longer "exceedingly beautiful" (טובת מראה מאד),[8] it is not part of her characterization anymore, which tells us that her physical appearance matters less to the narrative. Fourth, instead of being identified as "wife"[9] and "daughter,"[10] now Bathsheba is known as mother.[11] These four aspects of her characterization in Kings are related. As mother, she does exercise power and authority over her son, and once he takes the throne, she enjoys the position of power as queen mother in the court.[12] In Kings, her physical appearance is less important for her characterization and for the plot than it was in Samuel. Now, it is what she says and does that will drive the narrative.

Before we look directly at the text in Kings, it is important to review the textual and chronological interval between Bathsheba's last ap-

7. That Solomon does not accede to Bathsheba's request, though, may be mustered as evidence towards Bathsheba's lack of authority. Then again, it could also be that Bathsheba's request provided the pretence for Solomon to kill the main contender to the throne. This is another gap about her that reminds us of what a complex character she is.

8. Sarai's physical beauty does not seem to diminish with age, for example.

9. Bathsheba was called Uriah's wife in 2 Sam 11:3, 26; 12:9, 10, 15, and David's wife in 2 Sam 12:24.

10. 2 Sam 11:3 recognized that Bathsheba was Eliam's daughter, and the analogy of the ewe-lamb with a daughter in 2 Sam 12:3 echoes the בת in her name.

11. The important connection is not to her husbands; it is to her son Solomon as mother. We must try to avoid anachronism by importing aspects of our own cultural and historical understandings of motherhood onto Bathsheba, and instead allow the biblical depiction of Bathsheba's relationship with Solomon to influence our understanding of motherhood. Klein compares Bathsheba with Tamar and Ruth, other mothers of kings who also make themselves objects of sexual desire, conceive after a single encounter, and whose children are either in direct line to, or become the future king. Lillian Klein, "Bathsheba Revealed," 57. The comparisons end, though, because for Tamar and Ruth, their story ends with the birth of their children. Bathsheba's story does continue on past the birth of Solomon. Her role as a mother is more extensive than that of Tamar and Ruth. Bathsheba acts to get her son on the throne, and to advise him once he is on the throne. She is also a wife, who reminds her husband of a promise that her son should take the throne, and a skilled rhetorician who argues persuasively. Therefore, even though Bathsheba is primarily a mother, her role goes beyond simply giving birth to Solomon.

12. The way that Solomon treats Bathsheba in 1 Kgs 2:19 has caused many to wonder if she is a *gᵉbîrâ*—a technical title for "mighty lady." The text never refers to her as such, as it does with Maacah in 1 Kgs 15:13. Cf. Gray, *1 & 2 Kings*, 265; Andreasen, "Role of the Queen Mother," 188; Solvang, *A Woman's Place*. Bowen concludes that while Bathsheba should be seen as an extraordinary woman who plays a pivotal role in the outcome of the succession, she is not a *gᵉbîrâ*. "Quest for the Historical Gᵉbîrâ," 606.

pearance in 2 Sam 12 and her reappearance in 1 Kings 1. This lengthy interval, during which Bathsheba has not been seen at all, is a tragic one: David's daughter Tamar is raped by her half-brother Amnon. Several of David's concubines are also raped by his son Absalom. Absalom kills Amnon for raping Tamar, and then Absalom is killed by David's general Joab after Absalom had attempted a political coup that drove David out of Jerusalem. Such a litany of tragedies in one family has been explained as the working out of the consequences given by Nathan in 2 Sam 12 for David's sins with Bathsheba and Uriah. For example, Eugene Peterson says regarding 2 Sam 13:1–22: "This is the first installment of Nathan's prophesied consequence of David's sin against Bathsheba and Uriah: 'I will raise up trouble against you from within your own house' (12:11). Trouble indeed: David's virgin daughter violated; David's firstborn son a rapist. David's violation of Bathsheba is now being played out before his own eyes in his own home in Amnon's violation of Tamar; soon his murder of Uriah will be reproduced in Absalom's murder of Amnon."[13]

Bar-Efrat even more pointedly writes, "Amnon's abuse of Tamar is to be interpreted as David's retribution for his behavior towards Bathsheba."[14] Wesselius, however, makes a distinction between punishment and consequences: "Punishment for sin and the consequences of an action are not the same thing. Part of what is described is punishment and part is the unavoidable consequences of David's behavior . . . Three of David's sons, Amnon, Absalom, and Adonijah, died violent deaths, and all, including Solomon, seemed to have learned more from David's example of behaving as if he was above the law than they did from David's repentance."[15]

---

13. Peterson, *First and Second Samuel*, 191. An important distinction between the stories of David and Bathsheba in 2 Samuel 11–12 and Amnon and Tamar in 2 Samuel 13 is the way the text makes it clear that Amnon raped Tamar, as discussed in the previous chapter. For example, Amnon and Jonadab conspire to get Tamar to come to Amnon's inner chamber (הַחֶדֶר in 2 Sam 13:10, the same word that is used in 1 Kgs 1:15. Cf. note 60). Tamar clearly tells Amnon "no" in 2 Sam 13:12–13, but he nevertheless overpowers her and "forces" (עָנָה) her. After the rape, Amnon's response is one of hatred (שִׂנְאָה) in 2 Sam 13:15, while Tamar mourns (2 Sam 13:19–20). These emotions and responses of Amnon and Tamar are missing in David and Bathsheba's account. The gaps in our text highlight the difference. It is obvious that Tamar was wronged; it remains a mystery regarding Bathsheba.

14. Bar-Efrat, *Narrative Art*, 282.

15. Wesselius, "Joab's Death," 345.

If 2 Sam 13–24 is causally connected to 2 Sam 11–12 in any way, then even though Bathsheba as a character is not present, her presence still echoes throughout the latter chapters of 2 Samuel. Moreover, how we understand Bathsheba's role in 2 Sam 11 affects (and may be affected by) the way we read 2 Sam 13–24. Those who see Bathsheba as a catalyst for the tragedies that visit David's family might be tempted to further scapegoat her. Others may see Bathsheba as included among the many victims who were affected by David's actions and choices.

But Bathsheba is even more directly connected to 2 Sam 13–24 when we remember her identification in 2 Sam 11:4 as "the daughter of Eliam." Second Samuel 23:34 has told us that Eliam is the son of Ahithophel the Gilonite, who is Absalom's advisor in the coup against David. Using the same verb that David repeatedly used in 2 Samuel 11–12,[16] Absalom "sends for" (שלח) Ahithophel in 2 Sam 15:7; the same verse tells us that Ahithophel was David's counselor. Second Samuel 16:23 explains, "as if one had inquired at the oracle of God, so was the counsel of Ahithophel with both David and with Absalom." Indeed, when David hears that Ahithophel is among Absalom's conspirators, David prays, "Please, YHWH, frustrate the counsel of Ahithophel." (2 Sam 15:31) Ahithophel is the one who advises Absalom to go and lie with David's concubines in 2 Sam 16:21. And, in 2 Sam 17:1–3, Ahithophel asks permission from Absalom to go and kill David by himself, saying, "and I will strike the king alone" (והכיתי את־המלך לבדו).

Ahithophel is not explicitly linked to Bathsheba by the text, but their connection has not gone unnoticed. David Daube discusses the fact that Ahithophel advocates for Absalom to sleep with his father's concubines, saying that such "atrocious handling" of the concubines must have had a serious motivation. "It can be traced: he is the paternal grandfather of Bathsheba (2 Sam xi 3, xxiii 34), once treated by the king with the same ruthlessness."[17] Wesselius similarly suggests that "the reason why Ahithophel hated David" lies in what David had done to his granddaughter.[18] Interestingly, Wesselius titles the section where he talks

---

16. And that Bathsheba used in 2 Sam 11:5 to announce her pregnancy.

17. Daube, "Absalom and the Ideal King," 320. "When he now advocates the atrocious handling of the concubines, there must be special, weighty motivation. It can be traced: he is the paternal grandfather of Bathsheba (2 Sam xi 3, xxiii 34), once treated by the king with the same ruthlessness." Ibid.

18. Wesselius, "Joab's Death," 350.

about the connection between Ahithophel, Absalom, and Bathsheba as "Bathsheba's revenge," not "Ahithophel's revenge."[19] Baruch Halpern is another scholar who sees connections between Bathsheba and Ahithophel, although he acknowledges that the link between Bathsheba and Absalom's revolt is complex.[20] He writes,

> Ahithophel defected from David and supported Absalom's attempt to seize the crown. Yet he was the grandfather of Bathsheba. Ahitopel had nothing to gain from an upheaval if Solomon had a natural claim on the throne . . . Solomon's great-grandfather joined Absalom's cause in order to advance the family fortunes . . . Bathsheba will have remained in Jerusalem with David's harem, if she was in it during that episode. She will have been treated well, because of her grandfather's position, and probably her father's, in the ranks of Absalom's supporters. After the collapse of Absalom's coalition, she evidently set to work conspiring to set her son, and Uriah's, on the throne, as a measure of vengeance for her grandfather's death and, again, probably her father's.[21]

Thus, although Bathsheba is not explicitly mentioned in 2 Samuel 15 and following, her family connection makes her still present.[22]

Additionally, the connection to Ahithophel lends further insight into Bathsheba. As her grandfather, he is nonetheless described as a very active man in 2 Sam 15–17, so Bathsheba correspondingly must have been very young when David took her.[23] This age differential between her and David places even more guilt on David and less possibility of responsibility on Bathsheba. In 1 Kings, even though we see a mature Bathsheba, she still will be much younger than the elderly David.

19. Ibid., 345.

20. Halpern, *David's Secret Demons*, 404.

21. Ibid., 402–5.

22. The text does not, however, ascribe feelings to Ahithophel, as Wesselius does. Halpern, in particular, seems to fill in the gaps with aplomb. For example, although Halpern believes that Bathsheba remained in Jerusalem as one of Absalom's supporters, the fact that Bathsheba is identified as a "wife" (אשה) in 2 Sam 12:24, and that 2 Sam 15:16 specifies that David is leaving behind his "concubines" (פלגשים) would indicate that Bathsheba is part of the household that leaves Jerusalem with David. Halpern does acknowledge that he is not drawing on direct textual evidence, as he qualifies his argument with words like *evidently* and *probably*.

23. In *b. Sanh.*, 69b, the rabbis worked out that Bathsheba could have been as young as six years old. Cf. chapter 5, n. 52.

1 Kings 1:1–10: The Context

Bathsheba is not present in the first ten verses in 1 Kings, but these opening verses set the context for her reappearance. First, as mentioned, David
has changed. The first four verses introduce a new woman into David's
life. Because of his age and his inability to get warm under coverings, his
servants decide to search for a human heater. They tell David that they
will seek a young woman (נערה בתולה), who will do three things:
she will stand before David, she will be his attendant (סכנת), and she
will lie in David's bosom, with the result that he will be warm. The one
who is found is Abishag, from Shunem.[24] First Kings 1:4 describes her
as "exceedingly beautiful" (יפה עד־מאד), and goes on to explain that
while she was David's attendant (סכנת) and served him (ותשרתהו),
David did not know her. A few things about Abishag have implications
for our understanding of Bathsheba's character. The nature of Abishag's
relationship with David is especially significant, as it provides a contrast
with the relationship between Bathsheba and David, and as it correlates
with Adonijah's request to Bathsheba that he be given Abishag as a wife.

Berlin suggests that Abishag is a replacement for Bathsheba in
David's life,[25] but a close examination of Abishag will highlight four differences between them. First, the text is careful to explain that David did
not know her. Whether this is done for the purposes of characterizing
David as old and impotent (an exceedingly beautiful young woman may
lie in his bosom, but he does not know her sexually[26]) or characterizing Abishag in reference to Adonijah's request for her (and Solomon's

24. Shunem is a town in the hill country of Issachar (Josh 19:18), which was where
the Philistines encamped during a Philistine-Israelite battle during Saul's reign (1 Sam
28:4). Elisha stays with a Shunnamite woman whose dead son he later revived (2 Kgs
4:8–27). Frolov connects Shunem, and even Abishag, with the Shulammite woman in
the Song of Songs. "*No Return* for Shulammite," 256–58. Although the man in Song of
Songs is not necessarily Solomon, it would add an interesting footnote to Adonijah's
request for Abishag if his brother Solomon ended up wooing her.

25. In reference to 1 Kgs 1:15, Berlin writes, "One can feel a twinge of jealousy pass
through Bathsheba as she silently notes the presence of a younger, fresher woman."
"Characterization," 225.

26. The term בתולה should not be translated only as "virgin," but rather as a young
woman who is of the age of marriage, analogous to the English word *girl*. Of course, that
could mean she is a virgin, but does not necessarily nor automatically mean that. Cf.
Wenham, "*BᵉTUᵃlAh*," 326. Walls prefers to translate the Ugaritic *btlt* as "maiden" rather
than "virgin," "since the primary significance of the term is as an age, social, and gender
designation." *Goddess Anat*, 79.

response to that request), is not entirely clear. But it marks a difference between Abishag and Bathsheba. The latter is clearly named as David's wife with whom he did have intercourse. Second, Abishag is an attendant, or a סֹכֶנֶת, for David. [27] The root of this word, סכן, means "to be of use, service, benefit," and occurs three times in the participle form: twice in the feminine participle form in reference to Abishag, and once in Isa 22:15 to refer to the servant in charge of the palace. [28] The word is related to the Akkadian *šaknu* and *šakintu*. Solvang explains, "The positions of *sōkēn* and *sōkenet* are well attested in Ugaritic, Aramaic and Akkadian texts . . . In none of these examples is there any indication of sexual activity as a component of the position." [29] But Abishag is never referred to as David's wife, in contrast to Bathsheba (2 Sam 11:27; 12:24). Adonijah will be the first one who uses the term wife (אִשָּׁה) to describe Abishag but not in relation to David. A third piece of information about Abishag is that she is "exceedingly beautiful" (יָפָה עַד־מְאֹד). [30] Abishag's beauty is one of the main reasons that Berlin supposes that Bathsheba, "who was once young and attractive like Abishag, is herself now aging," [31] feels replaced by Abishag, but the Hebrew words used to describe their respective appearances are different. Bathsheba is טוֹבַת מַרְאֶה מְאֹד (very beautiful in appearance). Fourth, the servants tell David that the young woman will "lie in his bosom" (וְשָׁכְבָה בְחֵיקֶךָ, 1 Kgs 1:2). That string of words recalls Nathan's parable about the intimacy between the poor man and his ewe lamb and remind us of Bathsheba, but the physical

27. Mulder believes that Abishag is the סֹכֶנֶת for Bathsheba, and is supposed to take Bathsheba's place at David's side. Mulder, "Sokènèt in 1 Kön 1:2,4," 53. He suggests that Bathsheba has become old and impotent, and doesn't fit the ideals of a queenship, which emphasized youth and beauty. Fokkelman, however, challenges Mulder, saying, "Introducing Bathsheba as the person who is or must be represented is not supported by the text; the text itself provides another description of Abishag's risk." Fokkelman, *Narrative Art*, 1:347 n. 4. Again, our understanding of Ahithophel's age and its implications for Bathsheba's age must also challenge Mulder's supposition that Bathsheba is old and impotent. Certainly, she is older, but that does not mean that she is old.

28. The hiphil form of the verb in Ps 139:3 means "to be familiar with"; perhaps this meaning causes people to assume that there is a level of intimacy between Abishag and David.

29. Solvang, *A Woman's Place*, 141.

30. This description of Abishag also fits Sarai, who is "exceedingly beautiful" (יָפָה הִוא מְאֹד) (Gen 12:14). Joseph (Gen 39:6), David (1 Sam 16:12; 17:42), Tamar (2 Sam 12:1), Absalom (2 Sam 14:25), and the lover and the beloved in Song of Songs (1, 4, 6) are all described using the word יָפֶה, "handsome/beautiful."

31. Berlin, "Characterization," 225.

closeness between Bathsheba and David was never described in those terms. Thus, Bathsheba's character may be evoked by Abishag's,[32] but the differences between the two women also remain.

Verses 1–4 describe David and introduce Abishag; vv. 5–10 set up the problem to be resolved in this text: who will sit on David's throne?[33] Adonijah, David's son, desires to become king, and declares that he will do so (1 Kgs 1:5). Adonijah was initially introduced in 2 Sam 3:4 in the list of David's sons, but only by name. Here, he is one of the main characters. Although Adonijah is the heir apparent to the throne,[34] the words that are used to describe him signal the text's disapproval of his actions. Verse 5 explains that Adonijah exalts himself (מִתְנַשֵּׂא), a word that connotes arrogance in other places where it is used.[35] Also, Adonijah's actions explicitly echo those of Absalom's when the latter attempted to overthrow his father. Both sons provided themselves with a chariot, horses, and fifty runners.[36] Moreover, Adonijah is supported by David's general, Joab, and

32. Another similarity between Bathsheba and Abishag is that Abishag is described as "young" (נַעֲרָה), as Bathsheba must have been in 2 Sam 11, although 2 Sam 11 never explicitly describes Bathsheba in that way.

33. In 1926, Leonhard Rost published his argument that 2 Samuel 9–20 through 1 Kings 1–2 is a unified literary composition, the theme of which is to answer the question, who will sit on the throne of David? Rost, *Succession to the Throne of David*. Thornton alternately reformulated the question of the Succession Narrative as, why was it Solomon who succeeded David on the throne? Thornton, "Solomonic Apologetic," 160. Critiques of Rost generally fall into two categories. The first is that 2 Samuel 9, or 10–12, is not connected with the rest of the Succession Narrative. For example, cf. Bailey, *David in Love and War*. Lawlor also argues on the basis of the phrase וַיְהִי אַחֲרֵי־כֵן (and it happened afterwards) that is found in 2 Sam 10:1 and also in 2 Sam 13:1, that 2 Sam 10:1—12:31 is a literary unit with a chiastic structure that centers around 2 Sam 11:27a, and 2 Sam 13:1 thus begins a new section. "Theology and Art," 193, 205. The second critique is that Rost determines unity more on the basis of content than linguistic connections or literary style. Cf. Miller and Roberts, *Hand of the Lord*. In her *The Wages of Sin*, Keys reviews Rost's successors and detractors. Römer and de Pury also review the history of scholarship around Rost's thesis in "Deuteronomistic Historiography," 125–28.

34. This assumption—that as the eldest son, he would take the throne—is supported by Ishida, who writes, "The principle of primogeniture had been accepted in the royal succession since the inception of the Hebrew monarchy." Ishida, "Adonijah the Son of Haggith," 171. According to 2 Sam 3:2, Adonijah is David's fourth son. Amnon and Absalom have died, but it is not clear what has happened to Chileab, who is called "Daluiah" in LXX and 4QSamª, and "Daniel" in 1 Chr 3:1. At any rate, Chileab is not present to contend with Adonijah for the throne.

35. This is the hithpael participle of נשׂא, and is also used pejoratively in Num 16:3; Ezek 29:15; Prov 30:32; and Dan 11:14.

36. The Hebrew, though, is not exactly the same. Second Sam 15:1 uses the word

Abiathar the priest, but he is not supported by Zadok the priest, Benaiah the soldier,[37] Nathan the prophet, Shimei, Rei,[38] or David's mighty men (1 Kgs 1:9). Therefore, for unspecified reasons, Adonijah lacks the support of some key people in his desire (or attempt) to take the throne. The text does not leave us wondering long about what will be done, and Bathsheba plays a part in the resolution.

First Kings 1:11–31 may be divided into five scenes on the basis of dialogue: (1) vv. 11–14, Nathan's speech to Bathsheba; (2) vv. 15–21, Bathsheba's speech to David; (3) vv. 22–27, Nathan's speech to David; (4) vv. 28–30, David's speech to Bathsheba; and (5) v. 31, Bathsheba's response to David. Bathsheba is the recipient of the speech in the first and fourth scenes, and David receives the speeches in the second and third scenes. Bathsheba is physically present in four of the five scenes, but the scene from which she is absent remains important for her characterization. As we consider Bathsheba's characterization in Kings, once again, the gaps will be important for what they tell us about her and what they leave unsaid. Even as we see how she has developed, we will also see how she remains mysterious and enigmatic—a complex character throughout the narratives about her.

1 Kings 1:11–14: Nathan's Speech to Bathsheba

One of the gaps in 1 Kgs 1:11–14 has to do with the nature of the relationship between Bathsheba and Nathan. Does he approach her as an equal, as someone subject to her, or as someone who is directing her? When he tells her what to do, is he motivated by genuine concern for her and Solomon, or is he taking control of the situation for a weak and impressionable woman? Or, is there a mixture of motives? When we evaluate the content of what Nathan says to Bathsheba, we will find some clues for how to fill in this gap, as well as further insight into her character.

Nathan begins by posing a question to Bathsheba, who is identified as "the mother of Solomon." He asks, "Haven't you heard that Adonijah son of Haggith has become king, and our Lord David does not know?"

מרכבה for "chariot," and סוסים for "horses," while in 1 Kgs 1:5 Adonijah's "chariot" is רכב and his "horses" are פרשים.

37. According to 2 Sam 8:18 and 20:23, he is the commander of the Cherethites and Pelethites. Later, he becomes the commander of Solomon's army.

38. It is not clear who Shimei and Rei are; because neither name comes with either a patronym or a title, the text may be corrupt. Viviano, "Rei," 5:665.

The first thing to notice is the language of mothers and sons. Cogan encourages us not to read the repeated mentions of Haggith as mother of Adonijah as a basis for us to posit "a rivalry between her and Bathsheba,"[39] but Haggith is only mentioned twice in 1 Kings: in 1:11 and in 2:13.[40] In the latter reference, it is not necessary to identify Adonijah; there are no other Adonijahs with whom he might be confused. Also, in both places where we read "Adonijah son of Haggith," we also read "Bathsheba mother of Solomon." Thus, there is something significant about mentioning these mothers and sons in tandem. Second Samuel 3:4 introduces the sons born to David by means of their mothers, so these women are from the start connected to their sons. Bodner suggests that Nathan intends to exploit this maternal rivalry;[41] the text itself contributes to the maternal rivalry by always referring to "Adonijah son of Haggith" and "Bathsheba mother of Solomon."

The question Nathan asks is answered: she has heard.[42] Evidence for that can be found in scene 2, when Bathsheba describes Adonijah's sacrificial feast to David without Nathan having told her about that detail. But Nathan also says that David does not know about Adonijah's machinations, which is reminiscent of 1 Kgs 1:4. David did not "know" Abishag, nor does he "know" that Adonijah has become king.[43] Yet, when Nathan talks to David in scene 3, he diplomatically tells David that it must be Nathan himself who does not know about David's desire to have Adonijah succeed him. Thus, Nathan is more honest with Bathsheba than he is with the king, which suggests some level of comfort with her. Of course, Nathan did not mince words with David in 2 Sam 12,[44]

39. Cogan, *1 Kings*, 157.

40. Nothing is known about Haggith other than her name. Even her mention in 2 Sam 3:4 is without any other identifying information. Three out of David's six wives listed in 2 Sam 3:4 have some other identifying information about them: Ahinoam is from Jezreel, Abigail is the widow of Nabal the Carmelite, and Maacah is the daughter of King Talmai of Geshur. Haggith, Abital, and Eglah are only listed with their name.

41. Bodner, "Nathan," 50.

42. Nathan begins with the same interrogative (הלוֹא) with which Bathsheba was named in 2 Sam 11:3. The JPS translation "you must have heard" reflects the definite sense of the particle suggested by BDB, discussed previously. Again, I prefer to keep the sense of the word as a question, as it reflects more subtlety and suggestiveness.

43. Seow writes, "This lack of knowledge on his part is telling, for the king was once assumed to have had great wisdom and the ability 'to know all things that are on earth' (2 Sam 14:20)." "1 Kings," 18.

44. Cf. 2 Sam 12:7–14. Why would Nathan want or need to deal more gently with the feeble David in Kings than he did with the powerful David in 2 Samuel? Or, is it

so Nathan's honesty at this point does not necessarily mean that he does not respect Bathsheba. But Nathan is not completely honest with Bathsheba; he uses hyperbole when he says that Adonijah has "become king."[45] It could be that Nathan does so for rhetorical purposes.[46]

After Nathan asks Bathsheba if she has heard about Adonijah, he asserts that she must act to save her life and the life of her son Solomon (1 Kgs 1:12). Is this also hyperbolic, or are the lives of Bathsheba and Solomon really at stake? Such dramatic language would undoubtedly be motivational. Then again, if there was an obvious rivalry between Adonijah and Solomon (and Haggith and Bathsheba), then when Adonijah took the throne, perhaps the threat to Bathsheba and Solomon would be real. First Kings 2, after all, records the way that Solomon put his own kingdom in order by killing those who had not supported him. In some ways, the reasons behind why Nathan says what he does are moot, for Bathsheba will act.

In 1 Kgs 1:13, Nathan tells Bathsheba, "Go in at once to King David, and say to him, 'Did you not, my lord the king, swear to your servant, saying: Your son Solomon shall succeed me as king, and he shall sit on my throne? Why then is Adonijah king?'" Is this a command, or a suggestion? The gap about Nathan and Bathsheba's relationship still remains open, but in this verse, it is superseded by a larger gap: nowhere is it recorded in Samuel-Kings whether or not David really did swear to Bathsheba that Solomon would become king.[47] There are multiple possibilities for filling this gap. First is the possibility that David did make that oath to Bathsheba, and somehow Nathan knows. David may have done it in front of Nathan, or he may have told Nathan about it, or Bathsheba may have told Nathan about it. Nathan's role in declaring God's favor

---

because David is elderly and feeble that Nathan feels the need to be more diplomatic towards him?

45. Nelson explains, "Adonijah's sacrifice meal was not necessarily the occasion for an unauthorized coronation, although the wily Nathan makes it out to be just that. It may have been only a way of building goodwill among his potential supporters." *First and Second Kings*, 16.

46. Bodner writes, "It is noteworthy that Adonijah has not become king at this point in the narrative, but this fictional elaboration by the prophet heightens the efficacy of his speech to Bathsheba." "Nathan," 50.

47. And because the text does not explicitly record such a promise from David, Brueggemann believes that David never made one. Brueggemann, *1 & 2 Kings*, 14. Seow is also skeptical, because of "the importance of such a tradition to the Davidic monarchy." "1 Kings," 19.

for Solomon in 2 Sam 11:25 certainly points to his interest in the child.[48] Another possibility is that David's addled and aged mind has forgotten the promise, and he needs to be reminded by Bathsheba and Nathan. The other possibility is that David never made such a promise; Nathan (or Bathsheba) has just invented one. The text does not proffer any motivations for Nathan to do so, but we remember Nathan's interest in Solomon from the time of his birth.

This narrative gap provides different possibilities for Bathsheba's character. If David made the oath to her, it suggests a level of favor for her son—and for her—that places her above his other wives. If Bathsheba was the one who invented the promise, it would be evidence towards characterizing her as conniving.[49] Perhaps Nathan invented the promise; if so, then there could be any number of reasons why Bathsheba is willing to go along with his invention.[50] No matter which interpretation is chosen, there are still questions and problems. For instance, if David is so senile that he cannot remember the promise he made to Bathsheba, then why is he able to understand that Adonijah is not the proper heir to the throne?[51] This is a gap that cannot be filled by reading Samuel-Kings; the

48. Alter believes that one might expect to read about David's vow to put Solomon on the throne during the report of Solomon's "God-favored birth." *David Story*, 366.

49. However, it would seem that if someone did invent this oath, Nathan would be the more likely candidate than Bathsheba, for it comes first from Nathan's lips.

50. David Marcus, for example, assumes Nathan did invent the promise, and believes that Bathsheba was willing to play a part in Nathan's invention to get back at David for what he did to her in 2 Samuel 11. "The impetus for Bathsheba to act in consort with Nathan to deceive David, it may be supposed, was that David had at one time deceived her." Marcus, "David the Deceiver," 167. Marcus argues that those whom David deceived would want to turn around and deceive him. "How did David deceive Bathsheba? A number of possibilities come to mind. David was prepared to abandon Bathsheba even before she announced her pregnancy; he was prepared to abandon her during her pregnancy (since he wanted to hide his paternity of the child). He certainly was prepared to abandon her had Uriah gone home . . . It is even possible that David did once promise Bathsheba regarding Solomon, but did not follow up on it. Any or all of the above would have been perceived by Bathsheba as deception on David's part. Added to the indignities which David had perpetrated on her (he had violated her wedlock, subjected her to a charge of adultery, forced her to suffer loss of husband and first child, and he had not mourned the death of that child), we have a number of explanations for her revenge . . . We are disposed to regard her as devious, seeing an opportunity to get rid of an always potentially dangerous rival to Solomon." Ibid., 167

51. Aschkenasy, *Woman at the Window*, 111. Aschkenasy also notes that when Nathan first mentioned this promise to Bathsheba, she did not protest or question it, which would suggest that David had promised her that Solomon would succeed him, 110.

question of whether or not David swore to Bathsheba that her son would be king remains ultimately unanswered.

However, in 1 Chr 22:9–10, David recounts to Solomon that God told him that Solomon would succeed him. First Chronicles 23:1 recounts, "And David was old, and full of days, and he made his son Solomon king over Israel." It makes sense that if God, indeed, told David that Solomon would be his successor, there would be no need to include the intrigues of 1 Kings 1–2.[52] But if we limit our reading to the narrative in Samuel-Kings, we must wait until scene 4 of 1 Kings 1 and David's response to Bathsheba to gain further illumination of both of their characters.

Nathan concludes his speech, and this scene, by telling Bathsheba that while she is "still speaking,"[53] he will come in to "confirm" her words. Aschkenasy asks, "If there was such a promise, why does the prophet have to confirm it?"[54] The word "confirm" is the piel form of מלא, which means to fill, fulfill, accomplish, or complete. Only in 1 Kgs 1:14 is it translated as "to confirm."[55] Bodner suggests, "The Hebrew verb מלא should be translated more literally as 'fill up' rather than 'confirm' (as RSV); 'confirm' has the sense of validating or authenticating what has been said hitherto, whereas Nathan's speech is designed to accomplish the intended effect of Bathsheba's discourse to David. Nathan's machination is not to corroborate her witness or verify her story, but rather to rhetorically finish what she begins."[56] Victor Sasson has identified the phrase as a technical juridical term in the Mesad Hashavyahu lawsuit,[57] which lends a level of seriousness to what Nathan proposes to do. Surely,

---

52. Again, Bathsheba does not really appear in Chronicles; she is turned into Bathshua, and both the narrative of 2 Samuel 11–12 and 1 Kings 1–2 is expunged. Yet, if Chronicles is read alongside Samuel-Kings, as the rabbis seemed to do, then there is no question that she or Nathan made up David's promise. Cf. chapter 5 for further discussion.

53. The Hebrew word is the piel participle of דבר, which is properly translated in a continual sense, especially with the preceding word "still" (עוד).

54. Aschkenasy, *Woman at the Window*, 110.

55. BDB, 570; *HALOT*, 584.

56. Bodner, "Nathan," 51 n. 21.

57. Sasson, "An Unrecognized Juridical Term," 57–63, and "A Matter to Be Put Right," 115–20. Yabneh/Yavneh Yam is the name of the archeological site adjacent to Mesad Hashavyahu on the Mediterranean coast, and the ostracon was found at the latter.

the question of who will take the throne is a weighty one, and Nathan's witness may be a way to make sure the law is followed.

Different interpreters have taken different sides concerning the relationship between Nathan and Bathsheba, for as we have seen, evidence could be mustered for different directions. Aschkenasy writes, "Although Natan and the uninitiated reader may think that the prophet is manipulating her, perhaps the opposite is right. By playing the helpless mother, Bathsheba empowers Natan to take a bolder, more decisive action in her favor and force the issue on David."[58] Brueggemann, however, believes that "Nathan gives Bathsheba her lines to speak to David; he scripts the entire scenario."[59] An interpretation that better accounts for the narrative evidence is that Nathan's "advice" is not dictatorial but sincere, and Nathan is unable to amend the situation on his own. As previously noted, Nathan is honest with Bathsheba about David's situation of not knowing. Moreover, there are a number of people with whom Nathan could collude—Zadok, Benaiah, Shimei, Rei, or the fighting men—but he goes to Bathsheba. If that is not a sign of their equality, it must be a sign of the significance of the relationship between David and Bathsheba. If it appears that Nathan needs Bathsheba's assistance, the language about his "filling" her words would also suggest that that she needs his. Thus, there is a strong mutuality between Nathan and Bathsheba, which will be made more evident in their conversations with David.

1 Kings 1:15–21: Bathsheba's Speech to David

There is a gap about the exact nature of the relationship between David and Bathsheba depicted in 1 Kgs 1:15–21. Both intimacy and formality can be seen, and we must also remember the differences in their respective ages. One clue as to the nature of their relationship is found in the location in which they meet. The text specifies that Bathsheba goes into the king's "chamber," or "bedchamber." Based on its use elsewhere in the Bible, this word (חדר) seems to connote two things: a place of privacy or a sanctuary, and a place where sexual encounters occur.[60] The Hebrew

---

58. Aschkenasy, *Woman at the Window*, 115.

59. Brueggemann, *1 & 2 Kings*, 20.

60. BDB, 293. *HALOT* translates it as "dark room," or "bedroom," 293. In Gen 43:30, Joseph goes into the חדר when he is overcome with emotion after seeing his full brother Benjamin. It is the refuge and hiding place for Ben-hadad in 1 Kgs 20:30, and the place where king Joash is hidden from his wicked grandmother Athaliah in 2 Kgs 11:2.

"can mean any sort of inner room lying outside the central court."[61] Fokkelman sees this location as significant for the relationship between David and Bathsheba. "Something of the intimacy between Bathsheba and her husband is reflected here, on the figurative level. This woman is able to draw nearest to David and this she does."[62] This location probably connects with David's age and infirmity (זָקֵן מ בָּאֵי, cf. 1 Kgs 1:1), as Nathan will also converse with David in the chamber (1 Kgs 1:23), for the text does not refer to David leaving. Yet, unlike with Nathan, Bathsheba's entrance into the chamber is unannounced, suggesting that she does enjoy a particular closeness and privilege with the king.[63] When Bathsheba enters, she bows and does homage to David, though, so there is a level of formality between the two. That action can also be contrasted with Nathan, who will enter and bow, but will do so with his face towards the ground. Bathsheba will not do that particular action until later. Therefore, even though there is some element of formality in the way Bathsheba acts towards David, it is less so than in the relationships others have with him. Of course, the formality and intimacy that are both pictured in Bathsheba's presence in the chamber are not mutually exclusive. They illustrate the complexity of the relationship between Bathsheba and David, and some of the complexity of her character as well.

The other insight into Bathsheba's character may be found in her speech to David. While it does not differ significantly in content from what Nathan had told her to say, neither does she merely repeat Nathan's words to David.[64] The changes she makes confirm that Nathan is not just directing her. She is neither his puppet nor his parrot, but acts with her own initiative and intelligence. There are seven differences between what Nathan told Bathsheba to say, and what she actually says. First, Bathsheba

---

Qoheleth advises in Eccl 10:20 that one should not revile a rich man, even in one's חדר. In Judg 15:1, Samson asks permission from his father-in-law to go into the chamber (חדר) to see his wife when he is told that she has married another. Perhaps the text most closely linked to ours in terms of content and time is 2 Sam 13:10, and the חדר is the place where Tamar brings food to Amnon and where he rapes her.

61. DeVries, *1 Kings*, 15.

62. Fokkelman, *Narrative Art*, 1:355.

63. Abishag is also present, but she is there to serve (שרת) the king.

64. One word that is used in both Nathan's and Bathsheba's speeches is "maidservant" (אמה) to describe Bathsheba. Jepsen explains that this word is used "as a term of self-effacement in speech to royalty." "Amah und Schiphchah," 293–97. This term is different than the one used to describe Abishag; Bathsheba is not a סכנת.

makes into a statement what Nathan had formed as a question. He tells her to ask, "Did you not swear," where she says definitively, "you swore." Second, not only does Bathsheba tell David that he swore, but she adds the phrase "by YHWH your God." This raises the stakes for David: to swear by YHWH is a serious thing.[65] Bathsheba in 2 Samuel was following the ritual laws for purification, and this reminds us that she may well know of other laws for how to relate with YHWH. Third, Bathsheba is bolder with David than Nathan told her to be. Nathan suggested that she ask David why Adonijah has become king (1:13). Instead, she tells David of that news, and then tells him that he does not know about it. While Nathan had said to Bathsheba that David did not know of Adonijah's actions (1:11), he did not tell her to say that to David. Bathsheba is not treating David with kid gloves; if he has become senile, she calls his attention to that which he does not know. Fourth, Bathsheba goes on to give David details about what Adonijah has done: sacrificing animals and inviting certain people, details that were present in the narrator's account in 1 Kgs 1:9–10, but not in what Nathan told Bathsheba. But Bathsheba does not mention all the people not included by Adonijah. She names Solomon, but not Nathan, Benaiah, or the fighting men (cf. 1 Kgs 1:10). Fifth, when Bathsheba names Solomon as the person whom Adonijah did not invite to his feast, she refers to him as David's "servant" (עבד), a term that Nathan did not use in 1 Kgs 1:11–14.[66] It would appear that in reference to Solomon, Bathsheba does not try to emphasize his filial relation to David, but instead his loyalty in service. We may be reminded of the way Uriah was described as David's servant during the report of his death (2 Sam 11:21, 24). Solomon will not be referred to as David's son until 1 Kgs 1:33, after David has vowed to put him on the throne. Sixth, Bathsheba tells David that "the eyes of all Israel" are on him to tell them who will succeed him on the throne. Once again, this detail was not in what Nathan said to Bathsheba. Finally, Bathsheba tells David that when he dies, she and her son Solomon will be counted as offenders.[67] We see once again in Bathsheba's own words the importance

65. Leviticus 19:12 prohibits swearing falsely by YHWH's name, while Deut 6:13 and 10:20 prohibit swearing by the name of any god other than YHWH.

66. Nathan will, however, later refer to Solomon using the same term, which begs the question of how much he has told Bathsheba to say.

67. Although here Bathsheba speaks openly about David's death ("when my lord the king lies down with his fathers"), in v. 31 she will express hope that he will live forever. Cf. the discussion below.

of her position as mother.[68] And again, she does not appeal to David's paternity: Solomon is "my son," not "your son." Nathan had told Bathsheba that she needed to act in order to save her and Solomon's lives, but he did not tell Bathsheba to raise the issue of safety with David. Here is another point where Bathsheba does not follow a script.

Bathsheba's speech to David is another way that she is characterized in a generally positive manner. We can read in her words that she does not need to have her hand held by Nathan, but she has courage, wisdom, and intelligence. Her speech demonstrates her rhetorical prowess, perhaps fitting with the etymology of her name as "Daughter of an Oath."[69]

1 Kings 1:22–27: Nathan's Speech to David

What Nathan told Bathsheba in 1 Kgs 1:14 transpires; she is still speaking when Nathan enters in v. 22. The setting is not specified, but it would appear that David receives Nathan in the inner chamber described in 1 Kgs 1:15. Obviously, then, this is not an entirely private and intimate place. But, as mentioned before, Nathan is announced to David (1:23), while Bathsheba was not. Moreover, even though both Bathsheba and Nathan bow to David, he bows "with his face to the ground," something she does not do in 1:16, but will do in 1:31.[70] Bathsheba is not mentioned in this scene, and neither are there many gaps that are significant for her character. However, the differences between her speech to David in the previous scene, and what Nathan says to David here, underscore her independence and initiative in that she was not only doing what he told her to do.

The content of Nathan's speech is similar to Bathsheba's speech in the previous scene, but again, there are notable differences. Bathsheba said to David, "you swore by YHWH your God," and Nathan simply said, "you said."[71] Both Bathsheba and Nathan say that David had indicated

---

68. DeVries, however, sees in the grammar that Bathsheba is more worried about her own safety than that of her son. "Although a singular verb may often precede a compound subject, this styling expresses closely Bathsheba's evident concern first of all for her own safety, which naturally depends on that of Solomon." *1 Kings*, 15.

69. Cf. chapter 2, n. 58.

70. Because the text does not specify why she does it later, this is part of the openness of her character that remains in 1 Kings. It could be that she does it later in the presence of the others, as part of an act. It could also convey a depth of gratitude and a pledge of loyalty.

71. Translations often render this as "you must have said," or "surely you said." There

that one of his sons would be king after him and would sit on his throne (יִמְלֹךְ אַחֲרִי וְהוּא יֵשֵׁב עַל־כִּסְאִי), but Bathsheba names Solomon, while Nathan names Adonijah. And although both discuss Adonijah's sacrificial meal, Nathan adds the detail that it happened "today," and lets David know that "they are eating and drinking before him and they say, 'Long live the king Adonijah'" (1 Kgs 1:25). The list of the people who were and were not invited is also slightly different. Both Bathsheba and Nathan say that "all the sons of the king" and Abiathar the priest were included, but only Bathsheba tells David that Joab was also invited.[72] Nathan tells David "the chiefs of the army" were invited (1 Kgs 1:25), but he does not mention Joab by name. Both Bathsheba and Nathan tell David that "Solomon your servant" was not invited to the feast, but Nathan adds three more names: himself, whom he describes to David as "your servant," Zadok the priest, and Benaiah son of Jehoida. As previously mentioned, Nathan's whole strategy seems to be to assume the best for David, that David really did intend for Adonijah to take the throne, and he (Nathan) is the one who had not been told about the king's decision. But Nathan may also be asking if David had told Solomon who would take the throne; both Nathan and Solomon are identified as "your servant," and 1 Kgs 1:27 simply says, "you did not make known to *your servant* who would sit on the throne."[73]

1 Kings 1:28–30: David's Speech to Bathsheba

David's response in 1 Kgs 1:28 to Nathan's speech is not to summon Adonijah, or Solomon, but to ask for Bathsheba. We can fill the textual gap by assuming that she left when Nathan entered; there would be no need for her to be called if she was still present. When she comes, she

---

is no auxiliary verb present in the Hebrew, but inserting it helps to smooth out what Nathan is suggesting.

72. As mentioned about 2 Sam, there seems to be some sort of dynamic to the relationship between Bathsheba and Joab. Though neither of them directly interact with each other in the text, they are connected by Uriah.

73. In other places where people use the term "your servant," it usually refers to the speaker, unless the other "servant" is identified by name (cf. 2 Sam 11:21). Potiphar's wife calls Joseph "your servant" in Gen 39:19, though, without using his name. There is also a *Kethib/Qere* in 1 Kgs 1:27; the *Kethib* is in the plural, referring to the entire council privy to information about the succession, while the *Qere* is in the singular, and is supported by LXX. In that sense, whether singular or plural, Nathan would be included in the "servant" or "servants."

does not bow down in obeisance, as she and Nathan had done previously, but she stands before David (ותעמד לפני המלך). This is the same string of words used to describe Abishag's "standing" before David in 1 Kgs 1:2.

Whereas in scene 1 it was not at all clear if David had indeed sworn to Bathsheba about Solomon taking the throne, here there is no ambiguity about his decision, as David says, "By the life of YHWH who ransomed my soul from all distress: for just as I swore to you by YHWH, God of Israel, saying, 'Solomon your son will be king after me, and he will sit on my throne in my place,' thus I will do this day" (1 Kgs 1:29–30). Solvang says, "There is no way to establish for certain that David did make such an oath prior to 1 Kgs. It is only possible to confirm that he *took responsibility* for having made such a commitment *to Bathsheba*."[74] Not only does David swear "by YHWH," as Bathsheba told him he had (1 Kgs 1:17), but there are a couple of additions to that brief phrase of hers. First, he begins his oath with "By the life of YHWH who ransomed my soul from all distress," adding the phrase that is common in the psalms to express God's deliverance and salvation.[75] He also specifies that he swears "by YHWH God of Israel," where Bathsheba told David "you swore by YHWH *your* God." Therefore, he is not only repeating what she had told him.

In David's vow, Solomon again is not described as David's son, but as Bathsheba's son. Therefore, David's words suggest that he is not primarily motivated by his parental responsibility to Solomon, but rather by his faithfulness to his promise made in the name of YHWH to Bathsheba. There is also a sense of the immediacy of the vow David does make to Bathsheba. He declares that it will happen "this day" (היום הזה). These verses are significant for Bathsheba's overall characterization. Although David is feeble and old, he still has the final say as to who will replace him on the throne. However, Bathsheba has developed into having a position of authority over him, as he listens to what she says. He also listened to Nathan, but there was something significant for David about having Bathsheba present when he made his announcement. Here, therefore, is a clear example of how David and Bathsheba's rising

---

74. Solvang, *A Woman's Place*, 148.

75. God's "redemption of the soul" is mentioned in Pss 34:22; 49:15; 55:19; 69:19; 71:23, and David used that exact phrase (חי־יהוה אשר־פדה את־נפשי מכל־צרה) in 2 Sam 4:9 upon hearing that Saul is dead.

and falling have been in counterpoint with one another. In 2 Samuel 11, he sent for her and she came—she did what he commanded her to do. In 1 Kings 1, he calls for her (קְרָא), and she comes, but this time he does what she has told him to do. We can see that although she remains the minor character, she also has the power to contribute substantively to her own son's rise to power.

1 Kings 1:31: Bathsheba's Response to David

But in the final scene of this section, 1 Kgs 1:31, we see that Bathsheba is still complex and enigmatic. She is the only actor in this scene, but since there are no explanations for her actions and words, she still could be characterized in any number of ways. Her actions mirror those of Nathan when he came in to see David in 1 Kgs 1:23, as she "bows down" (קָדַד). But Nathan showed his respect to David immediately when he came before him, while Bathsheba, in this second entry, waits to show such respect until David has made good on his promise. Not only does Bathsheba bow, but she does so with her "face to the ground" (אַפַּיִם אָרֶץ), as Nathan did in 1 Kgs 1:23. The text does not explain why she bows to David at this point and in this manner. Bathsheba could be sincerely appreciative that David will keep the promise he made, and so she bows to him in a posture of gratitude.[76] Or, she could be going through the motions of respect and homage as a final step in the plan to convince David to put Solomon on the throne. Even if she and Nathan did convince David that there was a promise, she might still be genuinely grateful that their plan succeeded. The gesture could mean different things and have different implications for her character, depending on whether there really was a Davidic promise about Solomon as the next king. And as previously discussed, based on the text of Samuel-Kings, we do not know the answer to that question.

Similarly, there is no way to determine Bathsheba's tone in her statement, "May my lord the king David live forever." Brueggemann, for one, believes that her wish "is less than earnest."[77] Bathsheba's words are grammatically different from the other places in this chapter where people wish a long life for the king (1:25 for Adonijah and 1:34, 39 for Solomon), but the exact string is used often in later texts addressing for-

---

76. Cf. David's humble, grateful response to God in 2 Sam 7.

77. Brueggemann, *1 & 2 Kings*, 16.

eign kings (Dan 2:4; 3:9; 5:10; and Neh 2:3). It is also in contrast to her matter-of-fact comment that David would "lie down with his fathers" in v. 21. Seow suggests that her statement is "surely not an expression of hope for David's physical immortality, but a wish that David would live on through his lineage upon the throne, as promised by the deity in Nathan's oracle (2 Sam 7:12–16)."[78] The potential irony in this statement here also points to her complexity—she could be honestly hoping for David's long life, but she also may be eager for his death.[79] Although speech often gives us insight into characters, as Bathsheba speaks, key aspects of her character remain undefined.

After her actions and words, Bathsheba fades away from the scene. In v. 32, David requests that Zadok the priest, Nathan (who seems to have, like Bathsheba, left when the other entered the room), and Benaiah be sent to him. If Bathsheba is still present in the inner chamber when David issues the commands for Solomon's coronation, there is no indication of her presence. She will not reappear until 1 Kgs 2:13. In the interim verses, Solomon rides on David's mule to Gihon[80] and is anointed king. Therefore, in v. 39, the oath that David swore to Bathsheba is finally fulfilled. The text explains that the sound of music and merriment after Solomon's anointing is so great that "the earth is split open by the sounds" (1:40). When Adonijah and his guests hear of what has happened, he and his guests are afraid, but Solomon promises that Adonijah will be safe from harm if he remains worthy and does not act wickedly. First Kings 2:1–12 describes David's last words of instruction to Solomon, which includes advice about dealing with David's friends and foes. First Kings 2:10 records David's death, 2:11 is a summary of the length of his rule, and 2:12 states that Solomon sat on the throne of David and his rule was firmly established.

1 Kings 2:13–18: Bathsheba and Adonijah

Bathsheba in 1 Kings 2 interacts with Adonijah and Solomon, the contender for the throne and the one who ultimately received the throne. It is appropriate to separate out those encounters into two scenes. In the

78. Seow, "1 Kings," 19.

79. He does die, too—in the narrative space of just thirty-one verses.

80. Gihon is a public place, so everyone knows that he has become king in contrast to the relative privacy of the place where Adonijah held his feast, En-Rogel. Cogan, *1 Kings*, 161.

first one, 1 Kgs 2:13–18, Adonjiah comes to Bathsheba with a request that she ask Solomon to give him Abishag as a wife. This scene has two gaps, both of which have possibilities for Bathsheba's character. The first gap is why Adonijah chooses to come to Bathsheba, and the second gap is why she responds as she does.

In terms of the first gap, there must be something about Bathsheba that makes Adonijah approach her. Is she safe—or safer than others, at least? Does he believe she can be manipulated? Does he assume she has the power to make such decisions?[81] In 1 Kgs 2:13, he is identified as "Adonjiah son of Haggith," and she is identified as "Bathsheba, mother of Solomon" (1 Kgs 2:13). As previously noted, there is some sort of rivalry between these mothers and sons,[82] and at this point, Bathsheba and Solomon are the ones who have come out as the victors. Bathsheba speaks first, asking if his visit is friendly. "The implication of the question is that the rivalry between the two parties had not dissipated, which suggests that this conversation took place not long after Solomon took the throne."[83] That she even asks such a question, though, belies her naïveté—she knows enough to be cautious. Adonijah's reply is affirmative, and he asks if he might have a word with her. She then commands him to "speak."

Adonijah begins his request in 1 Kgs 2:15–16 by telling Bathsheba, "You know" (יָדַעַתְּ). This is in marked contrast with David in the previous chapter, who thrice was described as not knowing: once in reference to Abishag, once when Nathan described David to Bathsheba, and once to his face by Bathsheba. Bathsheba is someone who does possess knowledge, and Adonijah is aware of it. Adonijah then says that "all Israel" looked to him to rule. Bathsheba used similar (hyperbolic?) language when she told David that the eyes of "all Israel" were on him to declare who would take the throne. Yet, Adonijah's hyperbole is more extreme. We know the people who did not support his regency: Zadok, Benaiah, Nathan, Shimei, Rei, and David's warriors (הַגִּבּוֹרִים, 1 Kgs 1:8). But if Adonijah exaggerated in his statement that all Israel wanted

---

81. Cushman argues that Bathsheba does function as a gebîrâ in 1 Kings 1–2 (cf. note 12), since one of the particular roles of a gebîrâ like Šibtu, wife of King Zimri-Lim of Mari, was as administrator of the palace household with special authority over the harem. "Politics of the Royal Harem," 330.

82. Walsh, *1 Kings*, 47.

83. Cogan, *1 Kings*, 175.

him to be king, he is properly, or diplomatically, reverent when he ascribes Solomon's ascendance to the will of YHWH. Alter explains that
Adonijah tries to have it both ways in his speech to Bathsheba: "On the
one hand, the kingship really was his, and he enjoyed popular support;
on the other hand, he is prepared to be reconciled with the idea that it
was God's determination that the crown should pass on from him to his
brother. There may be a note of petulance here: Adonijah speaks of his
situation as though he deserved some sort of consolation prize."[84]

Adonijah has set the stage for his request, which he then asks
Bathsheba not to refuse. She once again responds with brevity, commanding him again, "Speak." This is a wonderfully brief response. She
has not committed herself to anything. Of course, we once again have
no idea as to her tone: she could be amused, frightened, suspicious, or
intrigued. Because she has not refused to *hear* his request, Adonijah proceeds, urging her to ask Solomon to give him Abishag as a wife. Adonijah
concludes by expressing his confidence that Solomon will not refuse her
request (1 Kgs 2:17).

We can see from Adonijah's words that he believes Bathsheba is the
person who can get Abishag for him as his wife. His perspective on her,
as evident in his language, both gives us insight into her character and
helps close up the gap as to why he would approach her. First, he believes
that she has the power to make this happen. He was less confident that
she would accede to his request than he is that Solomon will accede to
her request. Second, Adonijah is not afraid of Bathsheba, which is probably why he would approach her instead of Solomon, whom he does
fear (cf. 1 Kgs 1:50–53). But third, even if he is not afraid of her, he still
respects her. That respect can be seen in the way Adonijah asks her not
to turn her face from him (1 Kgs 1:16).

But if Adonijah's words help us understand why he would approach
Bathsheba and also lends insight into her character, the second gap in
this scene—why Bathsheba responds to Adonijah as she does—is far
less understandable. What Bathsheba says to Adonijah in 1 Kgs 1:18 is,
"Good. *I* will speak concerning you to the king." Although this is not as
terse as her previous one-word answers to him, it is still enigmatic. What
does she mean by the word *good* (טוב)? Is his request a good one? Is
what will happen to him "good" for Solomon? Is she simply indicating,
"All right, I will do this"? Seow points out how she is not agreeing to relay

---

84. Alter, *David Story*, 377.

the petition itself, but only that she will speak to Solomon "about you" (עָלֶיךָ).[85] Nancy Bowen acknowledges the openness of the text as far as Bathsheba's intent when she agrees to intercede for Adonijah. "What cannot be determined is if Bathsheba is acting in good faith or with cunning deviousness."[86] Remember that her first question to Adonijah demonstrated that she was not completely naïve regarding him; therefore, we read her awareness into her character here. But neither does she have to be sinister in order to proceed as she promised Adonijah she would.

1 Kings 2:19–24: Bathsheba and Solomon

We do not have to wait long for Bathsheba to act: in the following verse, she goes to Solomon to speak to him "concerning Adonijah." This second scene in 1 Kings 2, between Bathsheba and Solomon, takes place in vv. 19–24, and as with Bathsheba's character up to this point, there are still gaps about her. The first one is the exact nature of her relationship with her son. When she goes to Solomon, he arises to meet her, and he bows to her.[87] However, she does not bow to him. Not only does she not show Solomon the same obeisance that she did David (1 Kgs 1:15), but Solomon sets a throne for her on his right. Other texts illustrate how that location is a position of honor.[88] Here, too, is evidence of Bathsheba's continued development. In 1 Kings 1, she was "mother of Solomon." Now, in 1 Kings 2, she has become "mother of the king." Her maternal relationship with her son (for example, in v. 20, Solomon calls

---

85. Seow, "1 Kings," 32.

86. Bowen, "Quest for the Historical Gebîrâ," 605.

87. The LXX variant, which will be discussed in further detail in the following chapter, refers to Solomon kissing his mother instead of bowing down to her. But Gray explains, "The queen-mother in the ancient Near East enjoyed great respect, and a royal epistle among the Ras Shamra texts (Gordon UT, 1965, 117, 5), where the king declares 'At the feet of my mother I bow down,' seems to authenticate the MT over against the G variant." *1 & 2 Kings*, 105.

88. For example, the divine craftsmen are honored when they are "seated on the right hand" of Baal in the Ugaritic Myth of Baal: 2.5.46–48. Driver, *Canaanite Myths*, 99. The queen sits at the right hand of the king in Ps 45:10, and YHWH tells the king to sit at his right hand in Ps 110:1. Psalm 110:1 is frequently quoted or alluded to in the NT to refer to Jesus in various ways. Cf. Hay, *Glory at the Right Hand*. Jesus' location at the right hand of God is viewed as an expression of exaltation (e.g., Acts 2:33–35; 5:31), evidence of his divine sonship (e.g., Matt 22:44 [cf. Mark 12:36, Luke 20:42–43], Matt 26:64 [cf. Mark 14:62], Luke 22:69), and the reason that he is able to intercede for us (e.g., Rom 8:34).

her "mother")[89] has become intertwined with the more political role of Queen Mother. The increased power and authority can be seen by her placement at Solomon's right hand.

Bathsheba begins her speech to Solomon in 1 Kgs 2:20 by telling him that she has "one small request." Perhaps she is trying to minimize something that is more major, or perhaps she honestly believes this request is not a large one; the text does not specify. However, it is worth noting that once again, Bathsheba does not merely follow a script that was given to her by a man; she adds the adjective *small* to Adonijah's request from 1 Kgs 2:16.[90] Solomon encourages her to ask, and in response to her injunction not to refuse her, he promises that he will not refuse.

Bathsheba spells out what Adonijah wishes, saying, "Give Abishag the Shunammite to Adonijah your brother as a wife" (1 Sam 2:21). It is noteworthy that she adds the identification "your brother" to his name, but again, her motives for doing so are left open. Perhaps she wants Solomon to be benevolent to one of his family members,[91] or perhaps she is well aware that this brother was, and apparently still is, a contender for the throne. Clearly, Solomon is aware of his fraternal connection to Adonijah, as his answer to Bathsheba makes clear: "he is my elder brother."[92] Solomon's assertion in 2 Kgs 2:20 that he will not refuse his mother's request turns out to be ultimately rhetorical, because in 2 Kgs 2:22, he does refuse it. In contrast with David, "who passionately vowed to accede to Bathsheba's request, Solomon reprimands his mother for making the request,"[93] saying, "Why do *you* ask Abishag the Shunammite for Adonijah? Ask for him the kingship, for he is my older brother, and the priest Abiathar and Joab son of Zeruiah are for him." The text did not refer to Abishag as David's wife, and made it clear that David did not sleep with her. But, based on Solomon's response, it would seem that Abishag was close enough to David that Adonijah's request is still tantamount to a bid for power.

---

89. Cogan, *1 Kings*, 176.

90. Adonijah said, "One request, one, I am asking from you; do not turn your face." 1 Kgs 2:16.

91. Cf. Fokkelman, *Narrative Art*, 1:395.

92. Solomon also identifies Abiathar and Joab as Adonijah's supporters. Adonijah, Abiathar, and Joab die in 1 Kgs 2:25–34, in the order in which Solomon names them in 1 Kgs 2:22.

93. Aschkenasy, *Woman at the Window*, 113.

Bathsheba once again fades from the scene towards the end. Where Solomon "spoke to his mother" in 2:22, starting in 2:23, Solomon makes a vow that is directed to God. The text does not tell us that Bathsheba leaves, but as we saw with both Bathsheba and Nathan in the previous chapter, a description of someone leaving should not necessarily be expected. After Solomon sarcastically tells his mother to "request the kingship" for Adonijah, he vows that Adonijah will die. Solomon's vow is worth looking at in slightly closer detail. First of all, the narrator tells us that "Solomon swore by YHWH." Bathsheba described David's vow as "by YHWH your God" (1:17), and David referred to his vow as "by YHWH, God of Israel" (1:30), but there are no other descriptors of YHWH in what Solomon says. Then, Solomon takes on a self-imprecatory oath, saying, "Thus may God do to me and thus may he add." In v. 24, Solomon recounts the history of his own succession and connects it to 2 Samuel 7 and 1 Kgs 2:4 before he vows that Adonijah will die. As Adonijah did before him, Solomon also ascribes his ascension to the throne to God. Finally, Solomon says that Adonijah will die "this day" (1:24). The last place where that timing was specified, David said that he would fulfill his promise to Bathsheba "this day." It happens; the end of our pericope tells us that Adonijah died.

It would appear that Bathsheba's role in the drama of David's story and her own son's succession has come to an end. Although she played an important role, especially in Solomon's ascendancy, she is still a minor character. But though minor, she remains quite complex. We heard many more words from her in Kings than in Samuel, which was an indication of her development. However, even though she spoke more in Kings, the mysteries of many of her motives still remain. In fact, with so many words and so little definitive explanation, her complexity is highlighted even more in Kings.

We also can witness development in the relationships Bathsheba has with others from 2 Samuel to 1 Kings. Nathan, David, and Solomon all reappear in 1 Kings to interact with Bathsheba, but there is a change in the nature of many of those relationships. Nathan did not speak to Bathsheba in 2 Samuel, only about her. In 1 Kings, Nathan speaks directly to her, and it would seem that he needs her as a partner in his own plan. Previously, David was the one who told others what to do, as illustrated in the way he sent for people throughout 2 Sam 11–12. In 1 Kings, he is being told what to do by Bathsheba, which shows a change in both of their positions.[94] Solomon was just born when 2 Samuel 12 ended, so Bathsheba's interaction with him is clearly different in 1 Kings. In their relationship we see that he respects her and defers to her—and yet still he will refuse the request she presents to him.

As in Samuel, here too Bathsheba continues to be characterized in a generally positive manner. One important conclusion can be made from Bathsheba's speeches: she does not only, or merely, say what other men tell her to say, but adds her own words to what they have suggested. Therefore, she displays a certain amount of intelligence and independence. Moreover, she is not naïve, especially where her own son is concerned. On the other hand, Solomon's decision to kill Adonijah is not necessarily something which she plotted or in which she participated.

What we do know about Bathsheba is that her role in the plot of the larger story comes to an end in 1 Kings 2. She is not mentioned again after 1 Kgs 2:22 when Solomon has been placed on the throne and has the motivation to make his kingdom secure. Perhaps this happens because as he begins to rise she will fall (or, at least, fade away), repeating the theme of characters rising and falling that has been seen throughout this pericope. Gunn and Fewell say that while we long for an ending to resolve things for us, sometimes the ending itself leaves things ambiguous.[95] Donald Juel, who asserted that "no point in a story is as significant for appreciation and interpretation as its ending,"[96] explains that an ending "can achieve closure, pulling together loose threads from a story, or it can resist closure, refusing to answer burning questions posed in the course of the narrative."[97] In many ways, the ending of Bathsheba's story does both. It achieves closure and ends with resolution concerning Solomon's kingdom, but it also resists closure, leaving things open regarding Bathsheba. We have not had all our burning questions answered, nor will we, for she is never to be mentioned again in the text. The form and content of the MT agree: Bathsheba is a character who is open throughout, and whose death itself is the final gap in her characterization.

94. It is not that David never tells people what to do in 1 Kings, for he gives the command to place Solomon on the throne (1 Kgs 1:30–35) and tells Solomon precisely what to do to set the kingdom in order (1 Kgs 2:1–9). The contrast between David and Bathsheba in 2 Samuel and 1 Kings is all the more significant then, for in the latter texts he does not tell her what to do, and she tells him what to do.

95. Gunn and Fewell, *Narrative Criticism*, 105–6.

96. Juel, *Master of Surprise*, 107.

97. Ibid., 110.

4

Versions of Bathsheba

THE PREVIOUS CHAPTERS HAVE SHOWN THAT BATHSHEBA IN THE MT IS a minor, complex, generally positive,[1] but also evolving character as the reader moves from Samuel to Kings. This chapter will explore how those four aspects of her characterization continue and experience modification as we consider the way in which Bathsheba is portrayed in the Septuagint (LXX), the Syriac Peshitta, and the Aramaic Targumim. We will see that even as the different versions make changes to the text of the MT, the qualities in Bathsheba's character remain consistent, and her characterization in the MT will be confirmed by these translations.

Two sometimes opposing goals of translation are fidelity to the original text and freedom to express the ideas of the text in the new language. Walter Benjamin expresses it as follows: "The task of the translator consists in finding the particular intention toward the target language which produces in that language the echo of the original."[2] Benjamin

---

1. Again, "generally positive" is in some ways a moral judgment, and in part should be seen in contrast to David. It also can be understood *via negativa*: I mean that Bathsheba is not stupid, not seductive, not scheming.

2. Benjamin, "Task of the Translator," 258. The challenge that comes in producing an echo of the original while still working with the new language has been noted for some time. In the introduction to Ecclesiasticus, the grandson of Joshua Ben Sirach (2nd century BCE) writes, "You are urged therefore to read with good will and attention, and to be indulgent in cases where, despite our diligent labor in translating, we may seem to have rendered some phrases imperfectly. For what was originally expressed in Hebrew does not have exactly the same sense when translated into another language. Not only this work, but even the law itself, the prophecies, and the rest of the books differ not a little as originally expressed." In a letter to Rabbi Samuel Ibn Tibbon dated September 30, 1199, Maimonides explained that literal translation is not preferable. "Whoever wishes to translate and purposes to render each word literally, and at the same time to adhere slavishly to the order of the words and sentences in the original, will meet with much difficulty. This is not the right method. The translator should first try to grasp the sense

also notes that a translation of a text is a positive sign that the life of a given literary work will continue beyond its origin.[3] G. Thomas Tanselle's insight that a text is not merely aesthetic but is also in some ways a utilitarian object leads him to suggest that changes made to the text may help it to function better.[4] Although he is discussing textual emendations and not just translations, the principle still applies—a text that is translated into a new language will function better for the people who speak that language and do not speak the parent language. Therefore, while a new version hopes to remain faithful to the original, changes are inevitable. Yet, it is not despite of, but very much in and through the changes from the MT that we still see Bathsheba characterized as complex, generally positive, and showing development.

Because the primary interest in this study is the character of Bathsheba, who will remain our focus in this chapter, I will not provide an exhaustive catalogue of general techniques of characterization applied to all characters throughout the LXX, the Peshitta, and the Targumim. Neither will this chapter provide a comprehensive study of tendencies in

---

of the subject thoroughly, and then state the theme with perfect clarity in the other language. This, however, cannot be done without changing the order of the words, putting many words for one word, or vice versa, so that the subject be perfectly intelligible in the language into which he translates." Löwy, *Miscellany of Hebrew Literature*, 222. In the Talmud, b. *Qid.* 49a, t. Meg 3:41, we read, "Whoever renders a verse literally is a liar; and whoever adds to it, he is a blasphemer and a reviler."

Nida's *Towards a Science of Translating* credits Etienne Dolet (1509–1546) with publishing the first formulation of a theory of translation. Dolet's fundamental principles of translating included: "1. The translator must understand perfectly the content and intention of the author whom he is translating. 2. The translator should have a perfect knowledge of the language from which he is translating and an equally excellent knowledge of the language into which he is translating. 3. The translator should avoid the tendency to translate word for word, for to do so is to destroy the meaning of the original and to ruin the beauty of the expression. 4. The translator should employ the forms of speech in common usage. 5. Through his choice and order of words the translator should produce a total overall effect with appropriate 'tone.'" *Towards a Science,* 15–16. Nida points out that throughout the millennia, two basic conflicts about translation remain. "These fundamental differences in translation theory may be stated in terms of two sets of conflicting 'poles'; (1) literal vs. free translating and (2) emphasis on form vs. concentration on content." *Towards a Science,* 22. Nida also points out how there are special theological problems in translating biblical texts, as there are differences of opinion about issues of inspiration versus philology, tradition versus contemporary authority, and theology versus grammar. *Towards a Science,* 26.

3. Benjamin, "Task of the Translator," 254.

4. Tanselle, *Rationale*, 19.

the different versions, each of which is worthy of its own, careful attention.[5] Yet, I will pay attention to some general tendencies of each version in order to prevent overinterpretation of Bathsheba's character.

For example, 2 Sam 11:26 of the MT reads, "When the wife of Uriah the Hittite heard that her husband was dead, she mourned for her master." Instead of using two different nouns for Uriah, "husband" and "master," the Targum and the Peshitta repeat the same word, בעל/ܒܥܠ, "master."[6] Leveling out different words throughout a given verse, however, is a translation tendency in both the Targum and the Peshitta,[7] so it is not much grist for the hermeneutical mill. This particular example demonstrates how some of the tools of textual criticism will need to be utilized in this chapter as I consider the final form of the versions, and the character of Bathsheba portrayed in each. Yet, I will not be doing strict textual criticism; my methodology will be literary criticism. According to Tanselle, the two forms of criticism—literary and textual—cannot be separated.[8] I would emend his assertion to say that the two can be distinguished, but they are often interrelated. As Hens-Piazza affirms, "new literary criticism does not deny that there were many and complex stages involved in the text's composition."[9] My interest is less in how or why changes have happened from one version to another, although I will explain those as I can. But I will concentrate on the way those changes affect the shape of Bathsheba's character, in comparison and contrast with

5. General discussion of translation tendencies may be found in Tov, *Textual Criticism*. For the LXX, cf. Greenspoon, "Hebrew into Greek," 80–113; Jellicoe, *Septuagint and Modern Study*; Metzger, "Lucianic Recension," 1–41; Peters, "Septuagint," 1093–1104; Swete, *Introduction*; Wevers, "Interpretative Character and Significance," 84–107; and the Septuagint Commentary Series. For the Peshitta, cf. Dirksen, "Old Testament Peshitta"; Morrison, *Character of the Syriac Version*; Weitzman, *Syriac Version of the Old Testament*; Williams, *Studies in the Syntax of the Peshitta of 1 Kings*. For the Targumim, cf. Alexander, "Targum, Targumim," and "Jewish Aramaic Translations of Hebrew Scriptures," 217–53; Bascom, "The Targums"; Churgin, *Targum Jonathan to the Prophets*; McNamara, "Interpretation of Scripture in the Targumim," 167–97; Smolar and Aberbach, *Studies in Targum Jonathan*; and van Staalduine-Sulman, *Targum of Samuel*.

6. The Septuagint, though, has "husband" throughout v. 26.

7. Cf. Churgin, *Targum Jonathan*, 53–54, and Weitzman, "Interpretive Character of the Syriac Old Testament," 592. Another example of a tendency in a recension is that Lucianic tends to use personal names more than pronouns. It ought not to be over-emphasized that Lucianic refers to Bathsheba more by name than pronoun because Lucianic does this with all characters.

8. Tanselle, *Rationale*, 34–36.

9. Hens-Piazza, *Nameless, Blameless, and Without Shame*, 58.

the way she is portrayed in the MT. By doing these horizontal readings,[10] we will gain a deeper understanding of her character overall.[11]

This chapter will be structured by looking at each version separately. After giving some brief background information about the version, I will follow the general plotline of the narrative, noting where in the changes to the MT we see various nuances in Bathsheba's continuing complexity, generally positive characterization, and evolving development.

LXX Background Information

The first version to be considered is the Septuagint, and its primacy in this study is not accidental, for the Septuagint is one of the most important witnesses to the Hebrew Bible. Tov asserts that, along with the Qumran scrolls, the LXX is the most important non-Masoretic witness in textual criticism, especially for the books of Samuel and Kings.[12] Its name derives from the letter to Aristeas, which has attained legendary status, since most scholars believe now that it is only a legend, a pseudynomous letter, and only refers to the translation of the Pentateuch.[13] Yet, even though its origin is not as fantastic as the legend claims, the Septuagint is still understood to be the earliest complete version of the Hebrew Bible.[14] As such, its importance for text criticism is high.

Although its importance for the work of the text critic must not be minimized, the LXX is also important as a witness to the history of interpretation. As the title indicates, John Beck's *Translators as Storytellers*

10. Berlin, *Zephaniah*, 8.

11. Greenspoon explains that the method of study that focuses "maximal attention on a minimal number of words," is still helpful, for "the data obtainable through such multi-leveled analysis often far exceed the seemingly grander results of more far-ranging, but inevitably more superficial, examinations." "Hebrew into Greek," 99.

12. Tov, "Textual Criticism (OT)," 403. Peters explains, "On the purely formal level, any Hebrew text retroverted from the Greek Bible will in fact predate by several hundred years the complete ms on which our Hebrew Bible is based." "Septuagint," 1102. Similarly, Conybeare and Stock state, "Never has a translation of any book exercised so profound an influence upon the world as the Septuagint version of the Old Testament." *A Grammar of Septuagint Greek*, 20.

13. The legend has it that seventy-two elders, representing each of the twelve tribes, were sequestered in individual rooms to translate the Torah from Hebrew into Greek. After seventy-two days, they all emerged with identical translations, which confirmed the inspired nature of their translation.

14. Swete, *Introduction*, 434. The Dead Sea Scrolls provide fragments of biblical texts which date earlier than the LXX, but a complete Hebrew Bible was not found at Qumran.

argues that the translators of the Septuagint were not merely slavish translators only interested in linguistics, but rather were interpreters and storytellers who were interested in the literary nature of the text. "No translation is free from interpretation. Since this is also true of the Septuagint, it stands as a witness to the translator's understanding of their text. Thus the Septuagint is not only a translation; it is also a 'commentary' which reflects the interpretation of its time. Such interpretation is motivated by both cultural and theological presuppositions."[15] Swete takes a somewhat critical position toward the interpretive tendencies in the Septuagint, but he nonetheless asserts that they are worth study. "It is never safe to neglect [the translators'] interpretation, even if in the harder contexts it is seldom to be trusted. Indirectly at least much may be learned from them; and their wildest exegesis belongs to the history of hermeneutics, and has influenced thought and language to a remarkable degree."[16]

---

15. Beck, *Translators as Storytellers*, 5.

16. Swete, *Introduction*, 446. Cf. Greenspoon, "We are cautioned against making too much of interpretive elements, theological and otherwise, in the Septuagint. We should likewise be aware of the danger of undervaluing the rich and unique evidence bequeathed to us by the first translators of the Bible." "Hebrew into Greek," 108. The warnings against overemphasizing the interpretive nature of the translations (of the Septuagint and other versions) are sounded particularly for the work of text criticism proper. Even Tov acknowledges that while many translations are only of limited value for textual criticism, those translations are important for exegesis. Tov, *Textual Criticism*, 15. Wevers similarly explains, "Translations which are free can be used for text critical purposes only with much caution . . . on the other hand, such translations are most useful for demonstrating how the translator understood the text." "Interpretative Character and Significance," 93.

Indeed, in the places where the LXX differs from the MT, it is quite possible that those differences do not represent a different parent text, but can be explained by the translators' work in attempting to render the Hebrew into Greek. Such a task is made more complicated by the fact that Greek and Hebrew are two very different languages which do not share similar syntactical structure or cognate vocabulary, as the other Semitic languages do. On the one hand, those places where there are differences in translations are especially interesting as evidence of exegesis. On the other hand, though, the places where there are similarities are just as significant. Greenspoon explains, "Researchers seeking interpretive elements in the LXX are naturally drawn to places where the Greek translators introduced such material either through the insertion of additional words or by the reinterpretation of material contained in their Hebrew Vorlage. If, however, we seek to understand fully the conceptual world of these translators, these divergences are only part, albeit an important part, of the study. Where translators were content to render their Hebrew in a straightforward manner, such passages were presumably consistent with their beliefs or presuppositions or thought patterns . . . These instances

Any discussion of the general translation tendencies of the LXX is complicated by the diversity of the texts and translators.[17] Metzger points out that the Septuagint is not a unified version of the Hebrew Bible, but rather "a collection of independent translations of the several books or groups of books made at different times and places. Of some books there was more than one translation, and even in the case of individual books, the hand of more than one translator can be discerned."[18]

Even to describe the Bathsheba texts in the same way is problematic because those texts are not all translated by the same group.[19] So, I will only note general characteristics of translation, modestly trying not to make too much of what is there. McCarter explains that in general there is a tendency in LXX in 1–2 Samuel and 1–2 Kings to translate somewhat woodenly. Manuscript A is non-idiomatic, while B is wooden, and the Succession Narrative in B is in καιγε, which makes the Lucianic witnesses also important.[20]

The term *Septuagint* has been used variously to refer to (1) the Greek translation of the Torah, (2) the critical text (which is the nearest thing to an Ur-text), to be distinguished from the various papyri and manuscripts, or (3) the multiple witnesses to the Septuagint.[21] Different

---

also need to be taken into account." "Hebrew into Greek," 85. Porter and Pearson echo Greenspoon's point about translations representing the ideas of the translator, and assert that those passages translated literally in LXX are just as important as those passages that are free paraphrases. "Isaiah through Greek Eyes," 542.

17. Wevers describes such an attempt as "foolhardy." "Interpretative Character and Significance," 95.

18. Metzger, "Lucianic Recension," 14.

19. The possibility was raised in the nineteenth century that there were different translators, or later revisers in Samuel. In 1884, Woods noted differences in vocabulary within the two books, in his *Light Thrown by the Septuagint Version on the Books of Samuel*. A few decades later, Thackeray argues, on the basis of vocabulary and syntax, that the four books of Kings can be divided into five separate units of translation: 1 Sam, 2 Sam 1–11:1, 2 Sam 11:2—1 Kgs 2:11, 1 Kgs 2:12–21:43, 1 Kgs 22—2 Kgs 25:30. "Greek Translators of the Four Books of Kings," 268–78. Olmstead and Redpath agreed with Thackeray's suggestions (Olmstead, "Earliest Book of Kings," 169-214; Redpath, "A Contribution," 606), and Kelly agreed strongly, saying, "there can be no question of the fact that a new translator began work at II Sam 11:2. The division of translation at II Samuel 11:1-2 may then be taken as one of the assured results of scholarship." Kelly, "The Septuagint Translators," 19. If their findings are correct, then the fourth act of Bathsheba's story, beginning with 1 Kgs 2:12, is translated by a different group.

20. McCarter, *Textual Criticism*, 89–90.

21. So Peters, "Septuagint," 1093–1094. Wevers has a slightly different triad of definitions: 1) the translation of Hebrew Torah into Greek in Alexandria, 2) the translation of

schools of thought and study divide and organize the Septuagint differently. The Göttingen version follows Paul Lagarde's eclectic methodology, which is based on Lagarde's convictions that all extant manuscripts of LXX are the result of *ein eklektisches Verfahren*, so the process of arriving at the Ur-text must accordingly be eclectic. The Cambridge version, edited by Alan Brooke and Norman McLean, is a diplomatic version[22] based on the uncial of Codex Vaticanus, supplemented with other uncials.[23] I have chosen to use the Cambridge edition for a very practical reason: the Göttingen volume on Reigns has not been published yet. So, where I refer to the LXX in this study, I am referring to the Cambridge version, based on Vaticanus. Where appropriate, I will also note daughter rescensions. Lucianic, in particular, provides some interesting contrasts with Vaticanus. Occasionally, I will also refer to the Old Latin witness.

Bathsheba in the LXX

As mentioned above, Bathsheba is presented in the LXX with the same overall characteristics as she has in the MT, and this consistency to her

---

the Hebrew canon into Greek, which is better referred to as Old Greek, to distinguish it from above, and 3) the Alexandrian canon, including not only the Greek version of Hebrew Scriptures, but also "deuterocanonical books." "Interpretative Character and Significance," 86.

22. In contrast to an "eclectic" edition (sometimes referred to as a "critical" text), a "diplomatic" one uses a single manuscript for its primary text, and adds other textual evidence in an apparatus.

23. Codex Vaticanus is one of the extant ancient Greek Bibles that contains both the OT and NT, and because of its scope, it is textually one of the best manuscripts available. Its appellation comes from the fact that it has been in the Vatican Library since at least 1475, when it was listed in a catalogue there. The date suggested is c. 350, and its origin is most likely Egypt. Its OT is similar to that used by Origen in his fifth column of the Hexapla, so therefore it was affected far less than other manuscripts by the influence of the Hexapla on the LXX. Cf. Parker, "Codex Vaticanus," 1074. The apparatus of the Cambridge version is tripartite: the first section gives only itacisms and small errors of the principle manuscript adopted in text together with other uncials cited in the manual edition. The second and main apparatus combines principal variants of all known uncials, selective cursives, and chief ancient versions together with the writings of Philo, Josephus, and other important early Christian writers. The third section embodies the Hexapla material. Jellicoe critiques the Cambridge edition for its apparatus, and the way it stresses the importance of B (i.e., Codex Vaticanus) and, in effect, that of the uncials as a whole. He instead is interested in paying more attention to the miniscules, or cursives, which he sees as "unjustifiably neglected." *The Septuagint and Modern Study*, 175. By contrast, he notes the way that the Göttingen edition has all the variants of Cambridge combined in a single main apparatus.

characterization may be seen not in spite of, but through, the textual changes. In regards to Bathsheba's generally positive characterization, the LXX closes some of the gaps that were present in the MT to emphasize that David was the one who took the initiative in seeing, seeking out, and sleeping with Bathsheba. Bathsheba in the LXX, therefore, is more clearly not to be blamed for bathing in the open, nor for seducing David.

While I demonstrated that in the MT of 2 Sam 11:2 David (and not Bathsheba) is on the roof, their respective locations are even more evident in the Greek. The Hebrew compound preposition מֵעַל is translated both times in v. 2 by either the Greek απο or επι, but not with a compound such as "from atop."[24] In the clause where the text describes David's seeing Bathsheba, the Greek word is απο, "from," not επι, "on." Other witnesses make David's position even clearer by putting the phrase "from the roof" in a different position. While the MT and Vaticanus explain "and he saw a woman bathing from the roof," Lucianic, Armenian, Sahidic, Syro-hex-j, and Theodotian have "and he saw from the roof a woman bathing." These Greek versions clarify the position of David vis-à-vis Bathsheba, by emphasizing that he is the one on the roof. Therefore, any possibility that Bathsheba might have been on the roof is ruled out in the Greek.

In v. 3, the LXX continues Bathsheba's generally positive characterization by using a Greek word that signals more intentionality in David's seeking after Bathsheba. Instead of translating the Hebrew דרשׁ with Greek εκζητειν, the Greek verb used is ζητειν, which more commonly translates בקשׁ.[25] The verb ζητειν (and בקשׁ) means "to seek or search for," or "to desire." The semantic nuances of the Greek suggest that David's interest in Bathsheba is more explicitly connected with his desire; at the very least, it's an unusual translation of דרשׁ.

Perhaps the most striking difference in LXX from MT comes in 2 Sam 11:4. The Greek says, "και εισηλθεν προς αυτην" (and he went in

---

24. The second time מֵעַל is translated, the LXX uses απο. The LXX in Judges 16:27 uses επι with the accusative (επι το δωμα) for "upon the roof." Conybeare and Stock, *Grammar of Septuagint Greek*, 85. Muraoka suggests that the Greek translation of מֵעַל should be επανω, as in Sir 45:12 (a crown of gold upon his turban). HRCS, Appendix 4, 294.

25. ζητειν does translate דרשׁ approximately forty times, but approximately 130 times it translates בקשׁ. Lucianic tradition has εξεζητησεν, from εκζητειν, the word used more typically to translate דרשׁ. Cf. Gen 9:5; Exod 18:15; Lev 10:16; Deut 4:29; 12:5, 30; 17:4, 9; 23:21; 1 Kgs 14:5; 2 Kgs 1:16; 22:13; etc. HRCS, 430–31.

to her), which differs from MT (and 4QSam[a])—"and she came to him."[26] In this language, David takes all initiative in the verse, and there is no activity on Bathsheba's part. He sent for her, he came to her, he lay with her. Bathsheba is not the subject of the verb "to come," she is merely the (or an) object. At first glance, this would also seem to be part of the way the LXX continues the trajectory from the MT in presenting Bathsheba in a generally positive manner. That is, as the LXX has it, the only thing Bathsheba does in 2 Sam 11:4 is to return to her house. Therefore, in that version she is not a willing participant in their liason, something the MT leaves somewhat more gapped, and that makes her positive insofar as it moves further away from any possibility that she desired to be with David. In other words, if she had seduced him, we would expect her to want to "come" willingly to him. But if this change regarding Bathsheba may present her more positively—insofar as we conjecture that she did not "come" willingly to David—it also presents her in somewhat more of a flattened perspective compared to the complexity of her character in the MT. For in this scenario, Bathsheba is more victimized by David than in the MT. Although the MT did not explain why Bathsheba went to David, the fact that she was the subject of that action lent to her slightly more complexity and mystery.

Another way the LXX flattens Bathsheba's character is in terms of the resonances of meaning in her personal name in Chronicles. When Bathsheba is named in 2 Sam 11:3, different manuscripts render her name in different ways: Alexandrian refers to her as Βηθσαβεε, but Vaticanus has Βηρσαβεε, and Lucianic has variations on the latter spelling, which Driver refers to as "the strange corruption."[27] It is to be expected that personal names go through slight changes from the Hebrew to the Greek.[28] However, 1 Chr 3:5 in LXX also names Bathsheba Βηρσαβεε,

---

26. We would expect the Greek και εισηλθεν προς αυτον, which does occur in mss c, s. The phrase is entirely omitted in mss h, a₂, and Ethiopic.

27. Driver, *Notes*, 222. One reason why Βηρσαβεε and its variants are strange is that Βερσαβεε also reflects the place name באר שבע. Cf. Josh 15:28; 19:2; Judg 20:1; 1 Reigns 3:20; 8:2; 2 Reigns 3:10; 17:11; 24:2, 7, 15; 3 Reigns 1:16; 4:24; 19:3; etc., HRCS, 40.

28. For example, within our narrative, Bathsheba's father is referred to by LXX[BAMN] as Ελιαβ, who, among others, is also David's eldest brother in 1 Sam 16:6. Lucianic names him Ηλα, as do some of the Old Latin manuscripts. Driver asserts that the use of the name Ammiel in 1 Chr 3:5 "supports MT against LXX Ελιαβ." *Notes*, 222. Bathsheba's husband, Uriah the Hittite, is glossed in 4QSama as [נ]ושא אש כלי יואב—Joab's weapon bearer—and also in Josephus (*Ant.* 7.131). However, the LXX evidence does not specify that connection between Uriah and Joab, and, according to 2 Sam 23:37 and 1 Chr 11:39, the arms-bearer for Joab is identified as Naharai the Beerothite.

and does not attempt a transliteration of the Hebrew בת־שׁוּע. In the LXX for Chronicles, Bathsheba is not "daughter of shame," or "daughter of help," which means that LXX Chronicles presents Bathsheba with less complexity than the Chronicler of MT does.

More differences between the LXX and the MT are found in 2 Sam 11:18–25, where the conversations between Joab, the messenger, and David take place.[29] The MT has Joab guessing that David will get angry, and it is Joab in the MT whose words connect the fate of Uriah with the fate of Abimelech in their deaths connected to a wall and a woman. In the MT, David does not get angry and does not mention the Abimelech episode. However, the LXX takes the words about Abimelech out of the mouth of Joab and puts them instead into the mouth of David in his conversation with the messenger. In the Greek of 2 Sam 11:22, the messenger and David say to one another exactly what Joab said in 2 Sam 11:19–21. Both Driver and McCarter affirm the LXX as based on an earlier Hebrew tradition because it makes more logical and text-critical sense.[30] This text illustrates the difference in methodologies between text criticism and literary criticism: text criticism affirms that the LXX represents an earlier tradition and the MT represents a later, corrupted tradition. Additionally, the changes between the versions do not just arise from translational license in moving from Hebrew to Greek, nor do they necessarily reflect an intentional theological change. Quite probably, they come from some sort of scribal error in the Hebrew tradition underlying the MT.

From a literary critical perspective, though, when we compare the final forms of MT and LXX, the differences highlight David's character and affect our understanding of Bathsheba's characterization. When David gets angry in the LXX tradition and mentions Abimelech, it seems as if he does not yet realize that Uriah was killed. Instead, it is as

---

29. Verse 21, where Joab connected Uriah and Abimelech, has only minor differences from the MT, having to do with different names in Greek from Hebrew. In the MT, Abimelech's father is identified as Jerubbesheth, while Lucianic and other manuscripts refer to him as Jerubbaal. Lucianic and other manuscripts also omit "Son of Ner."

30. Driver explains regarding LXX, "The addition is a necessary one: for as the text stands, the terms in which the messenger speaks in v. 23a are unexplained (note especially his opening words, Because etc., which presuppose a question to have been asked)." *Notes*, 224. McCarter notes that the MT inverts the original order of the speeches: "David becomes angry in v. 22 *before* the messenger has reported the bad news in vv. 23–24a!" *2 Samuel*, 283. Lucianic also supports the LXX here.

if he remains deeply concerned about the tactics being used only until he finds out that they resulted in Uriah's death. In this view of David, we can see more clearly the emotional shift that occurs in him: he goes from being angry to suddenly unconcerned once he finds out that Uriah has died. Therefore, David's single-mindedness in wanting Uriah killed is emphasized.[31] By making this desire of David's more transparent, the LXX shows David more negatively, and correspondingly, Bathsheba appears more positively.

Another way the LXX extends the MT's generally positive characterization of Bathsheba (as it shows David more negatively) is in the way it discusses the seriousness of what he has done. This happens in three ways in 2 Sam 12. The first is in v. 3, in Nathan's parable. The LXX of 2 Sam 12:3 uses three verbs to reflect the two MT verbs: קנה, "to get, acquire," is reflected by κτασθαι[32], but ויחיה, "to nourish, keep alive" is reflected by περιεποιησατο, and by εκτρεφειν.[33] Probably the latter two are variant renderings of piel of חיה;[34] the Old Latin omits περι–εποιησατο. Yet, the care that is reflected in this text is heightened by the use of the two words in LXX: not only does the poor man care for and raise the ewe lamb (as he does in the MT), but he also "kept it around his dwelling," περιεποιησατο, and he "raised it from childhood," εκτρε–φειν. Irenaeus has the interesting and more precise *nutriebat*; the poor man "was nourishing" the ewe lamb. Lucianic uses the pronoun αυτου another time, which specifies and reinforces the relationship between the poor man and the lamb: "and she was to him as *his* daughter," not just as *a* daughter (italics added). Therefore, the language in the LXX

31. In contrast, the MT does not record such a shift in David's emotions; in that version, he is more disengaged throughout. Of course, there is a distinct lack of emotions throughout 2 Sam 11 in the MT, which seems to be part of the narrator's strategy in emphasizing actions instead of feelings. (Cf. Yee et al., chapter 1, note 45.) We might wonder if David cares at all about military matters, according to the MT. When he was introduced in 2 Sam 11:1, he was just lounging on the roof at the time when kings are supposed to go to war.

32. As is typical: HRCS, 793.

33. Both of these verbs are unusual: περιεποιησατο translates as "he kept it around his dwelling," and it is a usual word choice. Cf. HRCS, 1125, 257 in the Hebrew appendix. Other places where LXX uses this are Gen 3:8; Exod 21:19; 2 Kgs 20:3; Esth 2:11; Job 38:16; Ps 11/12:8; Prov 6:22; 28:31. And only in this verse does εκτρεφειν translate the piel of חיה. HRCS, 443–44.

34. McCarter, *2 Samuel*, 294.

suggests even more than the MT that the lamb is precious to the poor man, which makes the rich man's crime even more heinous.

The second way the LXX heightens the seriousness of the crime in 2 Sam 12 is in the way it changes the amount of repayment that David suggests from the Hebrew "fourfold" to the Greek "επταπλα—σιονα" (sevenfold).[35] The former is what is mandated in the Book of the Covenant (Exod 21:37/22:1), and there are different possibilities for the increase to seven. De Vaux suggests that it is not to be taken literally, but simply to reflect perfect restitution.[36] Driver explains, "David speaking impulsively is more likely to have used the proverbial 'sevenfold' (cf. Prov. 6, 31), than to have thought of the law Ex. 21, 37."[37] Coxon notes the semantic connection between Bathsheba's name and the number seven and suggests that the play on words is intentional,[38] but that connection would not exist in the Greek, only in the Hebrew. Whatever the reason for the change in the LXX to "seven," the LXX suggests a greater level of responsibility and restitution than does the MT, and therefore emphasizes the gravity of the crime.[39]

The third way the LXX of 2 Sam 12 emphasizes the seriousness of David's actions is in the language it uses as Nathan describes what David has done, and this is especially evident in the different recensions. The translation of the Hebrew בָּזִית in v. 9 by εφαυλισας, "to take lightly/minimize," is translated in Lucianic and Old Latin with εξουδενωσας, which is a stronger verb, "to consider as nothing," or "nullify."[40] Moreover, Lucianic, Theodotian, and Old Latin also omit τον λογον, which makes the question even more pointed and forceful, directed to God—not "Why did you consider *the word of God* as nothing" but "Why did you consider *God* as nothing?" However, v. 10 in the Greek seems to backpedal somewhat. In the MT, the object of David's disdain, that which he considered

35. Lucianic, and Theodotian, Ireneas, and Josephus (*Ant.* 7.150) still follow the MT with fourfold: πετραπλασιονα, and πετραπλην.

36. De Vaux, *Ancient Israel*, 160.

37. Driver, *Notes*, 224–25.

38. Coxon, "A Note on 'Bathsheba,'" 247–50.

39. Schipper argues that the LXX is preferred because it allows for the punishment of wrongdoings that include murder, and not just theft. Since Schipper believes David sees Joab as the murderer, it follows that David would pronounce the "sevenfold" punishment on him. "Did David Overinterpret?" 390–91. Cf. chapter 2, n. 138.

40. The latter is the word used in the LXX in v. 10, although it translates the same Hebrew word, בָּזִית.

as nothing, is God—בִי בְזִתָנִי, "for you considered me as nothing." But the first common singular "me" has been omitted from B, and is not in Lucianic,[41] which makes the indictment against David weaker in v. 10. It is not that David considered God as nothing, but David rather obliquely just "considered as nothing" without an object. It is difficult to justify this change from the MT for theological reasons, though, because in the previous verse, Lucianic did not shy away from making a pointed statement about God. What happens in the final reading of the Greek and the Hebrew is a difference in the timing of their statement about David's sins. The LXX and Lucianic—the latter, in particular—emphasize from the start that David's sins against Bathsheba and Uriah are tantamount to considering God as nothing, while the MT builds to that conclusion.

Though I noted that in some cases Bathsheba's complexity is flattened by the LXX when it clarifies that David "came to her," and by not referring to her with the different name in Chronicles, it still presents her as complex. One place where her complexity is seen in the LXX is in the language it uses to describe her beauty. Like the Hebrew, the Greek affirms in 2 Sam 11:3 that Bathsheba is beautiful to see, but the specific words used in the different languages connect Bathsheba with different biblical women. The string of words καλω το ειδι is used elsewhere in the LXX to describe Rachel (Gen 29:17), Judith (Judith 8:7), and Susanna (1:31). The same description with σφοδρα (καλη τω ειδει σφοδρα) is used for Abigail (1 Sam 25:5) and Tamar (2 Sam 13:2). By contrast, however, the MT uses טובת מראה to refer to Rebekah (Gen 26:7), Vashti (Esth 1:11), and the young women in Esth 2:3, and the string טובת מראה מאד is only used in 2 Sam 11:2. Therefore, the LXX is somewhat more suggestive of a connection between Bathsheba and other women in David's court (Abigail and Tamar) by describing their physical appearance with the same words.

Abigail and Tamar are quite different from one another, though. In addition to describing her as beautiful, the text also describes Abigail as having good insight (1 Sam 25:3). She was the wife of a fool, but acted boldly to save her husband from death, and to save David from bloodguilt. David praised her for her discretion (1 Sam 25:33) and, after her husband died, made her his wife.[42] Tamar, on the other hand, was

41. HRCS, 500.

42. The other place Abigail appears in David's story is in 1 Sam 30, when she and another of David's wives, Ahinoam, have been taken captive by the Amalekites. David

raped by her half brother Amnon, and the text describes her as desolate (2 Sam 13:20). Though the LXX describes Bathsheba's appearance using the same words that it uses to describe Tamar and Abigail, the comparison only goes so far, and the other words do not apply to Bathsheba. Abigail is a heroine; Tamar a victim.[43] Bathsheba is not an Abigail, but neither is she a Tamar. Instead, her characterization falls somewhere in the middle of these other two characters, and her complexity and subtlety is seen in that she cannot be reduced to either hero or victim.

Another way we see Bathsheba's complexity in the LXX is by comparing the different recensions, specifically how Lucianic differs from Vaticanus in four main ways. The first is found in 2 Sam 12:24. Vaticanus adds to the MT "εισηλθεν" (he came to her), which creates an envelope structure in Vaticanus with 2 Sam 11:4, when David first came to her.[44] In contrast with Vaticanus, Lucianic has "ελαλησεν" (he spoke to her). Therefore, the envelope structure is missing in Lucianic, so David's actions here can be seen in contrast with his actions in 11:4: in 12:24, he comforts Bathsheba, and speaks to her; he does not lie with her. In fact, Lucianic contrasts with the MT and LXX even further when it changes the object and subject. In Lucianic, she lay with him (αυτου), whereas the LXX has "he lay with her" (αυτης).[45] Thus, in Lucianic we have a very different picture of what has happened: David comforts Bathsheba and speaks to her, and she is the one lying with[46] him. It might be asserted that Bathsheba, in this picture, is the one who initiates things sexually, but the syntax seems to demonstrate that she does so in response to what David has done (comforting and speaking with her).

---

pursues them, avenges them, and rescues them. While the text does not tell us about David's feelings towards Abigail, his actions suggest that he is unwilling to let her go.

43. Not only is Tamar sexually victimized by her half brother, but she is also victimized by her father David's silence. Van Dijk-Hemmes explains that Tamar's story is an example of the phenomenon of "blaming the victim." She writes, "Jonadab and David are almost unanimouslsy considered innocent . . . the exegetical pardon commonly meted out to David and Jonadab teaches us that the process of concealment continues. By declaring that only Amnon, the rapist, is the guilty party, other men can wash their hands in innocence." "Tamar and the Limits of Patriarchy," 145. Cf. Trible, *Texts of Terror*, 37–63, and Bar-Efrat, *Narrative Art*, 239–82.

44. The circumstances, however, in which David "comes" to Bathsheba are very different at the beginning and at the end of the chapter. This is discussed in more detail below, under the category of Bathsheba's development as a character in the LXX.

45. MT also reads, "he lay with her."

46. Vaticanus has εκοιμηθε, the aorist form of the verb "to lay," but Lucianic has κοιμαται, the present tense.

A second difference between Lucianic and the LXX is found not in Bathsheba's words, which remain virtually the same as they are in MT, but in the words of Nathan and Adonijah to Bathsheba. When Nathan tells Bathsheba what to say to David in 1 Kgs 1:13, in Lucianic he adds God as a guarantor to what David swore: you swore to your servant "by YHWH your God," κατα κυριος του θεου. Bathsheba will add God in v. 17, and from a text-critical perspective it makes sense that Lucianic adds this phrase in v. 13 under the influence of the subsequent verse. What this does exegetically for Bathsheba, though, is to have her simply parrot back to David exactly what Nathan told her to say. Lucianic also changes Nathan's general description of "rulers of strength" in v. 25 to του ιωαβ, specifying that Joab is there,[47] which was what Bathsheba noted. Cogan points out that the "Lucianic reading 'Joab, commander of the army,' adopted by some commentators, NEB, [RSV] and NRSV, levels the subtle differences in the various reports concerning the goings-on at En-rogel."[48] Once again, we can see the distinction between text criticism and hermeneutics. Lucianic amends a more difficult reading in order to level differences in the various reports from Bathsheba and Nathan. But by doing so, it makes Nathan's confirmation of Bathsheba's words more literal, and suggests less independence to what she has said.

A similar change is found in Lucianic of 1 Kgs 2:20, where Adonijah adds μικραν to μιαν for the request; he tells Bathsheba he is making "one small request." This language corresponds to Bathsheba's words in v. 20, when she tells Solomon she has one small request from him. Again, this is easy to explain from a text-critical perspective which wants to smooth out differences from verse to verse, but the final form in Lucianic has implications for Bathsheba's character. It could be that Bathsheba has picked up on the irony of this "small" request, and cannot help repeating the words Adonijah uses. But if Bathsheba repeats Adonijah's exact words, she is only saying what she has been told to say, and has less of her own independent voice. As it is, in MT and Vaticanus, Bathsheba shows some ingenuity and initiative in adding her own words to what Nathan and Adonijah suggest.

A third change in Lucianic is found in the vocabulary used to describe the location where Bathsheba meets with David in 1 Kgs 1:15. The word for "inner chamber" is ταμιειον, which is commonly used to

---

47. Josephus also attests to this, with τον στρατηγον ιωαβον. *Ant.* 7.131.

48. Cogan, *1 Kings*, 160.

translate חדר,[49] although it has the sense of storeroom, or an innermost, hidden, secret room. The Hebrew "can mean any sort of inner room lying outside the central court."[50] Lucianic, though, has κοιτωνα, the word for "bedroom." κοιτωνα is used to translate חדר in Judg 15:1; 2 Sam 4:7 and 13:10; Ezek 8:12; and Joel 2:16. While the word itself is neutral, these passages in which it occurs are often marked with violence, and at the least, do not have particularily positive connotations.[51] Is Lucianic's word choice meant to suggest that like those other references to the κοιτωνα, something sinful or violent will occur when Bathsheba enters David's bedroom? Is this Lucianic's way to raise the question of whether or not Bathsheba will tell the truth to David in his room? Any connection with these other passages is hard to prove, but the echoes with other stories may add to the complexity of Lucianic's characterization of Bathsheba.

The fourth place we see Bathsheba's complexity in Lucianic is in the words it uses to refer to her son Solomon. In 1 Kgs 1:19, Bathsheba does not identify Solomon as David's servant in Lucianic.[52] Therefore, in Bathsheba's words to David, Solomon is simply her son (vv. 17, 21). But when Nathan refers to Solomon in 1 Kgs 1:26, Lucianic has υιον instead of δουλον, emphasizing that Solomon is not just a servant like the others. Instead, he is different; he is David's son. Bathsheba's own relationship to Solomon is highlighted in Lucianic's account of her words to David, but David's filial relationship with Solomon is emphasized by Lucianic's account of Nathan's words to David. Additionally, with the clause referring to Solomon as servant left out of 1 Kgs 1:19 in Lucianic, there is an increased subtlety to Bathsheba's words that is lacking in other manuscripts. That is, if she does not say, "and Solomon your servant he did

49. HRCS, 1334.

50. De Vries, *1 Kings*, 15.

51. In Judg 15:1, Samson wants to visit his Philistine wife in the bedroom. When her father prevents him from doing so, Samson responds by setting fire to the Philistines' fields and crops. In turn, they retaliate by burning his wife and her father. Samson responds with more violence, killing a thousand with the jawbone of an ass. In 2 Sam 4:7, Ishbosheth is beheaded in his bedroom by Rechab and Baanah. 2 Sam 13:10 tells us that the bedroom is where Amnon rapes Tamar. The passage in Joel occurs after the Lord has asked the sinful people to return to him with weeping and fasting because they have incurred his wrath. This fast is to be so encompassing that even the bride will leave her bedroom. And the reference in Ezekiel is to condemn what the elders of the house of Israel are doing in the darkness in the "inner rooms of the carved figures" (משכיתו בחדרי).

52. MT and Vaticanus do have her referring to Solomon as David's servant.

not invite,"[53] she leaves out the information that Adonijah's alliance with Abiathar and Joab is against Solomon. Therefore, in Lucianic, Bathsheba emphasizes the oath (and her own relationship with Solomon), not what Adonijah has done to Solomon.

These four different types of changes in Lucianic demonstrate complexity in Bathsheba's character in this recension. She lies with him, not he with her (12:24). She goes to see David in the κοιτωνα, not in the ταμιειον. But basically, she says exactly what Nathan and Adonijah tell her to say, and therefore shows less independence and ingenuity than in other versions. And even though Solomon is referred to more as her son (not David's servant), he is also identified as David's son.

Bathsheba remains complex in Vaticanus, too. In Bathsheba's request to Solomon in 1 Kgs 2:20, the LXX adds a δη, which softens the imperative and turns it into a genuine request.[54] There is, however, no corresponding נא in the Hebrew, so in the MT, Bathsheba's request is more obviously a command. Does this change in the LXX imply that she does not expect Solomon to obey? Or, with this addition, does she give Solomon more reason to refuse to acquiesce (and also punish Adonijah)? Either interpretation is possible, and the LXX—as the MT has done—therefore points to Bathsheba's complexity.

The other quality we see in Bathsheba in LXX is in her development from Samuel to Kings, which also happens in three slightly different ways than it does in the MT. She develops in her relationship with David, in her role as mother, and in the power and status she has. First, we actually see this development in her happen in her relationship with David at the end of 2 Samuel; we do not have to wait until Kings to observe it. For, as mentioned above, in the LXX of 2 Sam 12:24, the string of words "and he came to her and he lay with her" is the same as in LXX 11:4. Therefore, LXX has an envelope structure that MT does not.[55] But although the string of words is the same in the Greek, the context for David's actions differs. When David came to Bathsheba and lay with her in 11:4, she was the wife of another, and David's motivations for his actions were—at best—unclear. But this second occurrence in 12:24 when he came to her and lay with her, she has been identified as his wife, and his "coming" and

53. Bathsheba tells this to David in MT and in Vaticanus, but the entire clause is simply missing in Lucianic.

54. Only MSS b and p omit the δη.

55. In the MT of 11:4 he does not come to her; she comes to him.

"laying with" follow on the heels of his comfort. By using identical words to describe David's actions and embedding them in different contexts, the LXX even more than the MT emphasizes that the relationship between David and Bathsheba has developed. That developed relationship has consequences for Bathsheba's character.

A second way Bathsheba has developed from Samuel to Kings is in the role and status she has, which may be illustrated by the way both Adonijah and Solomon approach her in LXX of 1 Kgs 2. When Adonijah comes before her in 1 Kgs 2:13, he bows to her (και προσεκυνησεν αυτη). MT does not record that Adonijah bowed to her, nor does Syrohexaplar. De Vries says that by adding that detail, the LXX is "attributing to the brazen Adonijah a more humble demeanor than the passage justifies."[56] Yet, as it stands in the LXX, Adonijah does know and respect court politics, and Bathsheba is seen in this chapter as a woman whose position and status demand a level of humility.

But while Adonijah bows to her in the LXX of 1 Kgs 2:13, Solomon kisses her. Only here in LXX does the word "kiss" translate שׁחה.[57] Martin Mulder suggests that the change may be connected with the opinion of the Alexandrine Jews that it was inappropriate for a king to bow to someone else.[58] According to Cogan, "whether this is a true variant or the translator's finesse in accommodating the king's action to Greek court etiquette is hard to say."[59] Other texts from the Second Temple period give some insight into when—and why—one person would kiss another. Josephus uses the noun φιλεμα (kiss) four times in the death scene at Masada when fathers bid farewell to their loved ones before they massacre them.[60] At least ten separate references to kissing are found in the story of *Joseph and Asenath*, and the range of meaning includes a

---

56. De Vries, *1 Kings*, 26.

57. HRCS, 747. This is the same verb used in 1 Kgs 1 to reflect Bathsheba and Nathan's actions towards David. Josephus follows this reading when he writes, "περι πλακεντος" (he embraced her); *Ant.* 8.7.

58. Mulder, *1 Kings*, 109.

59. Cogan, *1 Kings*, 176. Klassen writes, "There is no agreement on the origins or significance of this practice [of kissing] in Judaism or Christianity. Hofmann (1938) first gave the kiss major attention and concluded that its roots were animistic and that the holy kiss was a means of conveying power from one person to another. Blank (IBD 3:40) describes the holy kiss as a 'ceremonious greeting comparable to the practice reflected in the OT.'" "Kiss," 90.

60. *J.W.*, 7.391.

reverential greeting, an act done at a reunion, an erotic expression, and something done as part of a reconciliation.[61] *Gen. Rab.* 70 (45b) espouses that, in general, kissing is indecent, but gives three exceptions: "kissing someone to honor that person, or kissing upon seeing someone after a long absence, and the farewell kiss."[62] With those three choices, it would seem Solomon's kiss for Bathsheba is his way of honoring her. Yet, Rabbi Tanchuma adds that kissing relatives is also acceptable,[63] and therefore it could also be interpreted that Solomon kisses his mother because she is his mother. In this example, we see another potential gap, with implications for Bathsheba's characterization. Does Solomon's action signal honor and respect, or intimacy and familiarity? Because the kiss replaces the MT "to do homage," it would appear to be the former, highlighting that Bathsheba has developed into someone worthy of honor.

Overall, the picture we have of Bathsheba in the LXX does not differ substantially from that in the MT: she remains a minor character who is characterized in a generally positive manner, but retains her complexity and shows development from Samuel to Kings. While LXX supports this overall characterization of Bathsheba, it demonstrates it in different ways than the MT does.

Peshitta Background Information

The Peshitta makes few substantial changes in the texts of Samuel-Kings, but there are some differences from the MT and the LXX that also contribute to understanding and affirming Bathsheba's character as generally

61. Charlesworth, *The Old Testament Pseudepigrapha*, 2:177–247. In 4:1, Asenath greets her parents with a kiss, and in 4:7, her father kisses her. She is urged by her father to greet Joseph with a kiss (8:3), but Joseph says, "It is not fitting for a god-fearing man who blesses the living God with his lips . . . to kiss a foreign woman . . . but a god-fearing man will kiss his mother, and his sisters born of his mother, and the sisters related to him, and the wife he sleeps with, who bless the living God with their mouth. Similarly it is not proper for a god-fearing woman to kiss a strange man, for it is an abomination before God." (8:4–7) Asenath's male guardians kiss her when she is depressed (18:3), and when she converts to Judaism, Joseph kisses her three times, imparting the spirits of life, wisdom, and truth with each kiss. In 20:1–4, Joseph kisses Asenath (her hand?) and she his head. In 21:7, Pharoah "led their mouths towards each other and brought their lips together and they kissed each other." When Asenath met Jacob in 22:9, she kissed him, and she also kissed Simeon when she met him. Levi kissed her hand (28:14–15) when he recognized that she was interested in the life and not the death of the enemies.

62. *Gen. Rab.* 70.12.

63. Ibid.

positive, complex, and showing development. In terms of the nature of the Peshitta, Peter Dirksen claims, "To say that very little is known about the origin and early history of the Old Testament Peshitta will be one of the few statements about this translation which will go unchallenged."[64] Despite his caution, there are a few things that can and should be said about the version which has been known since the ninth century as the Peshitta. Its name comes from the feminine form of the passive participle of the root pšṭ, "to stretch out, to extend," but the meaning developed from "stretched out" to "simple, straightforward, obvious."[65] Thus the name could mean a simple version, or it could also mean "widespread," which would be analogous to *Vulgata*, the common text. Weitzman writes, "No analogy, however, can be found for such usage in Syriac, and so the meaning 'simple' may be preferred."[66]

The translation must predate the fourth-century Syriac fathers Aphrahat and Ephrem, who cite it extensively. Weitzman puts its date at circa 150–200 CE, thus making it the earliest translation of the whole canon into another Semitic language. "It is thus potentially an important witness to the biblical text, and at the very least shows how the Hebrew text was understood at a particular (if as yet unidentified) time and place."[67] There is much debate over whether the origin of the Peshitta was Jewish or Christian—and related questions of its provenance. The Peshitta frequently agrees with LXX, Lucianic, and Vulgate against MT. It can be described as an idiomatic but faithful translation.[68] General characteristics of the Peshitta are "those of a close and accurate, though not too servile, representation of the original. Paraphrase is occasionally employed—most frequently in the case of words or phrases which appeared to the translator to need elucidation, and here and there slight additions have been made to the text for the same reason."[69]

---

64. Dirksen, "Old Testament Peshitta," 255.

65. Cf. *pashut* (פָּשׁוּט) in Mishnaic Hebrew, which came to mean "straightforward."

66. Weitzman, *Syriac Version*, 3.

67. Ibid., 2. Cf. Williams, "While we cannot assume the Peshitta to be entirely idiomatic Syriac since it is clearly influenced by the syntax of the Hebrew, the Peshitta Old Testament is nevertheless the earliest lengthy corpus in Syriac." *Studies in the Syntax*, 4.

68. Weitzman, *Syriac Version*, 61.

69. Burney, *Notes*, xxxiii.

Bathsheba in the Peshitta

Like the LXX, some of the ways the Peshitta contributes to Bathsheba's generally positive characterization (that differ from the way the MT presents her as generally positive) are by emphasizing David's responsibility and culpability in their interaction. One of those is found when David first sees Bathsheba in 2 Sam 11:2. In the Peshitta, as in the MT and LXX, David sees Bathsheba when he is ܡܢ ܠܥܠ ܡܢ ܒܝܬ ܐܠܟܐ ܠܠ, "on the roof of the house of the king." In the Peshitta, however, there is no mention of a roof in juxtaposition with her.[70] The Syriac does not specify Bathsheba's location, such that she could be in her house, or she could be in a courtyard; but there is no suggestion that she is bathing on top of a roof. Therefore, David is even more firmly placed in the position of voyeur.

Another change in the Peshitta is found in God's rejoinder to David through Nathan in 2 Sam 12:8, which reads, "I gave to you your master's daughters, and made his wives lie down in your embrace; I gave to you the *daughters* of Israel and Judah." It is not difficult to imagine from a text-critical standpoint how "house," *byt*, was changed into "daughter," *bnt*. But with the language of the daughters, the Syriac emphasizes that David's sin has been committed against the women, and suggests that the problem is in the way David has treated them. YHWH does not just refer to the covenant with David in 2 Sam 7, where the promise of an eternal "house" was given; in the Peshitta, YHWH reminds David that he had been given wives, and if that were not enough, YHWH would have added more. While it is still theologically problematic to have God taking women from one person and giving them to another, this text stresses that David did wrong in taking Bathsheba from Uriah when he already had women. By highlighting this negative aspect of David's actions against women, the Peshitta makes Bathsheba less suspect and affirms her as generally positive.

In terms of Bathsheba's development as a character, 2 Sam 12:24 of the Peshitta has Bathsheba naming her son,[71] which may signal the way the story will have her doing more as it proceeds in Kings. The Peshitta also emphasizes YHWH's love for Solomon, translating the MT יהוה

---

70. McCarter suggests that because the other witnesses (MT, LXX) have the second "from the roof" in varying positions, Syriac's omission of the phrase "represents the primitive situation." McCarter, *2 Samuel*, 279.

71. ܩܪܬ, "she called." The same is true for the MT *Qere* and in the Targum.

בעבור—"for the sake of YHWH" or "with respect to YHWH"—with the Syriac ܡܛܠ ܕܪܚܡܗ ܡܪܝܐ, "because YHWH loved him."[72] Such an assertion in the Peshitta more clearly sets up the theological rationale for Solomon to take the throne of David in 1 Kings, and may implicitly affirm Bathsheba's role in ensuring that it happens.

As she is in the other versions, Bathsheba remains complex in the Peshitta. When Bathsheba warns David about what will happen to Solomon and her when he "lies down with his fathers" in 1 Kgs 1:21, she adds in the Peshitta that he will lie down ܒܫܠܡܐ "in peace." There are different possibilities for this addition. Perhaps this addition heightens the contrast with what she believes will happen to her and Solomon: they will be in trouble, while David is at peace. Perhaps this is another type of euphemism or formality of the sort found in 1 Kgs 1:31 when she utters, "May my lord the king live forever." Or perhaps it is a genuine affirmation that David will be in peace. Of course, there are also echoes of David's son's names: Solomon, *šlhm*, "peace,"[73] or Absalom, *'bšlm*, "my father is peace." The different possibilities remind us that we do not definitively know the character of Bathsheba; in the Peshitta, as in other versions, she is complex.

To sum up, the Peshitta makes it clear when David sees Bathsheba that he is the voyeur. It also emphasizes David's wrongs against women, including Bathsheba. Her role as mother includes naming her child. And the Peshitta tells us in different ways than the other versions do that she remains somewhat mysterious and complex.

Targum Background Information

It is axiomatic that any discussion of scriptural translation will involve issues of interpretation, but that axiom is particularly evident when considering the Targumim. This dual nature of translation and interpretation is suggested by the very name for the Aramaic translation of the Scriptures, for the quadrilateral root *trgm* can mean either to translate

---

72. McCarter translates this as, "by the grace of God." The Syriac's language of the love of God is supported by Vulgate, but McCarter says both of those versions are "interpretive." McCarter, *2 Samuel*, 298. That is precisely the point, though—Vulgate and the Peshitta have interpreted the text, most likely under the influence of Solomon's name "Jedidiah," to mean that God loves Solomon.

73. But cf. the discussion of the meaning of his name in chapter 2.

or interpret.[74] Daniel Patte asserts, "What the Targum is expressing in Aramaic is not Scripture by itself, but Scripture as already interpreted."[75] Hauser and Watson, however, note that in the Targumim, the interpretive element is stronger, more obvious and more expansive than we would expect to see in any modern translation. They compare the Targumim to a tel with various strata, explaining that an extant text may include as much as several centuries of targumic development. Often, they explain, the Midrash developed alongside targumic texts, and elements of the midrashic heritage worked their way into the Targumim.[76] Pinkos Churgin explains, however, that even though the targumist "does not pretend to present a minutely literal translation of the Hebrew text, his reverence for the letter and transmitted reading of the text must far have exceeded that of the Greek and Syriac translators."[77] In other words, translating a text in a literal or wooden manner is not the only indicator that the translator highly revered the written word. Although the targumist was free and sometimes expansionistic, the changes made to the original text were not done lightly or without consideration for its theological significance.[78]

A better understanding of the interpretive nature of a Targum may be found in its *Sitz im Leben*. "The Aramaic Targum had a permanent and definite function in the prescribed liturgy of the Synagogue, and its task was to render faithfully into the vernacular the written text read in public."[79] Yet, because the words of the written text, as well as their implications, are not always entirely clear, the targumist felt the need to expand the translation with explanations. Such a view is reflected in the Midrash that theoretically identifies the author of Targum Jonathan.

74. BDB, 1076; HALOT, 1787. The word is a *hapax legomena* in biblical Hebrew, found in Ezra 4:7. Cf. Akkadian *targumanu,* interpreter/translator.

75. Patte, *Early Jewish Hermeneutic,* 53. Of course, by using the noun "Scripture," Patte is already making an interpretive claim of a sort, namely, that these are sacred texts. In that way, there is no such thing as Scripture "by itself."

76. Hauser and Watson, "Introduction and Overview," 22–23.

77. Churgin, *Targum Jonathan,* 9.

78. A parallel may be seen with Peterson's *The Message.* It is hardly literal, and might be more accurately categorized as a commentary rather than a translation, for he often drastically departs from the Hebrew, Aramaic, and Greek of the Old and New Testaments. Yet Peterson explains his own deep love of Greek and Hebrew, and how he attempted to write it "for disaffected outsiders and bored insiders" of the faith. Cusick, "A Conversation with Eugene Peterson," 83.

79. Heinemann, "Early Halakhah in the Palestinian Targum," 118.

> Said R. Jeremia, others say R. Hiyya B. Abba, Jonathan b. Uziel said it. And Eretz Israel trembled 400 parasangs. A Bath Kol said: "Who is the one who revealeth my mysteries to the children of men?" Rose Jonathan b. Uziel and said: "I am the one who revealeth Thy mysteries to the children of men. It is revealed and known unto you that . . . I did it for Thy sake in order that strife may not come about in Israel." To the question of why no such occurrence accompanied the act of the Targum to the Pentateuch, the answer is given: "The Pentateuch is clear while the Prophets contain things some of which are clear, while others are obscure." *B. Meg.* 3a.[80]

Indeed, Churgin identifies the main exegetical principle of Targum Jonathan as an attempt to "render intelligible . . . that which is obscure."[81]

Not only did the targumist attempt to prevent misunderstandings of the obscure passages of Scripture; another concern was that certain parts of Scripture might offend those who read or heard them. "So an 'interpretation' of the text was needed to adapt it to the culture, developing religious beliefs, social forms and practices, intellectual environment, and broader external world of each successive generation during which the targums were used."[82] Smolar and Aberbach explain that the passages that contradicted rabbinic halakah had to be reinterpreted in light of those laws and customs. "Inevitably, accuracy and historical truth had to be sacrificed on the altar of halachic orthodoxy."[83]

Although the Midrash identifies the author as Jonathan ben Uziel, and the name has remained for identifying purposes, there has been much debate over the date and provenance for Targum Jonathan. Most

---

80. This reference is found in the Babylonian Talmud, but there is a lack of supporting corroboration in the Palestinian Talmud (*y. Meg.* 1.9). Moreover, most quotations from Targum Jonathan in talmudic and midrashic writings are attributed to Rab Joseph, so it is generally agreed that either the author is unknown, or that there are multiple authors. There is some variety in language and translation techniques from book to book. Sperber suggests that Targum Jonathan originated in some kind of school activity, in which there was broad agreement about translation techniques, but then individual translators would have had some flexibility in the way they carried out their individual translations. *Targum Jonathan*, 1.

81. Churgin, *Targum Jonathan*, 28.

82. Hauser and Watson, "Introduction," 23.

83. Smolar and Aberbach, *Studies in Targum Jonathan*, 1, 61. Van Staalduine-Sulman, however, points out that Smolar and Aberbach ignore Churgin's point that the halakah of Targum Jonathan is not completely in harmony with that of rabbinic Judaism. *Targum of Samuel*, 39.

scholars believed Palestine to be its place of origin, although Frankel argued that Targum Jonathan originated in Babylonia. Kahle followed Frankel, but with some nuance: he saw Babylonia as the place where Targum Jonathan was finally formed, but explained that there were older, non-mishnaic elements in Targum Jonathan that could be Palestinian in origin.[84] As for dating Targum Jonathan, Kahle believed Targum Jonathan to be relatively late, not finished before the fifth century CE. Churgin, followed by Smolar and Aberbach, believed that Targum Jonathan reached its final form in the time of Rabbi Aqiba. But when the Aramaic Genesis Apocryphon was found at Qumran, it showed linguistic similarities to Targum Jonathan, so the consensus was that a relatively early date needed to be accepted.[85] Abraham Tal (Rosenthal) argued that it was closely connected with Old Aramaic, and suggested that it be dated before the Bar-Kohkba revolt in 135 CE. Most scholars follow Tal, allowing for the possibility of insertion of later material into the text and some editing in Babylonia.[86]

Targum Jonathan has many specific translation features, tendencies, and characteristics that are worthy of attention and focus. Other studies, however, have already discussed them with the detail they deserve, and thus will not be repeated here in this monograph.[87] Overall, we can see

84. Van Staalduine-Sulman, *Targum of Samuel*, 46.

85. Ibid.

86. Harrington, *Targum Jonathan of the Former Prophets*, 3.

87. In Churgin's discussion of the translation features of Targum Jonathan, he noted that textual variations from the MT fell into three categories. First, there were differences in pointing from a time "when doubts still existed, as to the reading of certain words." *Targum Jonathan*, 57. An example of this from the Bathsheba texts is found in 1 Kgs 1:18 and 1:20. The MT in 1:18 reads, ועתה אדני המלך, but the Targum substitutes ואת for ועתה. The MT in 1:20 reads, ואתה אדני המלך, but the Targum substitutes וכען for ואתה. Second, he noted grammatical differences which pointed to the translator's tendency to eliminate discrepancies in number or in person in the sentence. This rule, however, was not always consistently followed. Third, Targum Jonathan would render in one and the same way sentences that were different from one another in different places. This third category of variations did not come from a different reading, but were instead of an interpretive nature. *Targum Jonathan*, 53–54. Frankel noted the following tendencies in Targum Jonathan: frequent substitutions of the passive voice for the active one, and plural for singular; avoiding repetition of an expression in one verse (for example, "to flee" in 2 Sam 4:4 is rendered with two different verbs in Targum Jonathan); similar expressions in separate verses are rendered identically; different expressions are used in regard to God and humans (for example, in 1 Sam 12:18, the Israelites fear *before* God and fear *from* the words of Samuel); every ambiguity is avoided, and especially theological ambiguity; and the deeds and words of biblical heroes are rendered decorously

the Targumim cleaning up that which is messy in the MT, clarifying that which is obscure, and bringing the biblical text into agreement with the laws and customs of the time. An awareness of these tendencies will prevent overinterpretation of some of the targumic features when comparing them to the MT.[88] With those tendencies in mind, we still see some important implications for Bathsheba's characterization in the changes that the Targum does make from the other versions.

Bathsheba in the Targum

In fact, with the targumic tendency to protect the biblical heroes, it then becomes all the more striking that some of the changes in the Targum emphasize David's responsibility and culpability with Bathsheba (and consequently, continue to affirm Bathsheba's characterization as generally positive). For example, two manuscripts[89] include an additional punishment for David after 2 Sam 12:12 and preceding 2 Sam 12:13. This punishment is known as a tosefta, literally a "supplement." In the Aramaic of 2 Sam 12:6, David responds to the "man who did this" by saying that he ought to restore the lamb fourfold (Aramaic: אַרבעא, "four"). That number corresponds to the MT, not to LXX's "seven." The tosefta, however, adds,

---

(for example, David's abusive language against himself [1 Sam 24:15; 26:20] is rendered euphemistically, but the same expression against Shimei, David's enemy [2 Sam 16:9] is rendered literally). Van Staalduine-Sulman, *Targum of Samuel*, 8–10. Apowitzer saw other tendencies in targumic interpretation, including divergent prepositions (for example, the Hebrew אֶל is often translated with Aramaic עַל); a substitution of plural for singular; the completion of a sentence by adding a subject or an object; the conversion of a rhetorical question into its answer; the naturalistic translations of metaphors (e.g., "seed" was translated into "sons" and "to snatch away our eyes" was translated into "to cause us trouble"); and halakic changes in order to protect the biblical heroes. Van Staalduine-Sulman, *Targum of Samuel*, 12–14.

88. For example, the Targum of 2 Sam 11:27 reads, "the thing that David had done was evil before (קֳדָם) the Lord." It is not particularly surprising that the Targum removes the anthropomorphizing "in the eyes of the Lord." Cf. van Staalduine-Sulman, *Targum of Samuel*, 549 n. 503. I mentioned another example at the beginning of the chapter: the way the Targum levels out lord/master throughout 2 Sam 11:26 instead of allowing the MT's use of two different nouns, husband and master.

89. The manuscripts are MS C and Codex Montefiori 7; collated in Kasher, תוספתות, 114.

ולמא דאמרת ישלחם על חד ארבע הכי תהוי
בדיל נפשיה דאוריה רביא ואמנון ואבשלום ואדניה
ארבע נפשן יפקון מבנך

"And why did you say he will restore concerning one, four? Thus it will be for you. Four lives will go forth from your sons, because of the life of Uriah; the boy, and Amnon, and Absalom and Adonijah."

This tosefta, which is echoed in *Yoma 22b*,[90] emphasizes how David's children will pay a price for their father's sin. That the Targum includes this highlights that David has done wrong, and specifies the consequences for his sin.

If the punishment for David is made more specific, the level of his sin is also somewhat amplified in the way the Targum uses more euphemisms than the MT to describe what David did. There is already a euphemism in the Hebrew text of 2 Sam 12:14, "to scorn the enemies of the Lord."[91] This is incorporated into the Aramaic.[92] But the Targum adds another euphemism in its translation of the Hebrew verb נאץ. Instead of translating it with an pa"el form of Aramaic רגז, "to incite,"[93] or רחק, "reject,"[94] or even בזז, "plunder" (1 Sam 2:17), which would be expected, the Targum replaces the Hebrew with the Aramaic פתח, "to open one's mouth."[95] A third way 2 Sam 12:14 softens what David has done is by further distancing sins against God. The Hebrew says, "enemies of the Lord," but the Aramaic has דסנאי עמא דיוי, "enemies of *the people* of the Lord." Targum Jonathan typi-

---

90. *B. Yoma* 22b stressed, though, that the punishment would come during David's life, referring to the reference in 12:11 "before your eyes." Thus, it replaces Adonijah with Tamar, and states that four of David's children will be "hit" in some way, not necessarily killed: the boy, Tamar, Amnon, and Absalom.

91. McCarter describes this statement as a euphemism. *2 Samuel*, 296.

92. Van Staalduine-Sulman explains, "TJon most probably recognized the euphemism and gratefully integrated it in its own euphemistic rendering." *Targum of Samuel*, 553–54.

93. Cf. Num 14:11, 23; 16:30; Deut 31:20; Isa 52:5; 60:14; Jer 23:17; 33:24.

94. Isa 5:24; Jer 14:21.

95. According to McCarthy, the Aramaic expression "to open one's mouth " in T Jon's translation must be complemented with "to Satan"—the expression is a description of uttering the ominous words and thereby inviting disaster, because Satan might hear the words and realize them. *The Tiqqune Sopherim*, 242.

cally maintains a division between God and humans,[96] and wants to present its biblical heroes in a positive light. When we remember those tendencies, it is not surprising that we see these changes in the text. If read literally, it might appear that what David has done is not so bad: "he caused the enemies of the people of the Lord to open their mouths." But here is where the tools of text criticism are very helpful. When we compare the Aramaic with the Hebrew, and see all the changes made, we can surmise that the reason they are present in the Targum is because David's sins are so serious.[97] Because there are no corresponding changes (or additions) in the Targum to reference what Bathsheba has done, we see that it continues to characterize her in a generally positive manner.

One manuscript gives a variant that adds to Bathsheba's complexity. In 2 Sam 12:24, the Targum has ועל לותה, "and he came to her," which is the same as recorded in the MT (ויבא אליה), but MS B has the reading ועלת לותיה, "and she came to him." Van Staalduine-Sulman wants to explain the difference as the translator's euphemizing,[98] but it could also be that the translator connects this action of Bathsheba with the action she took in 2 Sam 11:4, when she also "came to him." That could add a level of assertiveness to her not indicated in other versions.

One way the Targum highlights Bathsheba's development is in what it has to say about Abishag in 1 Kings. There is no mention of Abishag lying in David's "bosom," as the MT has. Smolar and Aberbach explain,

> No less embarrassing was the advice given by his courtiers to the aged and cold king David to let a young maiden "lie in your bosom, that my lord the king may be warm." The Talmud discusses the reason for David's failure to marry the "young maiden," Abishag, who had been chosen to lie in his bosom. It was not old

---

96. For example, cf. 1 Sam 28:16, where if the word *people* does not work, at least there is some distance from God as enemy in Aramaic: "He is in the aid of the man whose enemy you are" (דבביה היהי בסעדיה דגברא דאת בעיל). Van Staalduine-Sulman, *Targum of Samuel*, 172–73.

97. Interestingly, in 12:10, God tells David "you despised me" in Aramaic, just as the MT also has "you despised me" (בזה). When so many other things regarding God are euphemized, it is all the more striking that this statement about David's actions is left untouched, and it too shows how the Targum is unwilling to gloss over David's wrongdoings.

98. Van Staalduine-Sulman, *Targum of Samuel*, 555n551. That is, van Staalduine-Sulman believes that the translator of this manuscript is hesitant to refer to David coming to Bathsheba, and so ascribes that action to her; yet the rest of that manuscript does not shy away from expressing what David has done.

age or impotence that prevented him from marrying Abishag;
on the contrary, his virility was as strong as ever. But since he already had eighteen wives, he was not permitted, according to the
rabbinic interpretation of the Deuteronomic law of kingship, to
exceed this number. (Cf. T. B. Sanh 21a, 22a). TJ, however, softens the language of the original by omitting the royal "bosom":
". . . and let her lie *with* you."[99]

Also, instead of Abishag as the סֹכֶנֶת of David in the MT, the Targum
explains "she was brought near" to the king. By doing so, the Targum
has more distance between Abishag and David, and therefore in 1 Kings,
Bathsheba's closeness with David is more apparent. Another specific example of Bathsheba's closeness can be seen in the Targum's addition to
1 Kgs 1:15. The Targum has Bathsheba not enter merely "the inner chamber" (החדרה), as she does in MT, but "the inner chamber *of the house
of the bed*" (לאדרון בית משכבא).[100] While the Hebrew alluded to an
intimate or private space, the Aramaic makes that explicit and definite,
again highlighting the close relationship Bathsheba shares with David.
The Talmud will be even more explicit about the intimacy between
David and Bathsheba at this point in 1 Kgs 1, which will be discussed in
the next chapter.

The Targumim, like the LXX and the Peshitta, agree with the MT's
characterization of Bathsheba as generally positive, complex, and showing development from Samuel to Kings, as expressed in the changes
noted above. Interestingly, although the Targum has a tendency to protect biblical heroes such as David, it does not do so by ascribing blame
or responsibility to Bathsheba. That trajectory continues for the most
part with other early Jewish readings as well, to be discussed in the next
chapter.

---

99. Smolar and Aberbach, *Studies in Targum Jonathan*, 51.

100. Brockelmann, *Lexicon Syriacum*, 6. In Jastrow's *Dictionary*, he notes this word's
connection to the Akkadian *idrânu*, and translates it as "an enclosure, chamber, especially dark alcove or bedroom," 45.

5

Jewish Interpretations of Bathsheba

AFTER CONSIDERING BATHSHEBA IN THE MT, THE LXX, SYRIAC PESHITTA, and the Aramaic Targumim, we have seen that though there are changes from one text to the next, her characterization remains more or less consistent throughout. This chapter looks at the way she is depicted in Jewish postbiblical work, namely, that of Josephus, the Jewish Midrash, and the Talmud. While all translation has an element of interpretation in it, with Josephus, the Talmud, and Midrash we have a marked move from the realm of translation into interpretation and commentary. It is all the more significant, therefore, that these early interpretations of Bathsheba will largely confirm Bathsheba's characterization as minor, complex, generally positive, and showing development in her character.

That Bathsheba is a minor character does not change in Josephus, the Talmud, or the Midrash; and like the biblical text, these accounts remain more interested in David than in Bathsheba. However, the expansions they make to the biblical text do expand Bathsheba's character. One example of this will be seen in the Midrash, when Bathsheba's role as Solomon's mother extends to giving him advice after he builds the temple. The Midrash therefore also shows more development to Bathsheba's character as she continues to act with wisdom and authority beyond where her story ends in the biblical text.

Bathsheba remains a complex character in these interpretations, but her complexity is seen in different ways: in the biblical texts, Bathsheba's complexity was related to the gaps in the text, the places where we could not determine why she acted the way she did. This is true for the Talmud, which does not have Bathsheba doing or saying much. But her complexity in Josephus' account is demonstrated by his mixed assessment of her, as Josephus presents her as both possessing and lacking specific virtues. In terms of Bathsheba's characterization as positive, here is where we get different responses. On the one hand, neither Josephus nor the rabbis state that Bathsheba is to be blamed for the adultery, or see her as a seductress. Instead, they continue the biblical text's own perspective that David is at fault, and therefore, relative to David, Bathsheba is still characterized in these interpretations as generally positive. But on the other hand, it is hard to sustain the view that Josephus characterizes Bathsheba in a positive manner: while some of his specific descriptions of her are more generous than the biblical text, others paint her more negatively when the Bible left her open. In that way, his interpretation of her is one of the earliest examples of a long line of more negative characterizations of Bathsheba throughout the history of biblical interpretation.

Josephus

This chapter will begin with Josephus because he provides a bridge of sorts between the versions and the rabbinic interpretations. *The Antiquities* predates the Peshitta and Targumim,[1] and linguistically is related to LXX.[2] I chose, however, to locate Josephus in this chapter instead of the previous one because even though Josephus claims in his introduction to *The Antiquities* that he will "set forth the precise details of what is written in the Scriptures . . . neither adding nor omitting anything" (*Ant.* 1.17), he does add to and omit from the Scriptures as he retells biblical history. Therefore, Josephus' work is much more an interpretation or expansion than a version or translation. But because Josephus is much earlier than the rabbinic texts, we can observe a rough historical progression in the history of interpretation of Bathsheba by starting with his work and then moving to the Talmud and Midrash.

Quite probably, Josephus introduced his own details into *The Antiquities* for apologetic reasons,[3] as he was interested in answering the charges that Jews had failed to produce great men.[4] In particular,

---

1. The Peshitta can be dated c. 150–200 CE, and Targum Jonathan c. 135 CE.

2. Though it is also connected to a Hebrew text and the Aramaic Targumim. Feldman asserts that it is possible that Josephus employed a Jewish tradition of both the MT and the LXX, as well as using an Aramaic Targum for the *Antiquities*. "Mikra in the Writings of Josephus," 456–60. In reference to 2 Samuel 11, Begg sees that most often, Josephus aligns himself with the reading of Lucianic. "David's Sin According to Josephus," 61. Rajak notes that while Josephus' native languages were Aramaic and Hebrew, his acquisition of Greek was intentional and deliberate. *Josephus*, 47–64.

3. Feldman, "Josephus," 986.

4. Feldman, "Josephus' Portrait of Solomon," 103–67. In *Contra Apion*, a sequel to

Josephus builds up Jewish biblical heroes using qualities that would appeal to a Greek audience. He emphasizes the external qualities of good birth and attractive appearance, the four cardinal virtues of character—wisdom, courage, temperance, and justice—and the spiritual virtue of piety.[5] These virtues and qualities are sometimes illustrated indirectly by the character's actions, and other times are seen in the author's direct characterization. We will consider the additions and omissions to the biblical story about Bathsheba, with two goals in mind. First, we will look at how Josephus characterizes her, particularly with reference to these specific qualities and virtues. Second, we will reflect back on the biblical characterization of her and compare it with his.

Although Josephus has been referred to as misogynistic,[6] his portrayal of biblical women is somewhat more mixed than that.[7] It is

---

the *Antiquities*, Josephus attempts to defend the "antiquity" and "purity" of the Jews and to "convict our detractors of malignity and deliberate falsehood." *C. Ap.* 1.1–3.

5. Feldman, "Mikra in the Writings of Josephus," 486. Feldman himself considers these virtues in his many articles.

6. Feldman, "Josephus' Portrait of Deborah," 115–20. Some of Feldman's examples include Josephus' references to his own wives, the woman leader at Masada, the Hasmonean Queen Salome Alexandra, and several biblical women, including Eve and Deborah. Feldman also notes regarding Ruth that "Josephus devotes relatively little space to the Ruth pericope (114 lines in the Greek of the Loeb Classical Library version) as against 202 lines in the Septuagint text (in the Rahlfs text) . . . in Josephus's version the role of Ruth herself is very much reduced, in line with his general misogynistic attitude. In particular, Josephus's omission of her kindness (*hesed*, Ruth 1:8) towards others is noteworthy." "Reflections," 45.

7. Levison, for examples, notes, "Josephus accentuates Ruth's generosity by adding the detail that, when she had returned from gleaning the fields, Ruth brought her entire lunch, which she had saved, to Naomi. According to the biblical version, Ruth brought to Naomi only the leftovers (Ruth 2.18)." "Josephus's Version of Ruth," 35. Sterling, however, observes that Josephus has eliminated almost all the direct speech in his retelling of Ruth, with the exception of Boaz. He writes, "This means that Josephus has effectively muted Naomi and Ruth." "The Invisible Presence," 115. Brown notes a lack of consistency in Josephus' portrayal of four biblical women. "Deborah and Hannah . . . are considerably more negative than their biblical counterparts . . . Jephthah's daughter . . . does not differ significantly, and . . . the witch of Endor . . . is actually more positive . . . Deborah is denied leadership roles outside of the prophetic (spiritual) realm; Hannah is weak-minded, overly emotional, and subordinate to the males in the story. Jephthah's daughter exemplifies a model daughter and affords Josephus the opportunity to demonstrate emphatically that the God of the Jews 'does not take pleasure in human sacrifice.' Such parenetic and apologetic tendencies also led Josephus to develop the witch of Endor into the epitome of hospitality and generosity, as well as submission to authority, which are likewise Roman ideals." *No Longer Be Silent*, 214–15. Cf. Halpern-Amaru, "Portraits of Biblical Women in Josephus' *Antiquities*," 151–54, 163–64.

therefore not surprising that his picture of Bathsheba would be correspondingly mixed. She exhibits some of the virtues Josephus highlighted in other biblical characters as examples of their "good" character. Josephus demonstrates that Bathsheba possesses the virtues of temperance and piety, where the Bible only hinted at them rather than directly stating she possesses them. Josephus elevates Bathsheba's good birth and physical beauty beyond what is described in the Bible. But in terms of the virtue of wisdom, Josephus gives Bathsheba a mixed review. In her interaction with David regarding Solomon's succession (1 Kgs 1:11–31), she has more wisdom than she is allotted in the Bible, but in his picture of her interaction with Solomon regarding Adonijah (1 Kgs 2:12–24), Bathsheba has less wisdom than she does in the Bible. And there are some places where he assesses her more negatively than the Bible does. Specifically, Bathsheba in *The Antiquities* lacks the virtues of courage and justice—virtues that she arguably possesses in the Bible. Josephus' picture of Bathsheba is consanguineous with the complex characterization we have seen of Bathsheba up to this point.

The Greek virtue of temperance[8] is linked with modesty in Josephus' description of Saul (*Ant.* 6.63).[9] In Josephus' portrayal of Bathsheba she has more modesty and more temperance than she does in the Bible. According to Josephus, when David initially sees Bathsheba from his roof, she is "bathing in her house" (λουομενην εν τη αυτης οικια) (*Ant.* 7. 130), something not specified in the MT. That Josephus makes it clear that Bathsheba is not on top of her roof points to more modesty in his version. Josephus also makes it clear that David is the one who does not behave with temperance and modesty. When David first sees Bathsheba, Josephus writes that he is unable to control his desire: ητταται του καλλους της γυναικος, και της επιθυμιας κατσου δυναμενος, "he was captivated by the beauty of the woman and unable to restrain his desire" (*Ant.* 7. 130). Uriah provides a stark contrast with David in this regard: Josephus writes that even when drunk, he does not feel desire (επιθυμιας) for his wife—the same desire that David could not control. [10] Even when Josephus eulogizes David with a description of

8. Feldman, "Mikra in the Writings of Josephus," 492.

9. Ibid., 491.

10. Yet, when Abishag is introduced in 1 Kings, Josephus adds that Abishag's sleeping with David is a medical prescription (*Ant* 7.343), perhaps to remove any suspicion that there are other reasons for David to sleep with her.

David as temperate (σοφρων), he qualifies it by adding that David never did wrong "except in the matter with Uriah's wife" (*Ant.* 7.391). Thus, the usually temperate David is the one who lacks that virtue, not Bathsheba. In the description of David and Bathsheba's encounter, told in 2 Sam 11:4, Josephus omits any mention that "she came" to him. Instead, all the action is David's, who "sent for her and lay with her" (μεταπεμψαμενος αυτην συνερχεται) (*Ant* 7.130).

Another change between Josephus and the biblical text is a small detail he adds when David first sees her bathing. Josephus tells us she was washing herself with cold water (ψυχρω υδατι). That same phrase is used in Josephus' account of the Levitical purity laws (Lev 15:16; *Ant.* 3.264), when he explains that those who are ritually impure must wash with cold water (υδωρ ψυχρον) to cleanse themselves, which points to Bathsheba's piety—another virtue.

Josephus also elevates the external quality of physical appearance; a hero should be physically attractive.[11] Josephus emphasizes the physical beauty of many of the biblical figures, including Moses, Jacob, Saul, David, and Absalom, often adding to the descriptions found in the Bible. Both the biblical text and Josephus refer to Bathsheba's beauty,[12] but where the Bible simply notes once that she is exceedingly beautiful (LXX: σφοδρα, 2 Sam 11:2), Josephus adds that her beauty is superior to all others (πασων διαφερουσαν). He then goes on to explain that David is overpowered (ηττατat) by Bathsheba's beauty, and David does not have the strength to hold back his desire for her (και της επιθυμιας κατασχειν ου δυναμενος) (*Ant.* 7.130). So, while Bathsheba's beauty is noted once in the Bible, Josephus refers to it three times.

In terms of the cardinal virtue of wisdom, Josephus gives a mixed assessment of Bathsheba. Wisdom is exemplified by the hero's general insight, understanding, and sagacity, as well as the hero's ability to settle disputes and persuade people.[13] As Bathsheba was advised by Nathan the prophet, she approached David to persuade him to put Solomon on the throne instead of Adonijah. According to Josephus, "she recounted

---

11. Plato remarks in *The Republic* that so far as is possible, the philosopher-kings should be the most handsome people (7:535). Feldman, "Mikra in the Writings of Josephus," 488.

12. The Greek is remarkably similar: the LXX explains she is καλη τω ειδει; Josephus writes that she is καλλιστην το ειδος.

13. Feldman, "Mikra in the Writings of Josephus," 488–90.

to [David] all that the prophet had suggested. . . . She added that all the people were waiting to see whom he would choose king, and urged him to bear in mind that, if, after his death, Adonijah became king, he would put her and her son Solomon to death" (*Ant.* 7.350).

The Bible lacks any narrated mention that "she added" to what Nathan the prophet had told her to say. In the Bible, Bathsheba converses with David using direct discourse, and the information that she and Solomon may suffer[14] after David dies is simply included in her speech (1 Kgs 1:17–21). Even though we can see that Bathsheba does add to what Nathan had told her to say, Josephus makes that explicit. With Nathan's help, but also by her own rhetoric, Bathsheba is able to persuade David to place Solomon on the throne. On this occasion, therefore, she does demonstrate the persuasive characteristic of wisdom.

But when Bathsheba approaches Solomon to request that he give Abishag to Adonijah in *The Antiquities*, it seems that she lacks wisdom: she does not understand the implications of Adonijah's request, nor is she able to persuade her son. Josephus writes, "And Bersabe[15] promised to intercede for him zealously and to bring the marriage about, both because the king would wish to do him a favor and because she would earnestly entreat him" (*Ant.* 8.6). But her promise to bring about the marriage does not come true. Her insight into Solomon's motives is inaccurate. Even after Solomon reminded Bathsheba that it was a "sacred duty to do everything for a mother" (*Ant.* 8.8), he refuses her request. Not only does Solomon refuse Bathsheba's request, but according to Josephus, he "took offense at her words, and sent his mother away" (*Ant.* 8.9).[16] The biblical text attributes no motives to Bathsheba, and the ensuing ambiguity allows for the possibility that Bathsheba is, indeed, a woman as wise as a serpent, though she acts innocent as a dove. That is, we could imagine in the biblical text that the reason that she told Adonijah, "Good," in 1 Kgs 2:18 was that she knew Adonijah's request would give Solomon the

14. One of the differences between Josephus' version and the biblical version is found in the details of what will happen to Bathsheba and Solomon. In the LXX, she says, "I and my son Solomon will be treated as sinners (αμαρτωλοι)." This follows the MT הַחַטָּאִים (1 Kgs 1:21). According to Josephus, however, Bathsheba says that she and Solomon will be put to death (αναιρησει); *Ant.* 7.350.

15. The LXX name for Bathsheba, cf. chapter 4.

16. The biblical text does not specify how Bathsheba exits the scene in 1 Kgs 2; she could have left on her own.

reason he needed to kill Adonijah. In Josephus, however, the earnestness with which she promises to entreat Solomon would belie her wisdom.

Courage is another one of the virtues, but Josephus clearly states Bathsheba's lack of courage. Instead, he uses the word "apprehensive" (υφοραω)[17] to refer to Bathsheba. When she goes to Solomon to request that Adonijah be given Abishag in marriage, she asks him not to deny the favor. Then, Josephus explains that Solomon "added a word of reproach for the way she had begun in that she had not spoken with a sure hope of obtaining what she requested but had been fearful of being denied" (*Ant.* 8.8). When Solomon describes Bathsheba's lack of courage in the Bible, the words he uses are certainly not as specific as those he uses in Josephus. Of course, the biblical text does not explicitly state one way or the other whether Bathsheba is courageous or fearful. In this sense, therefore, the biblical text(s) are at least more open than Josephus regarding Bathsheba, and it would seem that they are holding out the possibility of being more positive or more generous in their characterization of her.

Josephus does not describe Bathsheba as unjust, but in some of the rewording in *The Antiquities*, it would seem that she lacks this virtue. Herodotus connected the virtue of justice with truth-telling,[18] and in Josephus' version, Bathsheba has a distinct lack of interest in telling the truth. Josephus expands upon Bathsheba's words in 2 Sam 11:5, so according to Josephus, "she became pregnant and sent to the king, asking him to contrive some way of concealing her sin, for according to the laws of the fathers she was deserving of death as an adulteress" (*Ant.* 7.131). In the biblical text in which, after Bathsheba conceived, she "sent and she declared to David, 'I am pregnant,'" she speaks the truth. In the *Antiquities*, she is more interested in hiding the truth than telling it. Moreover, as Josephus tells it, Bathsheba knows she deserves death, but she is unwilling to face the consequences of the laws of the fathers. She would rather subvert justice than submit to it. This is a major indictment, especially from a legal standpoint. Of course, he is reading a bit counter to the text and adding a detail that is not present in the text, but it is hard to read this modification of Bathsheba's characterization as positive.

Two other aspects to Josephus' work are notable for our understanding of Bathsheba. One is the addition he makes to the account of

17. This can also be translated as "fearful."
18. Feldman, "Mikra in the Writings of Josephus," 493.

David praying for the life of the first child. Josephus explains that David asks God to spare the life of the child "whose mother he so deeply loves" (σφοδρα γαρ εστεργεν αυτου την μητερα) (*Ant.* 7.155). The biblical text does not have any expression of David's feelings for Bathsheba until he comforts her (2 Sam 12:24), so by adding this information before the death of the child, Josephus increases the level of emotion between David and Bathsheba. The second thing to note about Josephus is that if his picture of Bathsheba is mixed, so too is his portrait of David. Feldman makes the point that Josephus felt that he had to be cautious in his portrayal of David in order not to offend the Romans.[19] Still, we must conclude that while Josephus' overall picture of Bathsheba is complex, his characterization of her in more negative terms than the biblical picture is one of the first.

Rabbinic Material

If Josephus adds to and interprets what the text says, the Talmud and Midrash will do so even more. The picture of Bathsheba we receive in the more expansive rabbinic material is interpretive in nature from the start.[20] What we will see in their picture of her will provide both an example of early interpretations of her and clues for us as to how we might interpret her today.

Scholars have noted the variety of characterizations of David in postbiblical Judaism. Jouette Bassler asserts, "From the chrysalis of rabbinic interpretation he emerged as a multihued individual, bearing scant resemblance to the biblical figure."[21] Bassler's comment may be a bit of an overstatement, for the biblical David is already a complex and mul-

---

19. Any reference to David in connection with the Messiah, for example, might be considered by the Romans as encouraging revolt against their rule. Feldman, "Josephus' Portrait of David," 129–33.

20. Sternberg references rabbinical readings as an example of "illegitimate gap filling." He writes, "The hypotheses they frame are often based on assumptions that have no relevance to the world of the Bible (e.g., that Jacob and Esau went to school), receive no support whatever from the textual details, or even fill in what the narrative itself rules out. Where there's a will, the midrash will always find a way." *Poetics*, 188.

21. Bassler, "A Man for All Seasons," 156. Bassler notes that Rosner's dissertation, *David's Leben und Charakter*, is an exhaustive study of this topic. Shimoff explains that both the Exilarch and the Patriarch claimed direct Davidic descent, and therefore those sages who wanted to support their political leaders would have a political interest in defending David's honor, while those who were at odds with those leaders were the ones who criticized David. "David and Bathsheba," 246–56.

tidimensional character.[22] But while some of the rabbinic texts clearly identify David's actions with Uriah and Bathsheba as sins, others tend to whitewash David, or at the least, give explanations and occasional rationalizations for his actions. When the nature of rabbinic texts is dialectical and dialogic, it is hardly surprising that their picture of Bathsheba is correspondingly multivalent. Daniel Boyarin explains, "The famous indeterminacy of midrashic reading—its allowance of several possibilities equally—will be understood as a figure for the possibility of several ways of filling in the gaps."[23] However, no talmudic and midrashic references place blame on Bathsheba. It might be expected that they would vilify Bathsheba when David is such an important and beloved figure. But the evidence shows that nowhere is Bathsheba viewed as a seductress, or in any way at fault for their encounter. Even those rabbinic texts that give reasons for David's actions do not excuse him by blaming Bathsheba.

This discussion will consider specific texts from the Talmud and Midrash about Bathsheba. The Talmud is a commentary on the Mishnah,[24] and summarizes the discussions and explanations of the Mishnah. While there are two distinct works known as the Talmud, the Babylonian Talmud has greater popularity and authority than the Jerusalem or Palestinian Talmud, so most references to the Talmud refer to the former.[25] The word *Midrash* comes from the Hebrew root דרש, "to ask, inquire, or seek out meaning," although it is a word that "has been used to designate both the activity of interpretation and the fruits of that activity."[26] I will be considering Bathsheba in the collections of midrashic material known as the Midrash Rabbah.

As I look at the specific texts, I will follow the general plotline of the Bathsheba texts. The rabbinic commentary begins even before David

22. See Brueggemann, *David's Truth*, and Bowman's "The Complexity of Character and the Ethics of Complexity," 73–97.

23. Boyarin, *Intertextuality and the Reading of Midrash*, 41.

24. The Mishnah is the six-part legal code formulated toward the end of the second century CE. The six parts of the Mishnah include: (1) agricultural rules, (2) laws governing appointed seasons (Sabbaths and festivals), (3) laws on the transfer of women and property along with woman from one man (father) to another (husband), (4) system of civil and criminal law, (5) laws for conduct of cult and temple, and (6) laws on preservation of cultic purity in temple and in certain domestic circumstances.

25. For this volume I primarily use the Hebrew-English edition of the Soncino Press Babylonian Talmud (ed. Rabbi Isidore Epstein).

26. Kugel, "Two Introductions to Midrash," 91.

meets Bathsheba, when Abigail predicts that their encounter will cause David to stumble. In reference to Abigail's comment in 1 Sam 25:31, "Do not let this be a stumbling block to you," *b. Meg.* 14b explains, "The word *'this'* implies that something else would be, and what was that? The incident of Bathsheba; and so it was eventually."

Abigail is not the only one to forewarn David of his future stumbling with Bathsheba. God also personally warns David ahead of time, according to *b. Sanh.* 107a, a text worth quoting in its entirety for the way it describes how David first saw Bathsheba.

> David said to God, "Sovereign of the Universe! Why do we say [in prayer] 'The God of Abraham, the God of Isaac, and the God of Jacob,' but not the God of David?" He replied, "They were tried by me, but thou wast not." Then, replied he, "Sovereign of the Universe, examine and try me,"—as it is written, *Examine me, O Lord, and try me.* He answered, "I will test thee, and yet grant thee a special privilege, for I did not inform them [of the nature of their trial beforehand], yet, I inform thee that I will try thee in a matter of adultery." Straightaway, *And it came to pass in an eveningtide, that David arose from his bed, etc.* R. Johanan said: He changed his night couch to a day couch, but he forgot the *halakah*: there is a small organ in man which satisfies him in his hunger but makes him hunger when satisfied. *And he walked upon the roof of the king's house: and from the roof he saw a woman washing herself; and the woman was very beautiful to look upon.* Now Bath Sheba was cleansing her hair behind a screen,[27] when Satan came to him, appearing in the shape of a bird. He shot an arrow at him, which broke the screen, thus she stood revealed, and he saw her. Immediately, *And David sent and enquired after the woman. And one said, Is not this Bath Sheba, the daughter of Eliam, the wife of Uriah the Hittite? And David sent messengers, and took her, and she came unto him, and he lay with her; for she was purified from her uncleanliness: and she returned unto her house.* Thus it is written, *Thou hast proved my heart; thou hast visited me in the night; thou hast tried me, and shalt find nothing; I am purposed that my mouth shall not transgress.* [Psalm 17:3] He said thus: "Would that a bridle had fallen into the mouth of mine enemy [i.e., himself], that I had not spoken thus."[28]

---

27. Rashi reads this word as "beehive."

28. The word יתמז, "I am purposed," is connected with the word זממא, "a bridle."

In this account, David is clearly in the wrong. God had told David that his trial would be in the area of adultery, so he cannot be excused for being caught off guard. Shulamit Valler says, "The moment Satan is introduced into the story, it changes into a story about God and Satan; hence, David can have no influence on the sequence of events."[29] I disagree with Valler's comment that David can have no influence on what happens. Even if the rabbis are giving us a sophisticated version of "the devil made me do it" story, this interaction is hardly analogous to the encounter between God and *hassatan* in Job 1–2, where Job genuinely does not have any influence on the sequence of events.[30] In fact, precisely because David was "informed" by God about the nature of his trial (whereas Job was not), he at least theoretically could choose not to fall into temptation. And even though Satan's presence and personification of the temptation might increase the level of temptation, that does not rob David of all ability to say no. Moreover, the Talmud specifies that Bathsheba was washing her *hair*, and not washing her *self*, so there is even less reason to suppose that she is naked and touching herself in an intimate way.[31]

Following the story in *b. Sanh.* 107a of Satan becoming a bird, Raba the sage gives different expositions. In the first exposition, David explains that he did not want to sin, but neither did he want to seem superior to God. The second one teaches that Bathsheba was predestined for David from the time of creation.

> Raba expounded: What is meant by the verse, *Against you, only You, have I sinned, and done this evil in Your sight, that You might be justified when You speak, and be clear when You judge?*[32] David

29. Valler, "King David and 'His' Women," 138.

30. Newsom points out that in Job *hassatan* is not "yet the Satan-with-a-capital-S of later Jewish and Christian literature." *The Book of Job*, 55.

31. Exum writes, "The intimacy of washing is intensified by the fact that this is a ritual purification after her menstrual period, and this intimacy, along with the suggestion of nakedness, accentuates the body's vulnerability to David's and our shared gaze." "Bathsheba Plotted, Shot, and Painted," 53. Martin argues for the connection between hair and sexuality in Greek thought ("Paul's Argument from Nature," 75–84), so it is possible that the Talmudic reference to her hair is a euphemism for her sexuality. Cf. Cosgrove, "A Woman's Unbound Hair," 675–92.

32. This reference is from Ps 51, a psalm with the superscription, "A psalm of David when the prophet Nathan came to him, after he had gone in to Bathsheba." The superscription invites the later Jewish interpretive tradition to read the narrative of 2 Sam 11–12 in an intertextual relationship with Ps 51, as is done here. Moreover, the rabbinic

pleaded before the Holy One, blessed be He: You know full well
that had I wished to suppress my lust, I could have done so, but
though I [could], let them [the people] not say, The servant tri-
umphed over his master.

Raba expounded: What is meant by the verse, *For I am ready
to halt, and my sorrow is continually before me?* [Psalm 38:18]
Bath Sheba, daughter of Eliam, was predestined for David from
the six days of Creation, but that she came to him with sorrow.
And the school of R. Ishmael taught likewise: She was worthy
[i.e., predestined] for David from the six days of Creation, but
that he enjoyed her before she was ripe.

Valler believes that Raba's expositions mitigate David's guilt. "The first
homily eradicates David's sin altogether. Whatever he did he did for the
glory of God, not for his own gratification. The second homily reduces
David's sin by teaching that Bathsheba was predestined for him from
the very beginning of the creation, and, in taking her from Uriah, David
put things back into their natural order (even though much pain was
involved)."[33]

I would modify Valler's statement; Raba does not eradicate David's
sin by the very fact that he refers to Ps 51:6 (ET 51:4), where David says,
"Against you alone I have sinned and I have done evil in your eyes"
(לך לבדך והרע בעתניך עשיתי). Raba's explanation for David's sin
does not eliminate that David did sin against God, but explains that the
sin was for God's glory.

Moreover, the Sanhedrin text goes on and explains that when David
asked God to take away any consequence for his sins, God refused to do
so and encouraged David to accept his punishment.

He pleaded before him, "Sovereign of the Universe! Pardon me
that sin completely [as though it had never been committed]."
He replied, "It is already ordained that thy son Solomon should
say in his wisdom, *Can a man take fire in his bosom, and his
clothes not be burned? Can one go upon hot coals, and his feet not
be burned? So he that goeth in to his neighbour's wife, whoseoever
toucheth her shall not be innocent.*" (Prov 6:27ff.)[34] He lamented,

tradition that David was the author of the whole book of Psalms means that any psalm
could be put alongside the narratives of David for interpretive purposes, hence the quotation of Ps 38:18 here in relation to David and Bathsheba.

33. Valler, "King David and 'His' Women," 139.

34. The reason for the reference to Proverbs is that Solomon was considered the author of the wisdom literature, so those texts provide an intertextual reservoir by which to

"Must I suffer so much!" He replied, "Accept thy chastisement," and he accepted it.

Rab Judah said in Rab's name: Six months was David smitten with leprosy, the *Shechinah* deserted him, and the Sanhedrin held aloof from him. "He was smitten with leprosy,"—as it is written, *Purge me with hyssop, and I shall be clean; wash me, and I shall be whiter than snow. (Ps 51:9)*[35] "The *Shechinah* deserted him"—as it is written, *Restore unto me the joy of thy salvation; and uphold me with thy free spirit. [Ps 51:14]* "And the Sanhedrin kept aloof from him"—as it is written, *Let those that fear you turn unto me, and those that have known thy testimonies.* How do we know that it was for six months? Because it is written, *And the days that David reigned over Israel were forty years: [107b] Seven years reigned he in Hebron, and thirty and three years reigned he in Jerusalem* (1 Kgs 2:11); whilst [elsewhere] it is written, *In Hebron reigned he over Judah seven years, and six months.* (2 Sam 5:5) Thus, these six months are not counted [in the first passage quoted], proving that he was smitten with leprosy.

David's punishment by leprosy is also mentioned in *b. Yoma* 22b. In both of these accounts, God makes it clear that David's sins will not be eradicated.

Another example of a Talmudic text that explains David's sin is found in *b. 'Abod. Zar.* 4b–5a: "David was not the kind of man to do that act [with Bathsheba], as it is written, *My heart is slain within me;*[36] nor were the Israelites the kind of people to commit that act [with the golden calf], for it is said, *O that they had such a heart as this always etc.* Why, then, did they act thus? [5a] [God predestined it so] in order to teach thee that if an individual hath sinned [and hesitates about the effect of repentance] he could be referred to the individual [David], and if a community commit a sin they should be told: Go to the community."[37]

---

interpret the stories and character of Solomon, just as the Psalms did for David.

35. Lev 4:4 specifies the use of hyssop for the purification of a leper.

36. Ps 109:22.

37. This text clarifies that David's sin was predestined by God, as if to say that David genuinely has no control over committing a sin if the sovereign God had predestined it. The previous example of Raba in *b. Sanh.* 107a also explained that Bathsheba was predestined for David by God. Eskola traces the idea of predestination, seeing it in the Wisdom of Solomon and then in the Rule of the Community from the Dead Sea Scrolls, particularly in its discussion of children of light and darkness. In regards to the predestination he sees in Wis, he writes that it solves the problem of theodicy, "the divine determination of God will eventually provide salvation for the righteous (Wisd. Sol. 4,17)."

Still, even though this text has an explanation for David's sin (namely, that he sinned to teach others about repentance and grace), it does not ignore the sinfulness of David's actions. The connection between David with Bathsheba and the Israelites with the golden calf is illuminating in comparing David's actions with the serious sin of Israel's idolatry. The Midrash Rabbah for Num 11:3 also refers to David's affair with Bathsheba as sin.[38]

In *b. Šabb.* 56a, there is an attempt to exonerate David from his guilt: "R. Shemuel b. Nahman said in R. Jonathan's name, Whoever says that David sinned is plainly mistaken, for it is said, 'And David behaved himself wisely in all his ways, and the Lord was with him.' Is it possible that sin came to his hand yet the Divine presence was with him? Then how do I interpret, 'Why have you despised the word of the Lord, to do that which is evil in his sight?' He wished to do (evil) but did not."

The tractate continues on, though, with another rabbi observing that R. Shemuel, who sought to exonerate David, was a descendant of David, and "seeks to defend him and expounds in David's favor." The latter rabbi does not agree with R. Shemuel's interpretation.

The specific location of a rooftop is warned against by R. Joshua b. Levi. In *b. Pesaḥ* 113a, he warns the men of Jerusalem not to practice immodesty, meaning not to frequent places where immodest sights are seen. Variant texts read specifically "do not frequent roofs."[39] In *b. Ned.* 20a, R. Aha says, "He who gazes at a woman eventually comes to sin, and he who looks even at a woman's heel will beget degenerate children."[40] It

---

"Paul, Predestination, and 'Covenantal Nomism,'" 400. "A basic feature in the theology of Second Temple Judaism was the problem of theodicy. It was solved by using the idea of God's judgment which would fall on the godless rulers. Since God was Almighty and the rule of the apostates was only transient the judgment had to be predestined. No sinner could avoid it. The normative Judaism, centered around the Temple, was perhaps able to live according to the traditional covenantal religion and neglect this antagonism. From the wisdom theology onwards the theology of religious movements was formed after the idea of predestination, however. Practically all Second Temple texts contain these basic features. This soteriology is not a simple convenantal nomism. It is based on soteriological dualism where the predestination of judgment is the key concept. We have to speak of a 'weak' predestination, though, because the fallen Israelites were able to avoid the coming wrath. The eschatological 'getting in' took place in repentance and in a commitment to the law of God." Ibid., 403. Cf. Flusser, *Judaism and the Origins of Christianity*, and Merrill, *Qumran and Predestination*, 27, 41.

38. "Before David had sinned in connection with that unnameable incident [with Bathsheba]," 420 in *Midr. Rabb. Num.*

39. *Pesahim*, 582n2.

40. R. Simeon b. Lakish (*b. Ned.* 20a) explains, "'Heel' that is stated means the un-

could be argued that this text explains that women are responsible for men's sin because of their appearance, but it could also be argued based on this text that even after a first glimpse of Bathsheba, David should have looked away.

Judith Baskin points out that there is a tradition within the Talmud that blames women for male lust.[41] B. Ta'an. 24a talks about R. Jose of Yokereth, who one day saw a man boring a hole in the fence so that he might catch a glimpse of R. Jose's daughter. "He said to the man, What is this? And the man answered: Master, if I am not worthy enough to marry her, may I not at least be worthy to catch a glimpse of her? Thereupon [R. Jose] exclaimed: My daughter, you are a source of trouble to mankind; return to the dust so that men may not sin because of you."

Therefore, with this Talmudic text as evidence, it could be inferred that David sinned because of Bathsheba. Moreover, R. Isaac b. Abdimi exegetes Genesis 3:16 in b. 'Erub. 100b by explaining that the part of Eve's punishment that says "*and your desire will be for your husband*" "teaches that a woman yearns for her husband when he is about to set out on a journey." Baskin writes that this "is said to refer to a woman's desire for her husband when he is away on a journey and she has no sexual partner . . . due to female dependence on male mastery. Yet for none of these disadvantages were men in any way culpable. All were considered either ordained by God at the outset of the human drama or were part of women's punishment for disobeying God."[42] Someone following this line of thought might conclude Bathsheba is punished with sexual desires that cannot be fulfilled when Uriah, her husband, is away, and furthermore, that she sought to entrap David so that those sexual yearnings might be fulfilled.

Thus, inferences do exist in the Talmud that Bathsheba has culpability in David's sin (b. Ned. 20a: David's gazing at Bathsheba led to sin; b. Ta'an. 24a: she is "a source of trouble" to David; and b. 'Erub. 100b: Bathsheba had yearnings for Uriah when he was away). However, it is important to note that nowhere does the Talmud explain away—or erase—David's sin by naming Bathsheba, or suggesting that Bathsheba made him do it. Satan, David, and God may vie for various degrees of

---

clean part, which is directly opposite the heel." It is interesting to read Aha's reference to the children: Solomon hardly turned out to be the ideal son.

41. Baskin, *Midrashic Women*, 32.

42. Ibid., 75.

responsibility, depending on the different texts, but the blame is never placed solely nor specifically on Bathsheba. In fact, in reference to Bathsheba's "coming to" (ותבא) David, we have noted how different interpreters have concluded from that verb that Bathsheba wanted to be with David. *B. Ketub.* 9a, however, explains that she came to David in "the occurrence that happened" under "compulsion."

Valler argues that "the talmudic interpreters do not hesitate to distort the actions and words ascribed to the female characters involved in [David's] life,"[43] and specifically mentions how the biblical text presents Bathsheba as someone who is not afraid to tell David about her unexpected pregnancy and who shows courage in fighting for the rights of Solomon. It is true that in the Talmud, Bathsheba does not speak to David about her pregnancy. Nor will she speak to him about his promise to put Solomon on the throne. In fact, within the plot of the story as it is represented in rabbinic material, she will not speak until the Midrash has her speaking to Solomon after he has built the temple. If speech is one of the ways we can understand and characterize characters, we know less about Bathsheba in the Jewish material than in the biblical text. But if the Talmud and Midrash have Bathsheba saying less than she does in the Bible, they have her doing more. Her character will continue to act in Solomon's life long after the biblical text has her fade away.

The Talmud is more dismissive of Uriah and flattens his character more than Bathsheba's character. In the biblical text, Uriah is a fascinating figure.[44] But the Talmud is not interested in considering such nuances, nor is it interested in the biblical contrast between David's sins and Uriah's righteousness. It is interested in David's sins, but not at the level of highlighting Uriah's contrasting faithfulness. One theme in the Talmud is that Bathsheba was not actually married to Uriah at the time when David took her and lay with her. This is found in *b. B. Meṣ.* 58b, which refers to Bathsheba as a "doubtful married woman"; that is, it is doubtful that she was married at the time to Uriah. This theme is repeated in *b. Ketub.* 9b[45] and *b. Šabb.* 56a: "For R. Samuel b. Naḥmani said

43. Valler, "King David and 'His' Women," 130.

44. Sternberg uses Uriah as an example of the gaps and ambiguity of 2 Sam 11, explaining that he might not know what has happened between his wife and David, or he might indeed know. *Poetics*, 199–213. Kim describes Uriah as someone who is a hybrid, who "ruptures the story." "Uriah the Hittite," 76. Kim also highlights Uriah's faithfulness and honor. Cf. chapter 2, note 64.

45. "Everyone who goes out into the war of the House of David writes for his wife a

in R. Jonathan's name: Every one who went out in the wars of the house of David wrote a bill of divorcement for his wife, for it is said, *and bring these ten cheeses unto the captain of their thousand, and look how thy brethren fare, and take their pledge* ['arubatham]. What is meant by *'arubatham*? R. Joseph learned: The things which pledge man and woman [to one another]."

In other words, the divorce would become valid in retrospect if the husband died. Since Uriah did die, Bathsheba was divorced from the time that Uriah left, and she was technically not married when David first encountered her. *B. Šabb.* 56 a continues, "*And thou hast slain him with the sword of the children of Ammon*: just as thou art not [to be] punished for the sword of the Ammonites, so art thou not [to be] punished for [the death of] Uriah the Hittite. What is the reason? He was rebellious against royal authority, saying to him, *and my lord Joab, and the servants of my lord, are encamped in the open field* [etc]."

That is, David is not to be punished for killing Uriah, because Uriah refused to obey David's commands that he go down to his house and sleep with his wife. Midrash Samuel also excuses David from Uriah's death—in part. One section raises the issue of whether or not David is responsible for the deaths that God brought about to his adversaries (including Saul, Nabal, and Uriah). This section begins with Ps 51:16 (ET 51:14) where David pleads for deliverance from bloodguilt, and then explains why each accusation of bloodguilt is mistaken.

> Regarding the death of Uriah, R. Joshua ben Levi said, *Uriah the Hittite; all the thirty-seven* (2 Sam 23:39). R. Jonah Boṣriah said, "They reduced him from his greatness for he was worthy to be appointed after thirty-six, and they appointed him after thirty-seven." R. Haninah bar Papa in the name of R. Haninah Safra said he brought it from her becoming pregnant: *why did you despise the word of the LORD, etc. and you killed him with the sword of the sons of Ammon* (2 Sam 12:9), but the rabbis say, "*you killed him.*" This teaches that he killed many righteous like that.[46]

This reference to Uriah within the larger section of text that excuses David from these deaths means that the rabbis who are named have ap-

---

deed of divorce, for it is written, *And to thy brethren shalt thou bring greetings and take their pledge* [1 Sam 17:18]."

46. *Midrash Samuel*, 122–23. While Midrash Samuel resembles most of the other haggadic midrashim both in diction and in style, it is merely a collection of sentences referring to the books of Samuel that are found in those other midrashim.

pealed to 2 Sam 23:39 as evidence that Uriah has been denigrated, and therefore David is not guilty of his blood. Yet, we also see that the anonymous "rabbis" say David did kill him, and in fact, killed many (other) righteous.

Indeed, the perspective that justifies David killing Uriah is not the only rabbinic word about Uriah's death. In *b. Yoma* 22b, R. Huna said:

> How little does he whom the Lord supports need to grieve or trouble himself! Saul sinned once and it brought [calamity] upon him. David sinned twice, and it did not bring evil upon him. What was the one sin of Saul? The affair with Agag. But there was also the matter with Nob, the city of the priests?—[Still] it was because of what happened with Agag that Scripture says: *It repenteth Me that I have set up Saul to be king.* What were the two sins of David? – The sin against Uriah and that [of counting the people to which] he was enticed. But there was also the matter of Bathsheba?—for that he was punished, as it is written, *And he shall restore the lamb fourfold*: the child, Amnon, Tamar and Absalom.[47]

R. Huna's point is subtle. He uses the word *sin* in reference to David's murder of Uriah. Yet, he also explains that this sin "did not bring evil upon him." And, the fact that R. Huna connects "the sin of Uriah" with the sin to which "he was enticed" may be a way of saying that David's murder was not so problematic. Also, the notation of the punishment could be understood in different ways: on the one hand, that David was *punished* means he had done wrong, but on the other hand, that David *was* punished means that it is over.

The Talmud also refers to David's sinfulness when it discusses Nathan's visit to David and his parable. In *b. Sukkah* 52b, Raba observes that Nathan uses three different words to refer to the visitor who comes to the rich man; he is identified as "the traveler" (הֵלֶך), then "the journeyman" (אֹרַח), and finally "the man (who came to him)" (אִישׁ הַבָּא אֵלָיו). Rashi and Kimchi discuss Nathan's use of the three words, and Rashi explains that the visitor is "the evil inclination" (יֵצֶר הָרַע). Kimchi concurs: "The wayfarer and the traveler refer to the (Evil) Inclination for the wayfarer and the traveler are one (and the same). And the rabbis of blessed memory expound it in this way that the Evil Inclination is first like a wayfarer who passes a man by and does not

---

47. Cf. the Tosefta to Targum Jonathan, discussed in chapter 4.

take lodging with him. But after this he is like a traveler who passes a man and does take lodging with him. And then he is like a house-holder in that he has power over the man."[48] Again, their explanations that David had been taken hold of by the "evil inclination" need not only be seen as evidence that David was not also responsible for his sinfulness.

The number of times the rich man is commanded by David to re-pay has already been discussed in previous chapters, but Kimchi and Ibn Ezra give another account. Kimchi explains that instead of "fourfold," the number should be "eight": "The thief must repay four sheep for a young sheep (שׂה), but in this case it was a rich man and he stole the ewe-lamb (כבשׂה) of the poor man and it was deemed right to fine him and make him pay twice what was necessary 'because he had done this thing.'"[49]

Also previously discussed is that there are a few possibilities about the identity of the lamb in the parable. B. Yoma 66b records the cryptic comments R. Eliezer makes concerning the lamb when some people ask him about someone in the world to come: "He replied, 'Have you asked me only about this one'? 'May one save the lamb from the lion'?—He said to them: 'Have you asked me only about the lamb'? 'May one save the shepherd from the lion'?—He said to them, 'Have you asked me only about the shepherd'?"

The text continues to say that R. Eliezer's evasiveness was not be-cause he wanted to divert them with counter-questions, but because he never said anything he had not heard from his teacher. That did not stop people from speculating about his obscure comments. Some understood the lion to refer to David as king, who had taken the lamb (Bathsheba, cf. 2 Sam 12:1–4) from her husband. Others saw the lamb in Uriah, whom the lion sent to his death.[50]

Although the Talmud does discuss the punishments for David's sins, Gen. Rab. 32.1 brings up Nathan's word of pardon to David from 2 Sam 12:13. David discusses the sinfulness of Doeg and Ahithophel,

---

48. Rashi explains: first to a *wayfarer* (הלך) who passes by on his way (עובר לדרכו), then to a *traveler* (ארח) who enjoys hospitality (נעשׂה אכסנאי) and then to a *man* (איש) who is a house-holder (בעל בית). Coxon, "A Note on 'Bathsheba,'" 248. Coxon has translated Rashi and Kimchi from מקראות גדולות (*Miqraoth Gedoloth*).

49. Coxon, "A Note on 'Bathsheba,'" 250. Coxon says, "Ibn Ezra also reached the figure eight in his calculations . . . In this case the law of Ex 22,3 applied and double payment (שׁנים ישׁלם) was exacted." Ibid.

50. Jung, *Yoma*, 311.

who "permitted incest and bloodshed . . . as they have acted so have I acted; yet what is the difference between me and them? Only that Thou hast shown me love and saidst to me, *The Lord also hath put away thy sin: thou shalt not die* (II Sam XII, 13)."[51] The difference between David's sins and those of Doeg and Ahithophel (whom the *Gen. Rab.* explains "will neither be resurrected nor judged") seems to be that God decided to show David favor and pardon. Once again, this does not excuse David's sins, but highlights God's mercy in light of David's sins.

Nothing specific is discussed in the Talmud about Bathsheba's giving birth to Solomon; it will not be until Solomon is an adult that the Midrash Rabbah will emphasize her role as his mother. There is a brief mention in *b. Sanh.* 101a that Bathsheba is Solomon's mother—"Bath Sheba . . . from whom issued Solomon"—and the granddaughter of Ahithophel. *B. Sanh.* 69b has an odd accounting of how the rabbis knew that in the earlier generations, a boy who was only eight years old was able to beget children. From the math, they conclude that Bathsheba must have been able to conceive when she was six years old, and eight when she bore Solomon.[52]

---

51. *Gen. Rab.*, 249.

52. "Now, whence do we know that in the earlier generations [a boy of eight years] could beget children? Shall we say since it is written: [i] [*And David sent and inquired after the woman, and one said:*] *Is not this Bath Sheba, the daughter of Eliam, the wife of Uriah the Hittite?* [2 Sam 11:3] And it is written, [ii] *Eliam, the son of Ahithophel the Gilionite* [2 Sam 23:34]; and it is written, [iii] *And he sent by the hand of Nathan the prophet; and he called his name Jedidiah* [afterwards Solomon] *because of the Lord* [2 Sam 12:25]; and it is written, [iv] *And it came to pass, after two full years* [after Solomon's birth], *that Absalom had sheepshearers* [2 Sam 13:23]; and it is written, [v] *So Absalom fled and went to Geshur and was there three years* [2 Sam 13:38]; and it is written [vi] *So Absalom dwelt two full years in Jerusalem, and saw not the king's face* [2 Sam 14:28]; and it is written, [vii] *And it came to pass after four years, that Absalom said unto the king, I pray thee, let me go and pay my vow, which I have vowed unto the Lord in Hebron* [2 Sam 15:7]; and it is written [viii] *And when Ahithophel saw that his counsel was not followed, he saddled his ass, and arose, and got him home to his house, to his city and put his household in order, and hanged himself* [2 Sam 17:23]; and it is written, [ix] *Bloody and deceitful men shall not live out half their days* [Psalm 55:24]. And it has been taught: Doeg lived but thirty-four years, and Ahithophel thirty-three. Hence deduct seven years, Solomon's age when [Ahithophel] committed suicide, which leaves [Ahithophel] twenty-six years old at his birth. Now deduct two years for the three pregnancies, leaving each eight years old when he begot a child. But why so? Perhaps both [Ahithophel and Eliam] were nine years old [at conception], Bath Sheba being only six years when she conceived, because a woman has more [generative]vitality; the proof being that she bore a child before Solomon?" In other words, Solomon's age is calculated as seven when Ahithophel committed suicide by comparing 2 Sam 13:23, 2 Sam 13:38, and 2 Sam 14:28: Absalom

The rabbinic material picks up again with Bathsheba in reference to her role in Kings, adding more to her. In comments on 1 Kgs 1, *b. Sanh.* 22a discusses both Abishag and Bathsheba and their relationships with David.

> What are the facts regarding Abishag?—It is written: *King David was old, stricken in years etc. His servants said unto him, let there be sought etc.* Further it is written, *They sought for him a fair damsel etc.;* and it is written, *And the damsel [Abishag] was very fair, and she became a companion to the king and ministered unto him.* She said to him, "Let us marry," but he [David] said: "Thou art forbidden to me." "When courage fails the thief, he becomes virtuous," she gibed. And he said to them [his servants], "Call me Bath-Sheba." And we read: *And Bath-Sheba went to the king into the chamber.* Rab Judah said in Rab's name: On that occasion Bathsheba dried herself thirteen times.

"Drying herself" is a euphemism for intercourse. Steinsaltz explains, "David demonstrated his potency by engaging in thirteen consecutive acts of sexual intercourse with his wife Bath-Sheba (as is alluded to by the thirteen words found in this verse)."[53] Quite probably, the rabbis wanted to disprove any ideas that David was impotent, and that was what motivated such a description of his sexual encounters with Bathsheba. David was interested in proving his virility with Bathsheba, and not with another one of his eighteen wives. In this instance, we see an elaboration of the relationship between Bathsheba and David, and that their sexual relationship continued until nearly the end of his life.

Midrash Rabbah to Eccl 4:9–12 explains that the "two who are better than one" mentioned in that verse refers to David and Bathsheba. The threefold cord in Eccl 4:12, which "cannot be easily broken," refers to David, Bathsheba, and Nathan together: "R. Judah says: [Two] refers to David and Bath-sheba, and A THREEFOLD CORD to Nathan the prophet who told her, *I also will come in after thee, and confirm thy words* (I Kings I, 14). When they came into David's presence, he agreed with

---

killed Amnon two years after Solomon's birth; he was exiled for three years and he then lived two years in Jerusalem before his rebellion, in consequence of which Ahithophel hanged himself soon after, so two, three, and two equal seven. Ahithophel and Eliam are understood to be eight years old when they father their children based on Ahithophel's age of twenty-six when Solomon died. They factor that the three pregnancies added up to approximately two years, so that twenty-four years are left for the three generations (Ahithophel to Eliam to Bathsheba), which gives eight years for each.

53. Steinsaltz, *Sanhedrin*, 60.

them and said, *Cause Solomon my son to ride upon mine own mule* (*ib.* 33)."[54] Connecting David, Bathsheba, and Nathan with the threefold cord suggests that together they are a powerful force in achieving Solomon's kingship. That Bathsheba and David together are the two (who are better than one) indicates that Bathsheba is integral to the relationship. If Nathan is the one who makes it strong and not easily broken, Bathsheba still is not simply an afterthought in their interrelationship.

In reference to 1 Kings 2, R. Jacob explains in *b. Sanh.* 22a that Abishag was not permitted to Adonijah, although she would have been permitted to Solomon to marry because Solomon inherited the throne and subsequently the rest of David's harem. Therefore, the Talmud supports the idea that Adonijah's request for Abishag was indeed tantamount to requesting the throne, as Solomon himself said (1 Kgs 2:22). The Talmud is silent, though, on whether or not Bathsheba should have known this.

In the biblical text, of course, Bathsheba disappears after she has asked Solomon to give Abishag to Adonijah. Not so in the rabbinic material; there are some fascinating glimpses of her role in Solomon's life after he has become king and after he has built the temple. In this way, there is more development to her character in the rabbinic material on Kings.[55]

One way Bathsheba is present later in the story is when the Talmud describes that it is not until after Solomon has built the temple that God finally forgives David for his sins with Bathsheba. *B. Moʿed Qaṭ.* 9a describes the exact moment of forgiveness of the "misdeed" against Uriah and Bathsheba.

> At the moment when Solomon wanted to bring the Ark into the Temple, the gates held fast together. Solomon recited [a prayer of] four and twenty [expressions of] intercession but had no response. He began [anew] and said: *Lift up your heads, O ye gates* [Ps 24:7, 9] and again he had no response. As soon as [however] he said: [*Now therefore arise O Lord God . . . Thou and the Ark of Thy strength . . .*] *O Lord, turn not away the face of Thine anointed, remember the good deeds of David Thy servant,* he was answered forthwith. At that moment the faces of David's foes turned [livid]

---

54. *Eccl. Rab.* 121.

55. Those rabbinic texts that deal with the biblical references in Samuel are still more interested in David, but in the Midrash in particular, there is more about Bathsheba after the death of David than there is in the Bible.

like the [blackened] sides of a pot and all became aware that the
Holy One, blessed be He, had pardoned David that misdeed.

Whereas *b. Mo'ed Qat.* focuses on the response from David's foes, when
this story is repeated in *b. Šabb.* 30a, the focus is on the joy of the Israelites
when they hear that God has forgiven David. In *b. Šabb.* 30a, God tells
David that the forgiveness for his sin with Bathsheba will not be made
known in David's lifetime, but in the lifetime of his son Solomon. The
tractate quotes from 1 Kgs 8:66, explaining, "'*And they went into their
tents*' [means] that they found their wives clean; '*joyful*,' because they
had enjoyed the luster of the Divine Presence; '*and glad of heart*,' because
their wives conceived and each one bore a male child; '*for all the goodness
that the Lord had shewed unto David his servant*,' that He had forgiven
him that sin; '*and to Israel his people*,' for He had forgiven them the sin of
the Day of Atonement."

Both versions of this story, though, indicate that David's sin with
Bathsheba was not forgiven until after his death. Also, there is no mention of God forgiving Bathsheba, suggesting that she does not need
forgiveness.

In contrast to the Talmud, which often only hints at Bathsheba, she
is a full character in the Midrash Rabbah, where her role as Solomon's
mother is emphasized. Such emphasis connects with the text of 1 Kings,
where she is identified primarily in relationship to her son. The way she
is characterized and described in the Midrash to Leviticus and Numbers,
though, is that she is the one who instructs and teaches her son. The
rabbis make this connection by identifying Solomon with King Lemuel
from Prov 31, and Bathsheba with the mother who teaches him.

Before we get to those texts, though, she is mentioned in the
Midrash to Song 3:11. On the day the tabernacle was set up, that verse
from Song of Songs was recited: "Look, O daughters of Zion, at King
Solomon, at the crown with which his mother crowned him on the day
of his wedding, on the day of the gladness of his heart." The tabernacle is
compared to a crown because it was designed as beautifully as a crown.

> R. Isaac said: I have searched through the whole Bible but have
> not been able to find anywhere the statement that Bathsheba
> made a crown for Solomon. R. Simeon b. Yohai asked R. Eleazar,
> the son of R. Jose: "Perhaps thou hast heard an explanation
> from thy father of 'Upon the crown wherewith his mother hath
> crowned him'? He replied: "Yes, it can be compared to a king

who possessed an only child—a daughter. He loved her so dearly, that he called her 'my daughter,' and when his love increased he called her 'my sister,' and finally 'my mother.' Similarly, the Holy One, blessed be He, first addressed Israel as 'daughter' . . . when He loved Israel more, He called them 'my sister' . . . and when he loved them even still more, he called them 'mother.'"[56]

In this analogy, therefore, not only is the tabernacle the crown, but Bathsheba and Solomon become symbols for Israel and God, respectively. The mother (Bathsheba) is Israel, Solomon is God, and Israel crowns God with the tabernacle.

The day of Solomon's wedding is connected with the day he completes the temple in the Midrash to Leviticus and Numbers. Again, Solomon is identified as King Lemuel, and Bathsheba with his mother. The passage from *Num. Rab.* 10.4 is slightly more detailed than the one from *Lev. Rab.*, and is worth reading in its entirety.

Why was Solomon called Lemuel? R. Ishmael said: On the selfsame night that Solomon completed the work of the Holy Temple he married Bathiah, the daughter of Pharoah, and there was great jubilation on account of the Temple, and jubilation on account of Pharoah's daughter, and the jubilation on account of Pharaoh's daughter exceeded that of the Temple; as the proverb says: "Everybody flatters the king." The reason why he was called Lemuel is because he cast off the yoke of the kingdom of heaven from his shoulders; as if to say *Lammah lo el*[57] . . . What did Pharaoh's daughter do further? She spread a sort of canopy above him and set therein all manner of precious stones and pearls which glittered like stars and constellations, and every time Solomon wished to rise he would see these stars and constellations, and so he went on sleeping until four hours in the day. R. Levi said: On that day the continual offering was sacrificed at four hours of the day. Now Israel were grieved, for it was the day of the dedication of the Temple, and they could not perform the service because Solomon was asleep and they were afraid to wake him, out of their awe of royalty. They went and informed Bathsheba his mother, and she came and woke him up and reproved him. Hence it is written, *The burden wherewith his mother corrected him* (Prov. XXXI, 1). R. Johanan said: This teaches that his moth-

56. *Ex. Rab.*, 579–80; cf. *Song. Rab.* 3.11, 173, *Num. Rab.* 12.8, 473.

57. אל לו למה: the letters lamed, mem, waw, aleph, and lamed form Lemuel's name. A literal translation would be, "why to him God," meaning, "Why should he have what is divine?"

er bent him over a column and said to him: "*What, my son* (*ib.* 2)! Everyone knows that your father was a God-fearing man. Now they will speak thus: 'Bathsheba is his mother; she brought him to it!' *And what, O son of my womb* (*ib.* 2)! All the other women of thy father's house, when once they had become pregnant, saw the king's face no more, but I forced my way through and entered, so that my son might be fair complexioned and active![58] *And what, O son of my vows* (*ib.*)! All the women of thy father's house, when they became pregnant, would make vows and say: 'May we have a son worthy of kingship,' but I made a vow and said: 'May I have a son diligent and learned in the Torah and worthy of prophecy!' *Give not thy strength unto women* (*ib.* 3), by going in pursuit of lewdness, for they confuse a man's mind; *He that keepeth company with harlots wasteth his substance* (*ib.* XXXIX, 3). *Nor thy ways to that which destroyeth kings* (*ib.* XXXI, 3). The Torah has given a warning, *Neither shall he multiply wives to himself* (Deut XVII, 17). Be cautious in these things, for they are the ruination of kings! *It is not for kings, O Lemuel* (Prov. XXXI, 4). What have you to do with kings who say, 'What use is God to us (*lammah lanu el*),' that you should copy their deeds? *It is not for kings to drink wine* (*ib.*). Why should you liken yourself to kings who drink wine and become intoxicated and indulge in all manner of lewdness? Do not according to their deeds! *Nor for princes to say: Where is strong drink?* (*ib.*). Shall he to whom all the world's mysteries are revealed, drink wine and become inebriated?" . . . She said to him: "Justice was entrusted to the royal house of David; as you read, *O house of David, thus saith the Lord: Execute justice in the morning* (Jer. XXI, 12). If you drink wine you will pervert the justice due to those who are afflicted; you will acquit the guilty and condemn the innocent."[59]

The text in *Lev. Rab.* 12.5 is similar, but adds the detail that when Bathsheba corrected Solomon, "She took her slipper and slapped him this way and that." Moreover, in *Lev. Rab.* 12:5, when Nathan prophesied that Solomon would be born, Bathsheba tells him, "every one [of his wives] said: 'If I bring Solomon into the world, I shall offer up all the sacrifices mentioned in the Torah, and now I stand with my sacrifices [ready] in my hands and you are sleeping!'"[60]

58. It was thought that cohabitation in the last three months of pregnancy was beneficial to the unborn child. Slotki explains, "The inferences in the text are drawn from the use of the expressions בר בטני 'pure one of my womb,'" *Num. Rab.* 353 n. 1.

59. *Num. Rab.*, 352–53.

60. *Lev. Rab.*, 159–60.

In these accounts, Bathsheba has a great deal of authority over Solomon. She is the only one in Israel who is not afraid to wake up her son and reprove him, even using physical force if necessary. The detail in *Num. Rab.* 10.4 indicates Bathsheba's closeness with David; she continues to have sexual relations with him even after she has become pregnant with Solomon. Moreover, Bathsheba is a woman of faith who is more interested that her son be "diligent and learned in the Torah and worthy of prophecy" than she is interested in his becoming king. She knows her Torah, quoting from the Deuteronomic law of the king to her son. And while she is concerned for her own reputation and the reputation of David, she nonetheless gives Solomon advice about how to live with integrity and rule with justice. In *Num. Rab.* 10.4, there is an alternate exposition that the "mother" who corrected Solomon was not Bathsheba, but the Torah.[61] The bulk of the textual evidence, though, is given to Bathsheba, who speaks with strength, power, and authority to encourage her son to act wisely. While some might explain Solomon's weaknesses as coming from his mother (cf. Ezek 16:45), with this text it would seem that if Solomon had listened to the advice of his mother, his wisdom would not be replaced by his folly.

Even as the postbiblical material is quite different from the biblical texts, it still supports some of the elements of Bathsheba's characterization that we have seen in those texts. She continues to be a complex character, and in some ways less is known about her in the Talmud and Midrash than in the biblical text. Josephus also presents her as complex: she is beautiful and modest, but also fearful, and not interested in truth-telling. This complexity must be taken into account as we assess whether or not Bathsheba is presented positively in these interpretations. The Midrash Rabbah for Leviticus and Numbers presents her as a strong character; her strength is seen through her words and actions. And even if the rabbinic material may attempt to soften or explain David's sins, nowhere is Bathsheba blamed as the "cause." However, it is hard to maintain that Josephus presents her as predominantly positive—she may be equal parts positive and negative, but she is not held up as positive by him. We do see, especially in the Midrash Rabbah for Leviticus and Numbers, that her role develops, and that as Solomon's mother, she enjoys a level of authority and power, especially in his life as king.

61. *Num. Rab.*, 355.

As I stated in the introduction, the reason I do not agree with "negative" interpretations of Bathsheba is that they do not represent the MT, nor the earliest versions. My hope is to encourage readers to go back to the text and ground their judgments about the character of Bathsheba in the text, as I attempted to do in chapters 2 through 4. As we have considered some of the earliest interpretations about her, we observed how, overall, they also largely support the characterization of Bathsheba already noted in the earlier texts and versions.

Our review of Bathsheba's character and characterization has come to an end. With this chapter, we see some consistency to the way that she is characterized, but we also note the beginning of some changes. The grand history of interpretation will continue to reshape, reinterpret and reinvent her, and in the process some things will be lost, added, and changed. Many questions still remain about Bathsheba, but perhaps it will be those questions that invite us as readers to return again and again to a story that refuses to be finalized and flattened.

6

Bathsheba Beyond the Text

Further Implications

By placing Bathsheba under a spotlight, and paying close attention to her character, we have seen a consistency in the way she is presented in the MT, as well as the early versions of the LXX, Peshitta, and Targums. In all of these texts, Bathsheba is characterized as generally positive, complex, dynamic, and evolving as her character moves from Samuel to Kings. The early Jewish postbiblical interpretations generally follow a similar trajectory of characterization, though Josephus marks the beginning of a change—namely, in seeing her more negatively than others. Bathsheba has not received such sustained attention before in any modern biblical work of scholarship, but it is my hope that more people will consider her character—as well as other minor characters in the text—in the future. For although she is undeniably a minor character in the story of David (and the story of the Old Testament as a whole), Bathsheba still plays an important function in the David narrative. Namely, her character helps us see the larger biblical story with greater insight as Bathsheba gives us an inverted mirror through which we can see David. At times there are great parallels between her story and his, and at other times her story and his story are in counterpoint with one another. Together, David and Bathsheba participate in a larger recurring pattern of relationships among biblical characters that exemplify how the Bible presents the ways of God and humans.

Bathsheba appears only twice in David's story, but at two of the most important points in David's biography. First, in 2 Sam 11–12, David is at the height of his power and his honor. He has been enthroned in Jerusalem, defeated the Philistines, taken care of potential rivals from the house of Saul, received the divine promise of 2 Sam 7, and Nathan has reported that he will have rest from all his enemies (2 Sam 7:1). Now at the apex of his power, he finally is able to ease off a little and rest when other kings are doing battle.

It is at this point in David's story that the relatively unknown Bathsheba appears. Upon first glance, it seems as if she is a pawn in David's chess game: if David has great power and agency and operates from a position of arrogance, authority, and privilege, Bathsheba is almost his opposite. She is largely (though not entirely) acted upon by David and has comparatively little power and agency.[1] Yet, though it would appear that David is in control, in actuality, the tangled web into which he enters with Bathsheba will become his own entrapment. For 2 Sam 11–12 marks a critical tipping point in David's biography.[2] The "house" motif that first appeared in 2 Sam 7 reappears now, when things begin to go wrong in David's house (cf. 2 Sam 12:10).

And Bathsheba's own reappearance as a character comes at David's lowest point in 1 Kings 1–2 when the formerly virile king cannot even keep his own body warm in bed, and is not interested (or able?) to have sexual relations with a young beautiful woman who lies in his bed. In 1 Kings 1–2, she is not used by David; rather, she has the power and authority to help her son take the throne. So, even though Bathsheba remains a minor character throughout David's story, she plays a critical role in marking both the high point of David's life and career as king, when he is at peace on the throne in Jerusalem, and the lowest point, when he is weak and near death.

In view of the larger David story, Bathsheba assumes a role David had played earlier. The youngest of Jesse's sons, he ended up unraveling the rule of the Philistines by a small stone to the forehead of the great giant Goliath. Similarly, Bathsheba's brief message to the great King David that "I am pregnant" (2 Sam 11:5), like the pebble that felled Goliath, sets in motion a series of events that grows into an avalanche of catastrophes—political, sexual, and familial—that afflict and weaken David's "house" over his lifetime. Bathsheba's story also parallels David's story in terms of irregular succession: Bathsheba is instrumental in placing Solomon on the throne, bypassing another son who is in some way more "legitimate"—Adonijah, the eldest living son. Saul's kingship also had

---

1. Though she does enjoy some power, agency, and voice in 2 Samuel; cf. chapter 2.

2. Brueggemann refers to 2 Samuel 11ff. as the place where the text presents "the painful truth of the man" David. *David's Truth*, 33–61.

passed in an irregular way to David, bypassing another son who was in some sense more "legitimate," that is, Saul's son Jonathan.

So, not only does the minor character Bathsheba serve as a counterpoint to David (weak when he is strong and strong when he is weak), but she also functions as a mirror of the earlier David, when what little power the weak have sets in motion the unraveling of the powerful. David was the youngest of the sons of Jesse (and thus the most unlikely one to become king)—and yet he was chosen, anointed by Samuel (1 Samuel 16). David used a stone and a slingshot to bring down God's enemy, Goliath, and he himself became exalted (1 Samuel 17). Bathsheba used a few words to announce her pregnancy, and God's beloved, David, was brought down as his "house" unraveled in a series of rebellions, rapes, murders, and tragedies. In 1 Kings, she who was once low is seated in an exalted place at the right hand of her son, King Solomon.

In that sense, both David and Bathsheba's characters echo Hannah's song, which opens the narrative of Samuel–Kings.[3] Hannah, the once-barren woman, sings of God who deals death and gives life, who casts down and lifts up, raising the poor and needy from the dunghill and setting them with nobles, granting them seats of honor, "for not by strength shall humans prevail" (1 Sam 2:10). Like Bathsheba, the woman Hannah marks the demise of Eli's house and the sons who should have ruled after him, and Hannah's own son Samuel is inserted into the place of power as the kingmaker who anoints first Saul and then David. Of course, this theological refrain repeats in the New Testament as well, as Mary will again affirm the way of God who brings down those who are high and raises up those who are low (Luke 2). As Bathsheba models this pattern, her function in the text is, as Springer says, "highly desirable to the work as a whole."[4]

Again, Bathsheba is presented as a predominantly positive character: not stupid or unaware, and not a seductress scheming to advance herself. Sakenfeld urges us to realize "that the negative portrayals of her that are familiar to us are not necessarily supported by the biblical text."[5]

---

3. Alter points out the way that Bathsheba's request to Solomon that Adonijah be given Abishag echoes the beginning of 1 Samuel, "One should note that this whole larger narrative begins when a woman who is to become a mother (Hannah) puts forth a petition (*she'eilah*, the same word used here)." *David Story*, 379.

4. Springer, *Rhetoric of Literary Character*, 14.

5. Sakenfeld, *Just Wives?* 75.

Yet, the very familiarity of those negative portrayals Sakenfeld discusses has come from somewhere. The negative interpretations of Bathsheba do not represent the text, nor the earliest translations and interpretations. So what happened in the history of interpretation to swing the pendulum towards a negative characterization of Bathsheba? This is an area for further study. Josephus appears to be one of the earliest extant examples of an interpreter who begins to portray Bathsheba's character more negatively than the biblical text. Katharine Rogers writes, "In the Biblical account, the emphasis is entirely on David's lust. But Christian preachers were to use the tale as a misogynistic text: obviously a holy man like David could not have committed mortal sin unless seduced, so Bathsheba must have seduced him."[6]

Sustained study of later postbiblical interpreters from ancient to medieval and modern times would help trace the varied ways in which Bathsheba is portrayed and thus give us a fuller picture of the postbiblical afterlife of this character.

This study of Bathsheba's character also gives insight into the hermeneutical process in general, especially as we recognize how many interpretations purport to be based on the text, but in fact may be more influenced by the history of interpretation than the text itself. One implication from this project is the importance of grounding an interpretation in the details, and as much as possible, in the fields of reference of the text. Or, at the very least, it is important to come clean about when an interpretation takes liberties with what is written in the biblical text. Then again, readers and interpreters are never entirely objective, but read and interpret from their own historical and cultural locations. That the interpretations about Bathsheba change should not be of surprise, but is worth closer examination.

I have tried to maintain a primarily purist approach to Bathsheba's characterization, affirming that she is complex and developing because the text presents her that way. Bathsheba exists as a character for us simply by virtue of her "purely" textual presence in Samuel-Kings.[7] But that "purist" insight into her character needs some qualification—this minor character does give us insight into real life. Most people, like Bathsheba, are complex. Most people, like Bathsheba, change and develop over time

---

6. Rogers, *Troublesome Helpmate*, 5.

7. A "purist" approach is in contrast to a "realist" approach, which assumes a character may be taken out of a piece of literature and treated as a "real" person. Cf. chapter 1.

as they age and are put into different positions and situations. We often assume or think we know how a given person will act, and that is especially true for those people about whom we know very little. We often are prone to judge people based on what little information we have about them, not taking the time to study closely the details we are given about their lives. As we read about Bathsheba and learn that she is more surprising, nuanced, and mysterious than we might initially think, we should be encouraged to be open to the possibilities of surprise, change, nuance, and complexity in the character of the people we encounter in our daily lives. Indeed, if this study changes—even slightly—the way that we interact with the real people around us, its implication and application will be profound.

Bibliography

Aharoni, Yohanan. *Excavations at Ramat Rahel*. Rome: University of Rome, 1962.

Aichele, George et al. *The Postmodern Bible*. New Haven: Yale University Press, 1995.

Albrektson, Bertil. "Difficilior Lectio Probabilior: A Rule of Textual Criticism and its Use in Old Testament Studies." In *Remembering All the Way: A Collection of Old Testament Studies Published on the Occasion of the Fortieth Anniversary of the Oudtestamentisch Werkgezelschap in Nederland*, edited by Bertil Albrektson, et al, 5–18. Oudtestamentische Studiën 21. Leiden: Brill, 1981.

———. *Investigations at Lachish: The Sanctuary and the Residency*. Tel Aviv: Gateway, 1975.

Alexander, Philip S. "Jewish Aramaic Translations of Hebrew Scriptures." In *Mikra: Text, Translation, Reading and Interpretation of the Hebrew Bible in Ancient Judaism and Early Christianity*, edited by Martin Jan Mulder, 217–53. Philadelphia: Fortress, 1988.

———. "Targum, Targumim." In *ABD* 6:320–31.

Alter, Robert. *The Art of Biblical Narrative*. New York: Basic, 1981.

———. *The David Story: A Translation with Commentary of 1 and 2 Samuel*. New York: Norton, 2000.

Amit, Yairah. *Reading Biblical Narratives: Literary Criticism and the Hebrew Bible*. Minneapolis: Fortress, 2001.

Andreasen, Niels-Erik A. "The Role of the Queen Mother in Israelite Society." *CBQ* 45 (1983)174–94.

Arbel, Daphna. "Questions about Eve's Iniquity, Beauty, and Fall: The 'Primal Figure' in Ezekiel 28:11–19 and Genesis Rabbah Traditions of Eve." *JBL* 124 (2005) 641–55.

Arpali, Boaz. "Caution: A Biblical Story! Comments on the Story of David and Bathsheba and on the Problems of the Biblical Narrative." *Ha-Sifrut* 1 (1968–69) 580–97; English Summary, *Ha-Sifrut* 2 (1969–71) 684–86.

Aschkenasy, Nehama. *Woman at the Window: Biblical Tales of Oppression and Escape*. Detroit: Wayne State University Press, 1998.

Auerbach, Erich. *Mimesis*. Garden City, NY: Doubleday, 1957.

Bach, Alice. "Good to the Last Drop: Viewing the Soṭah (Numbers 5.11–31) as the Glass Half Empty and Wondering How to View it Half Full." In *The New Literary Criticism and the Hebrew Bible*, edited by J. Cheryl Exum and David Clines, 26–54. JSOTSup 143. Sheffield, UK: Almond, 1993.

———. *The Pleasure of Her Text: Feminist Readings of Biblical and Historical Texts*. Philadelphia: Trinity, 1990.

Bahrani, Zainab. *Women of Babylon: Gender and Representation in Mesopotamia*. Routledge: London, 2001.

Bailey, Randall C. *David in Love and War: The Pursuit of Power in 2 Samuel 10–12*. JSOTSup 75. Sheffield, UK: Sheffield Academic, 1990.

Bakhtin, M. M. *Problems of Dostoevsky's Poetics.* Minneapolis: University of Minnesota Press, 1984.

Bal, Mieke. *Lethal Love: Feminist Literary Readings of Biblical Love Stories.* Bloomington: Indiana University Press, 1987

———. *Narratology.* 2nd ed. Toronto: University of Toronto Press, 1997.

Bar-Efrat, Shimon. *Narrative Art in the Bible.* London: T. & T. Clark, 2004.

Barnet, John A. *Not the Righteous but Sinners: M. M. Bakhtin's Theory of Aesthetics and the Problem of Reader-Character Interaction in Matthew's Gospel.* Journal for the Study of the New Testament Supplements 246. London: T. & T. Clark, 2003.

Barth, Karl. "The Strange New World within the Bible." In *The Word of God and the Word of Man,* 28–50. Translated by Douglas Horton. New York: Harper, 1957.

Barthes, Roland. *S/Z.* New York: Hill & Wang, 1974.

Bascom, Robert. "The Targums: Ancient Reader's Helps?" *The Bible Translator* 36 (1985) 301–16.

Baskin, Judith R. *Midrashic Women: Formations of the Feminine in Rabbinic Literature.* Hannover: University Press of New England for Brandeis University Press, 2002.

Bassler, Jouette M. "A Man for All Seasons: David in Rabbinic and New Testament Literature." *Int* 40 (1986) 156–69.

Beck, John. *Translators as Storytellers: A Study in Septuagint Translation Technique.* New York: Peter Lang, 2000.

Begg, Christopher T. "David's Sin According to Josephus." *Ancient Near Eastern Studies* 43 (2006) 45–67.

Bell, Catherine M. *Ritual Theory, Ritual Practice.* New York: Oxford University Press, 1992.

Benjamin, Walter. *Selected Writings: Volume 3, 1935–1938.* Edited by Howard Eiland and Michael W. Jennings. Cambridge: Belknap, 2002.

Berlin, Adele. "Characterization in Biblical Narrative: David's Wives." In *Beyond Form Criticism,* edited by Paul R. House, 219–33. Winona Lake, IN: Eisenbrauns, 1992.

———. *Esther.* Philadelphia: Jewish Publication Society, 2001.

———. *Zephaniah.* AB 25A. New York: Doubleday, 1994.

Besançon, Maria. *"L'affaire" de David et Bethsabee et la genealogie du Christ.* Saint-Maur: Parole et Silence, 1997.

Blount, Brian K. *Cultural Interpretation: Reorienting New Testament Criticism.* Minneapolis: Fortress, 1995.

Boadt, Lawrence. "Understanding the Mashal." In *Parable and Story in Judaism and Christianity,* edited by Clemens Thoma and Michael Wyschengrod, 159–88. New York: Paulist, 1989.

Bodner, Keith. *David Observed: A King in the Eyes of His Court.* Sheffield, UK: Sheffield Phoenix, 2005.

———. "Is Joab a Reader-Response Critic?" *JSOT* 27 (2002) 19–35.

———. "Nathan: Prophet, Politician and Novelist?" *JSOT* 26 (2001) 43–54.

Boer, Roland. "National Allegory in the Hebrew Bible." *JSOT* 74 (1997) 95–116.

Booth, Wayne. *The Company We Keep.* Berkeley: University of California Press, 1988.

Bowen, Nancy. "The Quest for the Historical Gebîrâ." *CBQ* 63 (2001) 597–618.

Bowman, Richard. "The Complexity of Character and the Ethics of Complexity: The Case of King David." In *Character and Scripture: Moral Formation, Community, and Biblical Interpretation,* edited by William P. Brown, 73–97. Grand Rapids: Eerdmans, 2002.

———. "Narrative Criticism: Human Purpose in Conflict with Divine Presence." In *Judges and Method: New Approaches in Biblical Studies*, edited by Gale A. Yee, 17–44. Minneapolis: Fortress, 1995.

Boyarin, Daniel. *Intertextuality and the Reading of Midrash*. Indiana Studies in Biblical Literature. Bloomington: Indiana University Press, 1990.

Brenner, Athalaya. *I Am . . . : Biblical Women Tell Their Own Stories*. Minneapolis: Fortress, 2005.

Bright, John. *The History of Israel*. 3rd ed. Philadelphia: Westminster, 1981.

Britt, Brian. "Davidmachine." *The Bible and Critical Theory* 6 (2010) 21.1–21.14.

Brockelmann, Carl. *Lexicon Syriacum*. Edinburgh: T. & T. Clark, 1895.

Brown, Cheryl Anne. *No Longer Be Silent: First Century Jewish Portraits of Biblical Women*. Louisville, KY: Westminster, 1992.

Brueggemann, Walter. *1 & 2 Kings*. Smyth & Helwys Bible Commentary. Macon, GA: Smyth & Helwys, 2000.

———. *David's Truth in Israel's Imagination and Memory*. 2nd ed. Minneapolis: Fortress, 2002.

———. *Theology of the Old Testament: Testimony, Dispute, Advocacy*. Minneapolis: Fortress, 1997.

Burchard, Christopher. "Joseph and Aseneth: A New Translation and Introduction." In *The Old Testament Pseudepigrapha*, edited by James H. Charlesworth, 2:177–247. 2 vols. Garden City, NY: Doubleday, 1985.

Burney, Charles F. *Notes on the Hebrew Text of the Books of Kings: With an Introduction and Appendix*. Oxford: Clarendon, 1903.

Byatt, A. S., and Ignês Sodré. *Imagining Characters: Six Conversations about Women Writers*. Edited by Rebecca Swift. London: Chatto, 1995.

Calvin, John. *Sermons on 2 Samuel*. Translated by Douglas Kelly. Vol. 1. Edinburgh: Banner of Truth Trust, 1992.

Chatman, Seymour. *Story and Discourse: Narrative Structure in Fiction and Film*. Ithaca, NY: Cornell University Press, 1978.

Churgin, Pinkos. *Targum Jonathan to the Prophets*. 1907. Reprint, New York: Ktav, 1983.

Claassens, L. Julianna. "Biblical Theology as Dialogue: Continuing the Conversation on Mikhail Bakhtin and Biblical Theology." *JBL* 122 (2003) 127–44.

Clines, David. "X, X ben Y, ben Y: Personal names in Hebrew Narrative Style." *VT* 22 (1972) 266–87.

Coats, George. "2 Samuel 12:1–7a." *Int* 40 (1986) 170–74.

———. "Parable, Fable and Anecdote." *Int* 35 (1981) 368–82.

Cody, Aelred. "Sin and Its Sequel in the Story of David and Bathsheba." In *Sin, Salvation, and the Spirit*, edited by Daniel Durken, 115–26. Collegeville, MN: Liturgical, 1979.

Cogan, Mordechai. *1 Kings*. AB 10. New York: Doubleday, 2001.

Cohan, Steven. "Figures Beyond the Text: A Theory of Readable Character in the Novel." *Novel* 17 (1983) 5–27.

Cohen, H. Hirsch. "David and Bathsheba." *Journal of Bible and Religion* 33 (1965) 142–48.

Conybeare, Frederick C., and St. George Stock. *Grammar of Septuagint Greek*. Grand Rapids: Zondervan, 1980.

Cosgrove, Charles. "A Woman's Unbound Hair in the Greco-Roman World, with Special Reference to the Story of the 'Sinful Woman' in Luke 7:36–50." *JBL* 124 (2005) 675–92.

Coxon, Peter W. "A Note on 'Bathsheba' in 2 Samuel 12:1–6." *Biblica* 62 (1981) 247–50.

Cross, Frank Moore. *Canaanite Myth and Hebrew Epic.* Cambridge: Harvard University Press, 1973.

Cross, Frank Moore, and David Noel Freedman. *Studies in Ancient Yahwistic Poetry.* Grand Rapids: Eerdmans, 197.

Cushman, Beverly. "   *JSOT* 30 (2006) 327–43.

Cusick, Michael J. "A Conversation with Eugene Peterson." *Mars Hill Review* 3 (1995) 71–90.

Daube, David. "Absalom and the Ideal King." *VT* 48 (1998) 315–25.

———. "Nathan's Parable." *Novum Testamentum* 24 (1982) 275–88.

Day, Linda, and Carolyn Pressler, editors. *Engaging the Bible in a Gendered World: An Introduction to Feminist Biblical Interpretation in Honor of Katharine Doob Sakenfeld.* Louisville: Westminster, 2006.

Delekat, Lienhard. "Tendenz und Theologie der David-Salomo-Erzählung." In *Das Ferne und Nahe Wort: Festschrift Leonhard Rost zur Vollendung seines 70. Lebenjahres am 30. November 1966,* 26–36. Berlin: Töpelmann, 1967.

Derby, Josiah. "A Biblical Freudian Slip: 2 Samuel 12:6." *Jewish Bible Quarterly* 24 (1996) 107–11.

De Vries, Simon J. *1 Kings.* Word Biblical Commentary 12. Nashville: Thomas Nelson, 2004.

Diamant, Anita. *The Red Tent.* New York: Picador USA, 1998.

Dijk-Hemmes, Fokkelein van. "Tamar and the Limits of Patriarchy: Between Rape and Seduction (2 Samuel 13 and Genesis 38)." In *Anti-Covenant: Counter-Reading Women's Lives in the Hebrew Bible,* edited by Mieke Bal, 135–56. JSOTSup 81. Sheffield, UK: Almond, 1989.

Dirksen, Peter B. "The Old Testament Peshitta." In *Mikra: Text, Translation, Reading and Interpretation of the Hebrew Bible in Ancient Judaism and Early Christianity,* edited by Martin Jan Mulder and Harry Sysling, 255–97. Philadelphia: Fortress, 1988.

Dirksen, P. B., and P. A. H. de Boer. *Judges–Samuel.* The Old Testament in Syriac according to the Peshitta Version. Part 2, fascicle 2. Leiden: Brill, 1978.

Dobbs-Allsopp, F. W. "The Delight of Beauty and Song of Songs 4:1–7." *Int* 59 (2005) 260–77.

Driver, Godfrey Rolles. *Canaanite Myths and Legends.* Edinburgh: T. & T. Clark, 1956.

Driver, Samuel Rolles. *Notes on the Hebrew Text of the Books of Samuel.* Oxford: Clarendon, 1890.

Eagleton, Terry. *Ideology: An Introduction.* London: Verso, 1991.

Eissfeldt, Otto. Review of *The History of Israel,* by John Bright. *JBL* 79 (1960) 369–72.

Empson, William. *Seven Types of Ambiguity.* Norfolk, CT: New Directions, 1953.

Epstein, Isidore, editor. *Hebrew-English Edition of the Babylonian Talmud.* Translated by Maurice Simon. London: Soncino, 1960.

Eskola, Timo. "Paul, Predestination, and 'Covenantal Nomism'—Re-assessing Paul and Palestinian Judaism." *Journal for the Study of Judaism in the Persian, Hellenistic and Roman Period* 28 (1997) 390–412.

Everhart, Janet S. "Serving Women and Their Mirrors: A Feminist Reading of Exodus 38:8b." *CBQ* 66 (2004) 44–54.

Exum, J. Cheryl. "Bathsheba Plotted, Shot, and Painted." In *Semeia 74: Biblical Glamour and Hollywood Glitz,* edited by Alice Bach, 47–73. Atlanta: Scholars, 1996.

———. *Fragmented Women: Feminist (Sub)versions of Biblical Narratives.* JSOTSup 163. Sheffield, UK: Sheffield Academic, 1993.

———. *Plotted, Shot, and Painted: Cultural Representations of Biblical Women.* Sheffield, UK: Sheffield Academic, 1996.

Feldman, Louis. "Josephus." In *ABD* 3:981–98.

———. "Josephus' Portrait of David." *Hebrew Union College Annual* 60 (1989) 129–74.

———. "Josephus' Portrait of Deborah." In *Hellenica et Judaica: Hommage à Valentin Nikiprowetzky,* edited by Andre Caquot, Mireille Hadas-Lebel, and Jean Riaud, 115–28. Leuven: Peeters, 1986

———. "Josephus' Portrait of Solomon." *Hebrew Union College Annual* 66 (1995) 103–67.

———. "Mikra in the Writings of Josephus." In In *Mikra: Text, Translation, Reading and Interpretation of the Hebrew Bible in Ancient Judaism and Early Christianity,* edited by Martin Mulder and Harry Sysling, 455–518. Philadelphia: Fortress, 1988.

———. "Reflections on John R. Levison's 'Josephus's Version of Ruth.'" *Journal for the Study of the Pseudepigrapha* 8 (1991) 45–52.

———. "Use, Authority and Exegesis of Mikra in the Writings of Josephus." In *Mikra: Text, Translation, Reading and Interpretation of the Hebrew Bible in Ancient Judaism and Early Christianity,* edited by Martin Mulder and Harry Sysling, 456–518. Philadelphia: Fortress, 1988.

Fererra, Fernando. "Theory and Model for the Structural Analysis of Fiction." *New Literary History* 5 (1974) 245–68.

Fischer, Alexander A. "David und Batseba: Ein Literarkritischer und Motivgeschichtlicher Beitrag zu 2 Sam 11." *ZAW* 101 (1989) 50–59.

Fischer, Irmtraud. *Women Who Wrestled with God.* Collegeville, MN: Liturgical Press, 2005.

Fitzmeyer, Joseph A. *The Genesis Apocryphon of Qumran Cave 1: A Commentary.* 2nd ed. Biblica et Orientalia 18A. Rome: Biblical Institute Press, 1971.

Flusser, David. *Judaism and the Origins of Christianity.* Jerusalem: Magnes, 1988.

Fokkelman, Jan P. *Narrative Art and Poetry in the Books of Samuel: A Full Interpretation Based on Stylistic and Structural Analysis.* 4 vols. Assen: Van Gorcum, 1981.

———. *Reading Biblical Narrative: An Introductory Guide.* Louisville: Westminster, 1999.

Forster, E. M. *Aspects of the Novel.* New York: Harcourt, Brace, 1927.

Foucault, Michel. *The History of Sexuality.* Vol. 1. New York: Vintage, 1980.

———. *Power/Knowledge.* Edited by Colin Gordon. New York: Pantheon, 1980.

———. "The Subject and Power." In *The Essential Foucault,* edited by Paul Rabinow and Nikolas Rose, 126–44. New York: New Press, 1994.

Fowler, Elizabeth. *Literary Character: The Human Figure in Early English Writing.* Ithaca, NY: Cornell University Press, 2003.

Fox, Everett. *Give Us a King! Samuel, Saul, and David.* New York: Schocken, 1999.

Fox, Michael. *Character and Ideology in the Book of Esther.* 2nd ed. Grand Rapids: Eerdmans, 2001.

Freedman, David Noel. "Dinah and Shechem, Tamar and Amnon." *Austin Seminary Bulletin Faculty Edition* 105 (1990) 51–63.

Fretheim, Terrence. *First and Second Kings*. Louisville: Westminster, 1999.

Fritz, Volkmar. "Die Syrische Bauform des Hilani und die Frage seiner Verbreitung." *Damaszener Mitteilungen* 1 (1983) 55–58.

Frolov, Serge. "*No Return* for Shulammite: Reflections on Cant 7,1." *ZAW* 110 (1998) 256–58.

Galling, Kurt. "Archäologischer Jahresbericht." *Zeitschrift des deutschen Palästina-Vereins* 55 (1932) 240–52.

Garsiel, Moshe. "The Story of David and Bathsheba: A Different Approach." *CBQ* 55 (1993) 244–62.

Gaventa, Beverly Roberts. *Mary: Glimpses of the Mother of Jesus*. Minneapolis: Fortress, 1999.

George, A. R. *The Babylonian Gilgamesh Epic: Introduction, Critical Edition and Cuneiform Texts*. 2 vols. Oxford: Oxford University Press, 2003.

Gerleman, Gillis. "Die Wurzel *shlm*." *ZAW* 85 (1973) 1–14.

Gesenius, Wilhelm. *Gesenius' Hebrew Grammar*. Edited by Emil Kautzsch, revised by Arthur Ernest Cowley. 2nd ed. Oxford: Clarendon, 1910.

Gilligan, Carol. *In a Different Voice: Psychological Theory and Women's Development*. Cambridge: Harvard University Press, 1982.

Gogel, Sandra Landis. *A Grammar of Epigraphic Hebrew*. Atlanta: Scholars, 1998.

Goldner, Virginia. "Ironic Gender/Authentic Sex." *Studies in Gender and Sexuality* 4 (2003) 113–39.

Gottlieb, Hans, and E. Hammershaimb. *Kings*. The Old Testament in Syriac according to the Peshitta Version. Part 2, fascicle 4. Leiden: Brill, 1978.

Gravett, Sandie. "Reading 'Rape' in the Hebrew Bible: A Consideration of Language." *JSOT* 28 (2004) 279–99.

Gray, John. *1 & 2 Kings: A Commentary*. Old Testament Library. Philadelphia: Westminster, 1970.

Gray, Mark. "Amnon: A Chip off the Old Block? Rhetorical Strategy in 2 Samuel 13:7–15: The Rape of Tamar and the Humiliation of the Poor." *JSOT* 77 (1993) 39–54.

Green, Barbara. *Mikhail Bakhtin and Biblical Scholarship: An Introduction*. Atlanta: Society of Biblical Literature, 2000.

Greenfield, Jonas C. "An Ancient Treaty Ritual and its Targumic Echo." In *Salvacion en la Palabra, Targum, Derash, Berith: In Memoria del Professor Alejandro Díez Macho*, edited by Domingo Muñoz Leon, 391–97. Madrid: Cristiandad, 1986.

Greenspoon, Leonard. "Hebrew into Greek: Interpretation In, By, and Of the Septuagint." In *A History of Biblical Interpretation*, edited by Alan J. Hauser and Duane F. Watson, 80–113. Grand Rapids: Eerdmans, 2003.

Greimas, Algirdas Julien, and Joseph Courtés. *Sémiotique: Un Dictionnaire Raisonné de la Théorie du Langage*. 2 vols. Langue, Linguistique, Communication. Paris: Hachette, 1979–1986.

Gunkel, Hermann. *Das Märchen im Alten Testament*. Tübingen: Mohr/Siebeck, 1921.

Gunn, David M. "Bathsheba Goes Bathing in Hollywood: Words, Images, and Social Locations." *Semeia* 74 (1996) 75–101.

———. "David and the Gift of the Kingdom (2 Sam. 2–4, 9–20, 1 Kings 1–2)." *Semeia* 3 (1975) 14–45.

Gunn, David M., and Danna Nolan Fewell. *Narrative in the Hebrew Bible*. Oxford Bible Series. Oxford: Oxford University Press, 1993.

Hackett, Jo Ann. "Violence and Women's Lives in the Book of Judges." *Int* 58 (2004) 356–64.

Halpern, Baruch. *David's Secret Demons*. Grand Rapids: Eerdmans, 2001.

Halpern-Amaru, Betsy. "Portraits of Biblical Women in Josephus' *Antiquities*." *Journal of Jewish Studies* 38–39 (1987–88) 148–164.

Hammond, Gerald. "Michal, Tamar, Abigail and What Bathsheba Said." In *Women in the Biblical Tradition*, edited by George J. Brooke, 53–70. Studies in Women and Religion 31. Lewiston, NY: Mellen, 1992.

Harrington, Daniel J., and Anthony J. Saldarini. *Targum Jonathan of the Former Prophets*. Aramaic Bible 10. Wilmington, DE: Glazier, 1987.

Harshav, Benjamin. *Explorations in Poetics*. Stanford: Stanford University Press, 2002.

Harvey, Dorothea Ward. "Bathsheba." In *The Interpreter's Dictionary of the Bible*, edited by George A. Buttrick, 1:366. 4 vols. Nashville: Abingdon, 1976.

Hauser, A. J., and D. F. Watson. "Introduction and Overview." In *A History of Biblical Interpretation*. Vol. 1, *The Ancient Period*, edited by A. J. Hauser and D. F. Watson, 1–54. Grand Rapids: Eerdmans, 2003.

Hausl, Maria. *Abischag und Batscheba*. St. Ottilien: EOS, 1993.

Hay, David. *Glory at the Right Hand: Psalm 110 in Early Christianity*. Nashville: Abingdon, 1973.

Hearon, Holly E., editor. *Distant Voices Drawing Near: Essays in Honor of Antoinette Clark Wire*. Collegeville, MN: Liturgical, 2004.

Heinemann, J. "Early Halakhah in the Palestinian Targum." *Journal of Jewish Studies* 25 (1974) 114–22.

Heller, Joseph. *God Knows*. New York: Knopf, 1984.

Hens-Piazza, Gina. *1–2 Kings*. Abingdon Old Testament Commentaries. Nashville: Abingdon, 2006.

———. *Nameless, Blameless, and Without Shame: Two Cannibal Mothers before a King*. Collegeville, MN: Liturgical, 2003.

Hochman, Baruch. *Character in Literature*. Ithaca, NY: Cornell University Press, 1985.

Honeyman, Alexander. "The Evidence for Regnal Names among the Hebrews." *JBL* 67 (1948) 13–25.

Iser, Wolfgang. *The Act of Reading: A Theory of Aesthetic Response*. Baltimore: Johns Hopkins University Press, 1978.

———. "Indeterminacy and the Reader's Response in Prose Fiction." In *Aspects of Narrative: Selected Papers from the English Institute*, edited by J. Hillis Miller, 1–45. New York: Columbia University Press, 1971.

———. "The Reading Process: A Phenomenological Approach." *New Literary History* 3 (1972) 279–99.

Ishida, Tomoo. "Adonijah the Son of Haggith and His Supporters: An Inquiry into Problems about History and Historiography." In *The Future of Biblical Studies: The Hebrew Scriptures*, edited by Richard Elliott Friedman and H. G. M. Williamson, 165–87. Semeia Studies. Atlanta: Scholars, 1987.

James, Henry. *Henry James: Selected Literary Criticism*. Edited by Morris Shapira. Harmondsworth, UK: Penguin, 1963.

Japhet, Sara. *1 Chronicles*. Old Testament Library. Louisville: Westminster, 1993.

———. *The Ideology of the Book of Chronicles and its Place in Biblical Thought.* Frankfurt: Lang, 1989.

Jastrow, Marcus. *A Dictionary of the Targumim, the Talmud Babli and Yerushalmi, and the Midrashic Literature.* New York: Judaica, 1996.

Jellicoe, Sidney. *The Septuagint and Modern Study.* Oxford: Clarendon, 1968.

Jepsen, Alfred. "Amah und Schiphchah." *VT* 8 (1958) 293–97.

Johnson, Marshall. *The Purpose of the Biblical Genealogies.* 2nd ed. Society for New Testament Studies Monograph Series 8. Cambridge: Cambridge University Press, 1988.

Joüon, Paul. *A Grammar of Biblical Hebrew.* Translated and revised by Takamitsu Muraoka. Subsidia Biblica 27. Rome: Biblical Institute Press, 2003.

Juel, Donald H. *A Master of Surprise: Mark Interpreted.* Minneapolis: Fortress, 1994.

Jung, Leo. *Yoma.* In *The Hebrew-English Edition of the Babylonian Talmud,* edited by Isidore Epstein. London: Soncino, 1989.

Kasher, Rimon. תוספתות תרגום לנביאים [*Targumic Toseftot to the Prophets*]. Jerusalem: World Union of Jewish Studies, 1996.

Keil, Carl F. *The Books of the Kings.* Edinburgh: T. & T. Clark, 1872.

Kelly, Balmer H. "The Septuagint Translators of 1 Samuel and 2 Samuel." PhD diss., Princeton Theological Seminary, 1948.

Kessler, John. "Sexuality and Politics: The Motif of the Displaced Husband in the Books of Samuel." *CBQ* 62 (2000) 409–23.

Keys, Gillian. *The Wages of Sin: A Reappraisal of the "Succession Narrative."* JSOTSup 221. Sheffield, UK: Sheffield Academic, 1996.

Kim, Hyun Chul Paul, and M. Fulgence Nyengele. "Murder S/He Wrote? A Cultural and Psychological Reading of 2 Samuel 11–12." In *Pregnant Passion: Gender, Sex, and Violence in the Bible,* edited by Cheryl Kirk-Duggan, 95–116. Semeia Studies 44. Atlanta: Society of Biblical Literature, 2003.

Kim, Uriah. "Uriah the Hittite: A (Con)Text of Struggle for Identity." *Semeia* 90/91 (2002) 69–85.

Kirk-Duggan, Cheryl A. "Slingshots, Ships, and Personal Psychosis: Murder, Sexual Intrigue, and Power in the Lives of David and Othello." In *Pregnant Passion: Gender, Sex, and Violence in the Bible,* edited by Cheryl Kirk-Duggan, 37–70. Leiden: Brill, 2004.

Kirsch, Jonathan. *King David: The Real Life of the Man Who Ruled Israel.* New York: Ballantine, 2000.

Klassen, William. "Kiss." In *ABD* 4:89–92.

Klein, Lillian R. "Bathsheba Revealed." In *Samuel and Kings: A Feminist Companion to the Bible,* edited by Athalya Brenner, 47–64. Sheffield, UK: Sheffield Academic, 2000.

Klein, Ralph W. *1 Chronicles.* Hermeneia. Fortress, Minneapolis, 2006.

Kren, Thomas. "Looking at Louis XII's Bathsheba." In *A Masterpiece Constructed: The Hours of Louis XII,* edited by Thomas Kren and Mark Evans, 41–61. Los Angeles: J. Paul Getty Museum, 2005.

Kugel, James. "Reuben's Sin with Bilhah in the *Testament of Reuben.*" *Pomegranates and Golden Bells: Studies in Biblical, Jewish, and Near Eastern Ritual, Law, and Literature in Honor of Jacob Milgrom,* edited by David P. Wright, David Noel Freedman, and Avi Hurvitz, 525–54. Winona Lake, IN: Eisenbrauns, 1995.

————. "Two Introductions to Midrash." In *Midrash and Literature,* edited by Geoffrey H. Hartman and Sanford Budick, 77–103. New Haven: Yale University Press, 1986.

Laniak, Timothy. *Shame and Honor in the Book of Esther.* SBLDS 165. Atlanta: Scholars, 1998.

Lapsley, Jacqueline. *Whispering the Word: Hearing Women's Stories in the Old Testament.* Minneapolis: Fortress, 2005.

Lawlor, John I. "Theology and Art in the Narrative of the Ammonite War (2 Samuel 10–12)." *Grace Theological Journal* 3 (1982) 193–205.

Leneman, Helen. "Portrayals of Power in the Stories of Delilah and Bathsheba: Seduction in Song." In *Culture, Entertainment and the Bible,* edited by George Aichele, 139–55. Sheffield, UK: Sheffield Academic, 2000.

Levenson, Jon. "Exodus and Liberation." *Horizons in Biblical Theology* 13 (1991) 134–74.

Levison, John R. "Josephus's Version of Ruth." *Journal for the Study of the Pseudepigrapha* 8 (1991) 31–44.

Linafelt, Tod. "Taking Women in Samuel: Readers/Responses/Responsibility." In *Reading between Texts: Intertextuality and the Hebrew Bible,* edited by Danna Nolan Fewell, 99–113. Literary Currents in Biblical Interpretation. Louisville: Westminster, 1992.

Löwy, Albert. *Miscellany of Hebrew Literature.* Vol. 1. London: Trübner, 1872.

Luther, Martin. *Luther's Works: Lectures on Genesis, Chapters 38–44.* Translated by Paul D. Pahl. St. Louis: Concordia, 1965.

Marcus, David. "David the Deceiver and David the Dupe." *Prooftexts* 6 (1986) 163–83.

Margolin, Uri. "Characters and Their Versions." *Fiction Updated: Theories of Fictionality, Narratology, and Poetics,* edited by Calin Andrei Mihailescu and Walid Hamarneh, 113–32. Toronto: University of Toronto Press, 1996

Martin, Troy. "Paul's Argument from Nature for the Veil in 1 *Corinthians* 11:13–15: A Testicle Instead of a Head Covering." *JBL* 123 (2004) 75–84.

Mazor, Yair. "'Cherchez la femme,' or Sex, Lies and the Bible: Exposing the Anti-feminist Face of the Biblical Text." *Scandinavian Journal of the Old Testament* 18:1 (2004) 23–59.

McCann, J. Clinton. "Psalms." In *NIB,* 4:639–1280.

McCarter, P. Kyle. *1 Samuel.* AB 8. Garden City, NY: Doubleday, 1980

————. *2 Samuel.* AB 9. Garden City, NY: Doubleday, 1984.

————. *Textual Criticism: Recovering the Text of the Hebrew Bible.* Guides to Biblical Scholarship. Philadelphia: Fortress, 1986.

McCarthy, Carmel. *The Tiqqune Sopherim and Other Theological Corrections in the Masoretic Text of the Old Testament.* Göttingen: Vandenhoeck & Ruprecht, 1981.

McNamara, Martin. "Interpretation of Scripture in the Targumim." In *A History of Biblical Interpretation,* edited by Alan J. Hauser and Duane F. Watson, 167–97. Grand Rapids: Eerdmans, 2003.

McNay, Lois. *Foucault and Feminism: Power, Gender, and the Self.* Cambridge: Polity, 1992.

Merrill, Eugene H. *Qumran and Predestination: A Theological Study of the Thanksgiving Hymns.* Studies on the Texts of the Desert of Judah 8. Leiden: Brill, 1975.

Metzger, Bruce M. "The Lucianic Recension of the Greek Bible." In *Chapters in the History of New Testament Textual Criticism*, edited by Bruce M. Metzger, 1–41. New Testament Tools and Studies 4. Grand Rapids, Eerdmans, 1963.

———. *The Text of the New Testament: Its Transmission, Corruption, and Restoration.* Oxford: Oxford University Press, 1968.

Meyer, Carole. *Households and Holiness: The Religious Culture of Israelite Women.* Minneapolis: Fortress, 2005.

Midrash Rabbah Ecclesiastes. Translated by Abraham Cohen. 3rd ed., volume 8. Edited by Harry Freedman and Maurice Simon. London: Soncino, 1983.

Midrash Rabbah Exodus. Translated by Simon Maurice Lehrman. 3rd ed, volume 3.Edited by Harry Freedman and Maurice Simon. London: Soncino, 1983.

Midrash Rabbah Genesis. Trans Harry Freedman. 3rd ed., volume 1. Edited by Harry Freedman and Maurice Simon. London: Soncino, 1983.

Midrash Rabbah Leviticus. Translated by Jacob Israelstam and Judah Slotki. 3rd ed., volume 4. Edited by Harry Freedman and Maurice Simon. London: Soncino, 1983.

Midrash Rabbah Numbers. Translated by Judah Slotki. 3rd ed, volume 5. Edited by Harry Freedman and Maurice Simon. London: Soncino, 1983.

Midrash Rabbah Song of Songs. Translated by Maurice Simon. 3rd ed., volume 9. Edited by Harry Freedman and Maurice Simon. London: Soncino, 1983.

Midrash Samuel. Edited by Solomon Buber. Jerusalem, 1965; reprint from photo-offset of Kraków, 1893.

Miller, J. Hillis. "Character in the Novel: A Real Illusion." In *From Smollett to James: Studies in the Novel and Other Essays Presented to Edgar Johnson*, edited by Samuel Mintz, Alice Chandler, and Christopher Mulvey, 277–85. Charlottesville: University Press of Virginia, 1981.

Miller, Patrick D., and J. J. M. Roberts. *The Hand of the Lord: A Reassessment of the "Ark Narrative" of 1 Samuel.* Johns Hopkins Near Eastern Studies. Baltimore: Johns Hopkins University Press, 1977.

Moore, Michael S. "Bathsheba's Silence (1 Kings 1:11–31)." In *Inspired Speech: Prophecy in the Ancient Near East: Essays in Honor of Herbert B. Huffmon*, edited by John Kaltner and Louis Stulman, 336–46. JSOTSup 378. London: T. & T. Clark, 2004.

Morrison, Craig E. *The Character of the Syriac Version of the First Book of Samuel.* Monographs of the Peshitta Institute of Leiden 11. Leiden: Brill, 2001.

Mudrick, Marvin. "Character and Event in Fiction." *Yale Review* 50 (1961) 202–18.

Mulder, Martin. *1 Kings.* Leuven: Peeters, 1998.

———."Versuch zur Deutung von sokènèt in 1 Kön 1:2,4." *VT* 22 (1972) 43–54.

Nelson, Richard D. *First and Second Kings.* Interpretation. Atlanta: John Knox, 1987.

Newsom, Carol. "Bakhtin, the Bible, and Dialogic Truth." *Journal of Religion* 76 (1996) 290–306.

———. *The Book of Job: A Contest of Moral Imaginations.* Oxford: Oxford University Press, 2003.

———. "The Book of Job as Polyphonic Text." *JSOT* 97 (2002) 87–108.

Newton, Adam. *Narrative Ethics.* Cambridge: Harvard University Press, 1995.

Nicol, George. "The Alleged Rape of Bathsheba: Some Observations on Ambiguity in Biblical Narrative." *JSOT* 73 (1997) 43–54.

———."Bathsheba: A Clever Woman?" *Expository Times* 99 (1988) 360–63.

————."David, Abigail and Bathsheba, Nabal and Uriah: Transformations within a Triangle." *Scandinavian Journal of the Old Testament* 12 (1998): 130–45.

Nida, Eugene. *Towards a Science of Translating: With Special Reference to Principles and Procedures Involved in Bible Translating.* Leiden: Brill, 1964.

Noldeke, Theodor. *Compendious Syriac Grammar.* London: Williams & Norgate, 1904.

Noll, Kurt L. *The Faces of David.* JSOTSup 242. Sheffield, UK: Sheffield Academic, 1997.

Noth, Martin. *Die Israelitischen Personnamen im Rahmen der gemeinsemitischen Namengebung.* Hildesheim: Georg Olms, 1966.

Nussbaum, Martha C. *Love's Knowledge: Essays on Philosophy and Literature.* Oxford: Oxford University Press, 1990.

Olmstead, A. T. "The Earliest Book of Kings." *American Journal of Semitic Languages and Literature* 31 (1915) 169–214.

Olson, Dennis. "Biblical Theology as Provisional Monologization: A Dialogue with Childs, Brueggemann and Bakhtin," *Biblical Interpreter* 6 (1998) 162–80.

Ostertag, Danielle. "La Veuve Dans le Plan Messianique de Dieu." *Foi et Vie* 83 (1984) 5–26.

Palmer, Alan. "The Mind Beyond the Skin." In *Narrative Theory and the Cognitive Sciences*, edited by David Herman, 322–48. Stanford: CSLI, 2003.

Parker, David C. "Codex Vaticanus." In *ABD* 1:1074–75.

Patte, Daniel. *Early Jewish Hermeneutic in Palestine.* SBLDS 22. Missoula, MT: Scholars, 1975.

Peters, Melvin. "Septuagint." In *ABD* 5:1093–1104.

Petersen, David. "Portraits of David: Canonical and Otherwise." *Int* 40 (1986) 130–42.

Peterson, Eugene. *First and Second Samuel.* Louisville: Westminster, 1999.

Petruso, Thomas. *Life Made Real: Characterization in the Novel since Proust and Joyce.* Ann Arbor: University of Michigan Press, 1991.

Pinsky, Robert. *The Life of David.* New York: Schocken, 2005.

Plato. *The Republic.* Translated by Paul Shorey. 2 vols. Loeb Classical Library. Cambridge: Harvard University Press, 1930–1935.

Polzin, Robert. *David and the Deuteronomist: 2 Samuel.* Indiana Studies in Biblical Literature. Bloomington: Indiana University Press, 1993.

Porter, Stanley, and Brook W. R. Pearson. "Isaiah through Greek Eyes: The Septuagint of Isaiah." In *Writing and Reading the Scroll of Isaiah: Studies of an Interpretive Tradition*, edited by Craig C. Broyles and Craig C. Evans, 2:531–46. 2 vols. Vetus Testamentum Supplements 70. Leiden: Brill, 1997.

Pressler, Carolyn. *The View of Women Found in the Deuteronomic Family Laws.* BZAW 216. Berlin: de Gruyter, 1993.

Price, Martin. *Forms of Life: Character and Moral Imagination in the Novel.* New Haven: Yale University Press, 1983.

————. "The Other Self: Thoughts about Character in the Novel." In *Imagined Worlds: Essays on Some English Novels and Novelists in Honour of John Butt*, edited by Maynard Mack and Ian Gregor, 279–99. London: Methuen, 1968.

Prince, Gerald. *Dictionary of Narratology.* Lincoln: University of Nebraska Press, 1987.

Pritchard, James B., editor. *Ancient Near Eastern Texts Relating to the Old Testament.* 3rd ed. Princeton: Princeton University Press, 1969.

Propp, Vladimir. *Morphology of the Folktale.* Austin: University of Texas Press, 1968.

Provan, Iain. *1 and 2 Kings*. New International Biblical Commentary: Old Testament Series. Peabody, MA: Hendrickson, 1995.

Pyper, Hugh S. *David as Reader: 2 Samuel 12:1–15 and the Poetics of Fatherhood*. Biblical Interpretation Series 23. Leiden: Brill, 1996.

Rad, Gerhard von. *Wisdom in Israel*. Translated by James D. Martin. Nashville: Abingdon, 1972.

Rajak, Tessa. *Josephus: The Historian and His Society*. Philadelphia: Fortress, 1983.

Rand, Herbert. "David and Ahab: A Study of Crime and Punishment." *Jewish Bible Quarterly* 24 (1996) 90–97.

Redpath, Henry A. "A Contribution towards Settling Dates of the Translation of the Various Books of the Septuagint." *Journal of Theological Studies* 6 (1907) 606–14.

Reich, Ronny. " Palaces and Residencies in the Iron Age." In *The Architecture of Ancient Israel: From the Prehistoric to the Persian Periods*, edited by Aharon Kempinski, Ronny Reich, and Hannah Katzenstein, 202–22. Jerusalem: Ahava, 1992.

Reisner, George, Clarence Fisher, and David Lyon, editors. *Harvard Excavations at Samaria, 1908–1910*. Cambridge: Harvard University Press, 1924.

Ricoeur, Paul. "Biblical Hermeneutics." *Semeia* 4 (1975) 29–148.

Rimmon-Kenan, Shlomith. *The Concept of Ambiguity: The Example of James*. Chicago: University of Chicago Press, 1977.

———. *Narrative Fiction: Contemporary Poetics*. 2nd ed. New Accents. London: Routledge, 2002.

Rogers, Katharine M. *The Troublesome Helpmate: A History of Misogyny in Literature*. Seattle: University of Washington Press, 1966.

Roitman, Betty. "Sacred Language and Open Text." In *Midrash and Literature*, edited by Geoffrey Hartman and Sanford Budick, 159–75. New Haven: Yale University Press, 1986.

Römer, Thomas, and Albert de Pury. "Deuteronomistic Historiography (DH): History of Research and Debated Ideas." In *Israel Constructs Its History: Deuteronomistic Historiography in Recent Research*, edited by Thomas Römer, Albert de Pury, and Jean-Daniel Macchi, 24–141. JSOTSup 306. Sheffield, UK: Sheffield Academic, 2000.

Rorty, Amélie Oksenberg. "Characters, Persons, Selves, Individuals." In *Theory of the Novel: A Historical Approach*, edited by Michael McKeon. Baltimore: Johns Hopkins University Press, 2000

Rosenberg, Joel. "The Institutional Matrix of Treachery in 2 Samuel 11." *Semeia* 46 (1989) 103–16.

Rost, Leonhard. *The Succession to the Throne of David*. Translated by Michael Rutter and David M. Gunn. Historica Texts and Interpreters in Biblical Scholarship 1. Sheffield, UK: Almond, 1982.

Rudman, Dominic. "The Patriarchal Narratives in the Books of Samuel." *VT* 54 (2004) 239–49.

Sakenfeld, Katharine Doob. *Just Wives? Stories of Power and Survival in the Old Testament and Today*. Louisville: Westminster John Knox, 2003.

Sasson, Victor. "A Matter to Be Put Right: The Yabneh-Yam Case Continued." *Journal of Northwest Semitic Languages* 12 (1984) 115–20.

———. "An Unrecognized Juridical Term in the Yabneh-Yam Lawsuit and in an Unnoticed Biblical Parallel." *Bulletin of the American Schools of Oriental Research* 232 (1978) 57–63.

Scarry, Elaine. *On Beauty and Being Just*. Princeton: Princeton University Press, 1999.

Schaberg, Jane, Alice Bach, and Esther Fuchs, editors. *On the Cutting Edge: The Study of Women in Biblical Worlds*. London: Continuum, 2004.

Schipper, Jeremy. "Did David Overinterpret Nathan's Parable in 2 Samuel 12:1–6?" *JBL* 126 (2007) 383–407.

———. *Disability Studies and the Hebrew Bible*. New York: T. & T. Clark, 2006.

Schwartz, Regina. "Nations and Nationalism: Adultery in the House of David." *Critical Inquiry* 19 (1992) 131–50.

Schwarz, Daniel. "Character and Characterization: An Inquiry." *Journal of Narrative Technique* 19 (1989) 85–105.

Seebass, Horst. "Nathan und David in 2 Sam 12." *ZAW* 86 (1974) 203–11.

Seow, Choon-Leong. "1 Kings." In *NIB* 3:1–296.

———. *Ecclesiastes*. Anchor Bible 18C. New York: Doubleday, 1997.

Shimoff, Sandra. "David and Bathsheba: The Political Function of Rabbinic Aggada." *Journal for the Study of Judaism in the Persian, Hellenistic and Roman Periods* 24 (1993) 246–56.

Simon, Uriel. "The Poor Man's Ewe-Lamb: An Example of a Juridical Parable." *Biblica* 48 (1967) 207–42.

Smith, Carol. "'Queenship' in Israel? The Cases of Bathsheba, Jezebel and Athaliah." In *King and Messiah in Israel and the Ancient Near East*, edited by John Day, 142–62. JSOTSup 270. Sheffield, UK: Sheffield Academic, 1998.

Smolar, Leivy, and Moses Aberbach. *Studies in Targum Jonathan to the Prophets*. Library of Biblical Studies. New York: Ktav, 1983.

Solvang, Elna. "A Woman's Place is in the House: Royal Women of Judah and Their Involvement in the House of David." PhD diss., Princeton Theological Seminary, 1990.

Sperber, Alexander. *The Former Prophets according to Targum Jonathan*. Leiden: Brill, 1959.

Springer, Mary Doyle. *A Rhetoric of Literary Character: Some Women of Henry James*. Chicago: University of Chicago Press, 1978.

Staalduine-Sulman, Eveline van. *The Targum of Samuel*. Studies in the Aramaic Interpretation of Scripture 1. Leiden: Brill, 2002.

Stamm, Johann J. "Der Name des Koenigs Salomo." *Theologische Zeitschrift* 16 (1960) 285–97.

Stark, Jürgen Kurt. *Personal Names in Palmyrene Inscriptions*. Oxford: Clarendon, 1971.

Steinsaltz, Adin, editor. *The Talmud: The Steinsaltz Edition*. Vol. 15, *Sanhedrin*. New York: Random House, 1996.

Sterling, Gregory. "The Invisible Presence: Josephus's Retelling of Ruth." In *Understanding Josephus: Seven Perspectives*, edited by Steve Mason, 104–71. Journal for the Study of the Pseudepigrapha Supplement series 32. Sheffield, UK: Sheffield Academic, 1998.

Stern, David. "Midrash and the Language of Exegesis: A Study of Vayikra Rabbah, Chapter 1." In *Midrash and Language*, edited by Geoffrey Hartman and Sanford Budick, 105–24. New Haven: Yale University Press, 1986.

Sternberg, Meir. *The Poetics of Biblical Narrative: Ideological Literature and the Drama of Reading*. Indiana Literary Biblical Series. Bloomington: Indiana University Press, 1987.

Sternberg, Meir, and Menakhem Perry. "Caution: A Literary Text! Problems in the Poetics and the Interpretation of Biblical Narrative," *Ha-Sifrut* 2 (1970) 608–83, English Summary 679–82.

Stone, Ken. *Sex, Honor and Power in the Deuteronomistic History.* JSOTSup 234. Sheffield, UK: Sheffield Academic, 1996.

Swete, Henry B. *An Introduction to the Old Testament in Greek.* New York: Ktav, 1968.

Tanselle, G. Thomas. *A Rationale of Textual Criticism.* Philadelphia: University of Pennsylvania Press, 1989.

Thackeray, Henry St. John. "The Greek Translators of the Four Books of Kings." *Journal of Theological Studies* 8 (1907) 262–78.

Thornton, T. C. G. "Solomonic Apologetic in Samuel and Kings." *Church Quarterly Review* 169 (1968) 159–66.

Tov, Emanuel. *Textual Criticism of the Hebrew Bible.* Minneapolis: Fortress, 1992.

———. "Textual Criticism (OT)." In *ABD* 6:393–412.

Trible, Phyllis. *Texts of Terror: Literary-Feminist Readings of Biblical Narratives.* Overtures to Biblical Theology. Philadelphia: Fortress, 1984.

Tull, Patricia. "Bakhtin's Confessional Self-Accounting and Psalms of Lament." *Biblical Interpretation* 13 (2005) 41–55.

Ussishkin, David. "King Solomon's Palaces." *Biblical Archaeologist* 36 (1973) 84–105.

———. "Solomon's Palace and Megiddo 1723." *Israel Exploration Journal* 16 (1966) 176–86.

Valler, Shulamit. "King David and 'His' Women." In *A Feminist Companion to Samuel and Kings,* edited by Athalya Brenner and Karla Shargent, 129–42. Sheffield, UK: Sheffield Academic, 1994.

Vaux, Roland de. *Ancient Israel: Its Life and Institutions.* Translated by John McHugh. New York: McGraw-Hill, 1961.

Viejola, Timo. "Salomo—der Erstgeborene Bathsebas." In *Studies in the Historical Books of the Old Testament,* edited by John A. Emerton, 230–50. Vetus Testamentum Supplements 30. Leiden: Brill, 1979.

Viviano, Pauline. "Rei." In *ABD* 5:665.

Walker-Vadillo, Mónica Ann. *Bathsheba in Late Medieval French Manuscript Illumination: Innocent Object of Desire or Agent of Sin?* Lewiston, NY: Mellen, 2008.

Walls, Neal. *The Goddess Anat in Ugaritic Myth.* SBLDS 135. Atlanta: Scholars, 1992.

Walsh, Jerome. *1 Kings.* Collegeville, MN: Liturgical Press, 1996.

Walters, Stanley. "Hannah and Anna: The Greek and Hebrew Texts of 1 Samuel 1." *JBL* 107 (1988) 385–412.

Waltke, Bruce, and Michael O'Connor. *An Introduction to Biblical Hebrew Syntax.* Winona Lake, IN: Eisenbrauns, 1990.

Watzinger, Carl. *Denkmäler Palästinas 1.* Leipzig: Hinrichs'sche, 1933.

Weinsheimer, Joel. "Theory of Character: Emma." *Poetics Today* 1 (1979) 185–211.

Weitzman, Michael. *The Syriac Version of the Old Testament: An Introduction.* Cambridge: Cambridge University Press, 1999.

Wenham, Gordon. "B^eTU^lAh: A Girl of Marriageable Age." *Vetus Testamentum* 22 (1972) 326–48.

Wesselius, Jan W. "Joab's Death and the Central Theme of the Sucession Narrative (2 Samuel 9–1 Kings 2)." *Vetus Testamentum* 40 (1990) 336–51.

Westbrook, Raymond. *Studies in Biblical and Cuneiform Law.* Paris: Gabalda, 1988.

Wevers, John W. "The Interpretative Character and Significance of the Septuagint Version." In *Hebrew Bible/Old Testament: The History of Its Interpretation*. Vol. 1, *From the Beginnings to the Middle Ages*, edited by Magne Sæbø, 84–107. Göttingen: Vandenhoeck & Ruprecht, 1996.

Whybray, Robert. *The Succession Narrative*. London: SCM, 1968.

Williams, Peter J. *Studies in the Syntax of the Peshitta of 1 Kings*. Monographs of the Peshitta Institute Leiden 12. Leiden: Brill, 2001.

Wilson, Rawdon. "On Character: A Reply to Martin Price." *Critical Inquiry* 2 (1975) 191–98.

Woods, Francis Henry. *The Light Thrown by the Septuagint Version on the Books of Samuel*. Oxford: Oxford University Press, 1885.

Wyatt, N. "'Araunah the Jebusite' and the Throne of David." *Studia Theologica* 39 (1985) 39–53.

Yadin, Yigael. *The Art of Warfare in Biblical Lands in the Light of Archaeological Discovery*. Translated by M. Pearlman. New York: McGraw-Hill, 1963.

Yamada, Frank. "Configurations of Rape in the Hebrew Bible: A Literary Analysis of Three Rape Narratives." PhD diss., Princeton Theological Seminary, 2004.

———. "Dealing with Rape (in) Narrative (Genesis 34): Ethics of the Other and a Text in Conflict." In *The Meanings We Choose: Hermeneutical Ethics, Indeterminacy and the Conflict of Interpretations*, edited by Charles Cosgrove, 149–65. JSOTSup 411. London: T. & T. Clark, 2004.

Yee, Gale A. "The Form-Critical Study of Isaiah 5:1–7 as a Song and a Juridical Parable." *CBQ* 43 (1981) 30–43.

———. "'Fraught with Background': Literary Ambiguity in 2 Samuel 11." *Int* 42 (July 1988) 240–53.

Zevit, Ziony. *Matres Lectionis in Ancient Hebrew Epigraphs*. Cambridge: American Schools of Oriental Research, 1980.

Index